THE ABOLITIONISTS
AND THE SOUTH

D1563893

THE ABOLITIONISTS
AND THE SOUTH, 1831-1861

Stanley Harrold

THE UNIVERSITY PRESS OF KENTUCKY

For Emily

Copyright © 1995 by The University Press of Kentucky
Scholarly publisher for the Commonwealth,
serving Bellarmine College, Berea College, Centre
College of Kentucky, Eastern Kentucky University,
The Filson Club, Georgetown College, Kentucky
Historical Society, Kentucky State University,
Morehead State University, Murray State University,
Northern Kentucky University, Transylvania University,
University of Kentucky, University of Louisville,
and Western Kentucky University.

Editorial and Sales Offices: Lexington, Kentucky 40508-4008

Library of Congress Cataloging–in–Publication Data

Harrold, Stanley.
    The abolitionists and the south, 1831–1861 / by Stanley Harrold.
        p.   cm.
    Includes bibliographical references (p.   ) and index.
    ISBN 0-8131-1906-5 ; -0968-x (acid-free)
    1. Antislavery movements—Southern States—History—19th century.
    2. Abolitionists—Southern States—History—19th century.
    I. Title.
    E449.H297   1995
    973.7'114'0975—dc20   94-40321

This book is printed on acid-free recycled paper meeting
the requirements of the American National Standard
for Permanence of Paper for Printed Library Materials. ♾ ⊕

CONTENTS

Illustrations follow page 118.

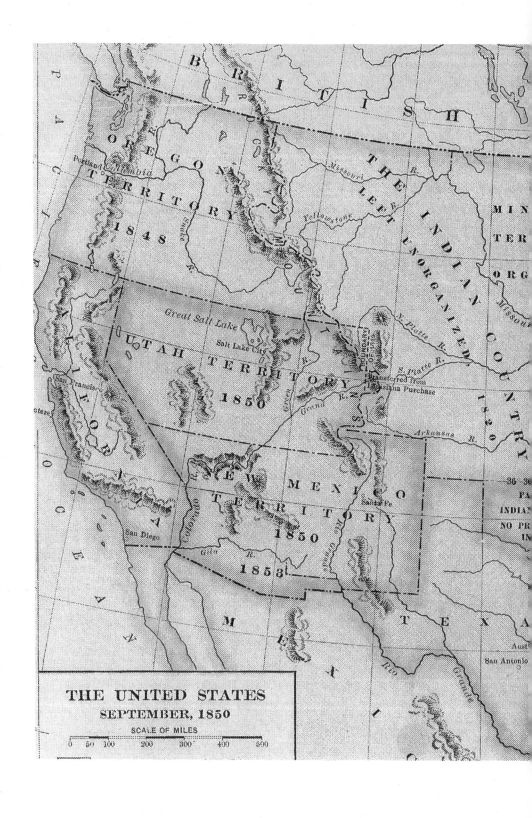

THE UNITED STATES

SEPTEMBER, 1850

SCALE OF MILES

0   50   100   200   300   400   500

ACKNOWLEDGMENTS

Writing history remains an individual effort, and I am responsible for the contents of this book. Yet the book would not exist without the contributions of a number of institutions and people.

Among the institutions, I thank the National Endowment for the Humanities, which funded a year of uninterrupted work, and South Carolina State University, which supplemented the Endowment's stipend. I am also indebted to the Institute for Southern Studies at the University of South Carolina for granting me several appointments that provided access to the services of the University's Thomas Cooper Library, including its essential interlibrary loan department. Also very helpful was Enda Corley-Smith of the South Carolina State University interlibrary loan department.

The staffs of several other libraries and archives provided help that was just as important. Roberta Zonghi of Boston Public Library and Gerald F. Roberts of the Berea College Archives deserve special mention. In addition, I thank the Historical Society of Pennsylvania, Boston Public Library, the New York Historical Society, Berea College, and Brown University Library for permission to quote from their manuscript holdings.

This book has also benefited from formal scholarly scrutiny. I presented an earlier version of chapter 2 at the annual meeting of the Southern Historical Association in 1989 and an earlier version of chapter 3 to the Southern Studies Colloquium at the College of Charleston in 1992. A shorter version of chapter 4 appeared in the winter 1993 issue of the *Radical History Review*, and I thank the *Review* for permission to publish a revised version here. Thorough readings for the University Press of Kentucky by William W. Freehling and James L. Huston improved the book.

Finally, I am deeply indebted to a number of friends who provided encouragement, help, comments on portions of the book, or all three. In alphabetical order they are: Herbert Aptheker, Merton L. Dillon, John d'Entremont, Lawrence J. Friedman, Judy B. Harrold, William C. Hine, John T. Hubbell, Seleta S. Byrd, James Brewer Stewart, and Vernon L. Volpe. These individuals have been very generous, and I am very grateful.

INTRODUCTION

This is a book about the American antislavery movement, the nation's most important reform movement of the nineteenth century. The antislavery effort contributed to the coming of the Civil War and affected issues of race in ways that continue to impact American society on the verge of the twenty-first century. Because of its importance, the antislavery movement has inspired countless studies. Many of them focus on the abolitionists—the men and women who were the most outspoken opponents of slavery. The purpose of this book is to clarify the characteristics and role of these individuals by analyzing their involvement in efforts *within the South* to destroy slavery.

The American campaign to end the enslavement of black people was part of an international effort in western civilization that had its roots in the industrial revolution and associated cultural developments of the eighteenth century. In the United States, in particular, there was significant progress against slavery following the War for Independence as northern states either abolished it or provided for gradual emancipation within their borders. During the same period the national government barred slavery from the Northwest Territory, and the United States Constitution enabled Congress to terminate the country's foreign slave trade by 1808.[1] But the Constitution also implicitly sanctioned slavery. In the cotton-growing states of the deep South and to a lesser extent in the mixed agricultural economies of the states of the upper South, human bondage continued to thrive. The international demand for cotton powered slavery's westward expansion and the formation of new slave states in the Southwest.

Consequently, the final struggle over slavery in the United States was geographically determined. Antislavery forces in the North challenged the proslavery forces of the South. Nevertheless, the advocates of African-American freedom faced considerable proslavery sentiment in the North, and, as this book emphasizes, slavery's southern defenders were ever fearful of abolitionist activities in their midst. The struggle reached its peak between 1831 and 1865. In the former year, William Lloyd Garrison initiated his newspaper, the *Liberator*, in Boston with a demand that slavery be immediately abolished, and in Virginia Nat Turner led the nation's largest slave revolt. In the latter year, the northern victory in the Civil War led to the total abolition of slavery in the country.

Northern abolitionists, like Garrison, used to be credited with sparking this most intense phase of the antislavery movement. The relationship of these dedicated reformers to the sectional controversy made them a perennially popular and controversial topic in American history. But, since the 1960s, a generation of historians has developed a more constricted interpretation of the abolitionists' significance.

Beginning with the abolitionists themselves, writers have distinguished between them and a broader antislavery effort. Although this distinction has not always been precise, historians during the past several decades have increasingly defined abolitionists quite narrowly as individuals who advocated—on the basis of moral principle—the immediate emancipation of the slaves and equal rights for blacks in the United States. Active membership in organizations pledged to these goals has become the chief means of identifying such persons.[2]

The abolitionists, according to this definition, were a small, vociferous portion of the larger antislavery movement. The movement also included a much more numerous group that concentrated its efforts against the extension of slavery into western territories while rejecting abolitionist demands for immediate northern action to end slavery in the southern states. The nonextensionists did not belong to immediate abolitionist organizations. They were chiefly motivated by political and economic considerations rather than by moral principles, although Christian precepts played a role, and many of them were as antiblack as antislavery. Many nonextensionists identified with the Free Soil party in 1848 and most of them became Republicans in the mid-1850s.[3] Accordingly, neither of these political parties was abolitionist. They were designed to stop the expansion of slavery and curtail the power of slaveholders in the national government, not to emancipate southern slaves immediately.

This precise distinction between immediate abolitionists and nonextensionists has been very useful in clarifying our understanding of who the abolitionists were, what their relationship to northern culture was, and how the antislavery movement developed. But, as historians have emphasized the distinction, they have inevitably narrowed perceptions of the influence abolitionists wielded over the antislavery movement and the sectional struggle as well. Once considered to have been at the center of the sectional controversy, abolitionists are now placed on its periphery. As the perception of abolitionist influence has contracted, historians—with some exceptions—have turned to analyzing the inner world of the immediatists.[4] During the last twenty years, historians have focused on the abolitionists as products of antebellum northern culture, who are valuable in achieving an understanding of that culture rather than as important players in the sectional struggle.

In the late 1980s, I began to explore the relationship between northern immediatists and antislavery action in the South—especially such action in the portions of the antebellum South that bordered on the free states. As several historians have recently emphasized, it was in the border slave states that human bondage was most vulnerable. Farmers from the Chesapeake to Missouri were increasingly planting crops, such as wheat and corn, that favored the employment of seasonable free labor rather than the maintenance of a year-round slave-labor force. Beginning in the eighteenth century, this fundamental economic development encouraged a willingness among many of the region's whites to question the utility of slave labor. It also encouraged individual manumissions, culminating in a growing free black population, and a long—if uneven—tradition of antislavery organization. Increasingly, too, the border South entered a northern economic orbit. The region developed cities, extensive rail systems, mercantile perspectives, and a significant foreign-born population, all of which weakened its ties to the cotton-growing South. Slaveholding interests continued to dominate the border region throughout the antebellum period. To be an abolitionist there was far more dangerous than it was in the North. Contemporaries, nevertheless, recognized that the border South—and portions of North Carolina and Tennessee as well—might prove receptive to a variety of antislavery strategies, and northern abolitionists vigorously pursued them.[5]

In undertaking this bisectional study, I aimed to gain a broader perspective on the scope of northern abolitionism, to shift focus away from the abolitionists as representatives of northern culture, and to assess their interaction with proslavery forces on slavery's home ground. Despite its limitations, I accepted the narrow definition of abolitionism in order to make the study as precise as possible concerning whose influence, ideas, and actions are being discussed.

As historian Ronald G. Walters demonstrates, one way of understanding the relationship between the abolitionists and the South is to analyze how they used the South and slavery as metaphors for social problems they confronted in the North. I was concerned instead with how those who acted against slavery in the South fit into northern abolitionism and how they helped shape abolitionist belief-systems, perspectives, customs, policies, and traditions—in other words, how they influenced the development of abolitionist reform culture.[6] As my investigation proceeded, I realized that it could also provide insights into the role of abolitionism in the coming of the Civil War.

This book attempts to modify current understandings of the abolitionists and their role in American history by challenging two major, mutually supportive perceptions concerning them. The older of these perceptions dates back to the early years of the twentieth century. It holds that, following an abortive propaganda campaign in the South during the mid-1830s, abolitionists concentrated their energies in the North and curtailed attempts to confront slavery on its home ground. The more recent is the view that abolitionists had negligible influence on the course of the sectional struggle. This perception takes two forms. The first portrays abolitionists as self-serving conservatives who used slavery as a symbol of national moral decline in a campaign to impose social order on the *North*. The second portrays them as seeking to purify only themselves from the sin of slavery by withdrawing into autonomous churches, parties, and cliques.[7]

In order to present an alternative model of abolitionist orientation, the chapters that follow integrate southern antislavery action into an understanding of northern immediatism during the three decades prior to the Civil War. The chapters' themes include the persistence of northern abolitionism in valuing direct confrontation with slavery in the South, the impact of action against slavery in the South on northern abolitionist reform culture, the role of northern immediatism in encouraging those who acted against slavery on its home ground, the relationship between the slaves and those whites who took such action, and the reaction of proslavery southern whites to abolitionist efforts in their section. Subsidiary themes include the cooperative spirit of blacks and whites in support of southern antislavery action and the impact such highly stressful action had on those who engaged in it. Contrary to several recent studies, I have found more commonality than disengagement between black and white abolitionists.[8] I have also discovered that—as one might expect—those who undertook dangerous and often illegal missions against slavery in the South paid a significant emotional price.

The first chapter of this book reviews the historical literature related to southern antislavery sentiment and provides a historiographical basis for what follows. The second and third chapters deal with northern abolitionist images of white and black southern opponents of slavery, and the relationship between the northerners and slavery's indigenous antagonists. They establish that northern abolitionists did not lose interest in direct antislavery action in the South after the mid-1830s. They also demonstrate that southern black rebels and southern white emancipators helped shape a northern abolitionist reform culture that undertook aggressive action against slavery in the South during the 1840s and 1850s.

The rest of the book explores various dimensions of this continued relationship between northern abolitionism and southern antislavery action. Chapter 4 analyzes the stature, influence, and abolitionist identity of northerners who gained renown for going into the South to rescue blacks from bondage. Chapters 5 and 6 are similar studies of those who undertook abolitionist missionary work in the South and those who attempted to establish northern colonies there. The seventh chapter traces the relationship between political abolitionism in the upper South and the northern immediatists. The eighth and final chapter explores the legacies of southern antislavery action in Civil War causation and in the struggle to establish black rights in the South during Reconstruction.

These chapters do not add up to a history of the antislavery movement in the South. Although a narrative account of southern abolitionism would be a worthwhile venture, the emphasis here is on analysis, and the organization is topical, not chronological. There is no attempt to mention every southern antislavery advocate, every event in the struggle within the South against slavery, or every northerner who went south for antislavery purposes. Nor is there an account of every southern antislavery organization. Rather, I have concentrated on individuals and groups who, while acting in the South, had close ties to northern immediatism and/or helped shape that movement's reform culture.[9] So there is no extended treatment of southern antislavery activists who had minimal ties to northern abolitionism, nor of the American Colonization Society (ACS), which—though nominally antislavery—was held by northern abolitionists and their southern allies to be fundamentally proslavery. Similarly, I treat the rise of small Republican parties in the upper South in the late 1850s only in relation to its impact on northern abolitionism and proslavery southern whites.

In contrast, the various northern abolitionist organizations, groups, and factions are at the core of this book, as are their respective perspectives on and engagement in southern antislavery action. Because historians do not agree on a common terminology for these entities, it is vital to explain the terms used in this book.

Among the more important of the abolitionist organizations was the American Anti-Slavery Society (AASS). Established in 1833, it enjoyed the support of virtually all immediatists until it shattered into several groups between 1837 and 1840. Of these groups, New Englanders who recognized the leadership of William Lloyd Garrison retained control of the society, although they represented a small minority in the movement. Usually called Garrisonians, these abolitionists by the early 1840s advocated the dissolution of the Union as the only effective means of withdrawing northern support from slavery and forcing emancipation. Garrison and many of his associates were nonresistants—pacifists who rejected all violent means including government action. They were unorthodox in religion, anticlerical, and generally distrustful of church organizations.

Such views caused considerable antagonism between them and a much larger group of immediatists who were orthodox Christians. These church-oriented or evangelical abolitionists included individuals who promoted abolitionism within the major church denominations as well as those who "came out" to establish independent abolitionist churches. From 1840 until the mid-1850s, church-oriented abolitionists were at least nominally united in the American and Foreign Anti-Slavery Society (AFASS), led by New York City businessman Lewis Tappan.

Closely associated with the church-oriented abolitionists were the political abolitionists, who were themselves divided into three regional factions. Beginning with the organization of the abolitionist Liberty party in 1840, the political abolitionists advocated organized political action against slavery, independent of the existing party system of Whigs and Democrats. The most strident of the political abolitionists supported the Gerrit Smith circle of upstate New York. Centered on Smith, a wealthy philanthropist, these abolitionists are referred to here as radical political abolitionists. They argued that slavery could never be legalized, that the United States Constitution—properly construed—prohibited slavery in the states, and that, therefore, the national government could abolish it in the South.

A more conservative faction of political abolitionists emerged in Cincinnati under the leadership of Gamaliel Bailey and Salmon P. Chase in the early 1840s. This faction recognized the sovereignty of the southern states over slavery within their bounds, advocated political action against slavery within the national domain, and called for moral suasion to encourage indigenous political action against slavery in the South. This faction led the bulk of Liberty abolitionists into the Free Soil party in 1848.

The third political abolitionist faction centered on evangelical Joshua Leavitt, who edited the weekly *Emancipator* in Boston. This faction was less ideologically coherent than the other two, but most of its leaders followed the Cincinnatians into the Free Soil party. By the mid-1850s former members of the Cincinnati and Boston factions of political abolitionists had much in common with the nonabolitionist but staunchly antislavery politicians of the Republican Party, who are usually called Radical Republicans.[10]

Other important abolitionist groups were the black abolitionists and the second-generation white immediatists. The blacks were actually the first abolitionists. They felt the injustice of slavery most keenly, had their own priorities, and tended to emphasize action over rhetoric. But they also identified as individuals with either the

Garrisonian, the church-oriented, or the radical political abolitionists. The second-generation white abolitionists, who embraced the cause amid resistance to the Fugitive Slave Act of 1850, cooperated with the Garrisonians but were more willing to employ violent means and to blend immediatism with Republican party politics than their predecessors.

Although the Garrisonians were less likely than other abolitionists to be directly involved in the South, each of these abolitionist groups and factions had a role in southern antislavery action and were in turn influenced by such action. They recognized that fundamental economic and demographic forces were transforming attitudes toward slavery among the people of the border region. They determined to hasten this transformation by encouraging indigenous southern abolitionism, by extending northern abolitionist efforts into the region, and by undertaking direct efforts in behalf of the slaves. Such activities helped shape the course of abolitionism and of the nation.

Throughout this book I have drawn upon recent studies of the antislavery movement to provide an intellectual framework for the interpretations I present. In attempting to integrate southern antislavery action into the existing portrait of that movement, I am indebted to the creative scholars who over the past thirty-odd years have achieved such a remarkably sophisticated understanding of the abolitionists. My hope is to build on that scholarship to present a portrait of the abolitionists' geographical orientation toward the South as well as of their role in that section and in the sectional conflict.

Chapter One

THE SOUTH IN ANTISLAVERY HISTORY

Now and then during the past century and a half historians have investigated the role of the border slave states in the development of the antislavery movement in nineteenth-century America. The subject is difficult to resist. In the tier of states stretching westward from Delaware to Missouri, northerners and southerners, slaves and free laborers, slaveholders and abolitionists met on what historian Barbara Jeanne Fields calls the "middle ground." Such a setting, where different economies, politics, cultures, and ethics mingled, has high potential for historical drama. In recent studies focused on the South, Fields, William W. Freehling, and Merton L. Dillon describe what that potential meant for black and white southerners in terms of race relations, political culture, and hopes and fears about emancipation. But in histories of the antislavery movement, the border region has become a deserted theater littered with discarded premises like so many crumpled playbills. Theories that the movement began in the upper South, that strong emancipationist sentiment existed there prior to the rise of immediate abolitionism in the North, that a northward diaspora of antislavery southerners helped shape the northern movement, that a creditable wing of northern abolitionism existed in the border region after 1831, and that a well-organized underground railroad helped slaves escape from it have all been dismissed or relegated to romance and legend.[1]

Several of these theories have been justly discarded. Others are more viable than is commonly supposed. All of them preserve an abolitionist perception that it was necessary to make progress against slavery in the South where it existed, rather than simply spreading antislavery sentiments among northerners who controlled no slaves.[2] This chapter explores the development of these various theories from their antebellum origins to their present status among historians. The aim of this exploration is to establish parameters for the substantive chapters, dealing with northern abolitionism and the South, which follow.

The abolitionists themselves were of two minds concerning the role of the South in the antislavery movement. Individual leaders contended simultaneously that the South was accessible to northern-based antislavery efforts and that it was not. Arguments that the movement began in the South and that significant antislavery sentiment continued to exist there supported hopes that various forms of moral suasion could lead quickly to general emancipation. Meanwhile portrayals of the South as a closed society that did not permit free discussion or dissent served to justify abolitionists and their allies in helping slaves to escape, advocating disunion or federal action against slavery, building sectional political parties, and eventually supporting a war to end slavery.[3]

The tendency of abolitionists to embrace conflicting views of the receptivity of southern whites to antislavery efforts is reflected in the frequency of paradoxical statements on that issue by historians of the sectional conflict. For example, Herman E. von Holst, writing in 1881 of the antebellum decades, held on the one hand "that the [white] masses [of the border region] everywhere still lay under the ban of slaveocracy, and would perhaps remain so till they were forcibly freed by an outside hand." On the other, Holst noted that the region had strong ties to the free states and commented, "Here and there the number of discerning ones was great enough to enable them to come forward openly, and to cause the slaveholders to look forward to the future with gloomy anxiety."[4] Holst's keen appreciation of the complexity of the forces affecting slavery on the middle ground anticipated the more recent studies of the issue. His embrace of a paradox reflects that complexity and helps to explain the abolitionists' bifurcated outlook and historians' shifting theories concerning southern antislavery action in the abolitionist movement.

During the first third of the twentieth century two giants of the profession, Albert Bushnell Hart and Gilbert H. Barnes, began the process of defining abolitionism as an essentially northern enterprise in its field of operation and in its origins. In 1906 Hart emphasized that after the mid-1830s, when abolitionist efforts to propagandize the South through a great postal campaign met fierce resistance, northern antislavery advocates concentrated on transforming public opinion in their own section in regard to slavery. Nearly three decades later Barnes accurately directed historians to explore the roots of American immediatism in the religious revivalism and organized benevolence that swept the North in the early nineteenth century. These insights, strengthened by more recent scholarship, led by the 1970s and 1980s to a pervasive view of abolitionism as a movement more concerned with the North than with the South, a movement in which slavery had acquired largely symbolic meaning in the context of northern psychological, social, and political development. At least one prominent historian concluded that abolitionism had no direct impact on the sectional conflict.[5]

According to this view, the movement in the United States for the immediate abolition of slavery, associated with William Lloyd Garrison's initiation of the *Liberator* in 1831 and the establishment of the AASS in 1833, was alien to the South and had a positive impact only on the North. The concept of an inaccessible South had become dominant, and interpretations that emphasized serious southern involvement in the antislavery movement appeared absurd.[6]

But an older tradition in historical literature suggested that the South was accessible to antislavery influences because immediate abolitionism had begun there. An artifact of antebellum optimism for peaceful change, never dominant and in most respects factually incorrect, this tradition reflects persistent efforts to find the meaning of the antislavery movement in the South.

In an early history of the movement, published in 1852, veteran abolitionist William Goodell recognized John Rankin of Tennessee as the pioneer formulator of the doctrine of immediate emancipation, which was at the heart of militant northern abolitionism from the 1830s through the Civil War. Goodell said that Rankin in the early 1820s had denounced the inherent sinfulness of slavery and advocated the "duty of its present abandonment." Following the war, Samuel J. May, an associate of Garrison, and Henry Wilson, a leading Radical Republican, made similar assessments of Rankin and other southern abolitionists of the 1810s and 1820s. Wilson linked northern abolitionism to earlier efforts of ministers in Kentucky and Tennessee, whom he said "proclaimed with great clearness and force the distinctive doctrines of modern abolition."[7]

For Goodell, May, and Wilson, as well as for the less partisan historians who followed them in the late nineteenth century, the chief conduit of antislavery activism from the South to the North was Benjamin Lundy. A northern-born Quaker, Lundy was the most active abolitionist in the South in the 1820s. He published his weekly newspaper, *The Genius of Universal Emancipation*, in Jonesboro, Tennessee, and Baltimore, and he organized local antislavery societies throughout the upper South. Impressed more by Lundy's moral tone than by his gradualism and affinity for schemes to expatriate freed slaves, early historians of abolitionism acknowledged his impact on the beginnings of the antislavery movement in New England and especially on its leader, Garrison, who briefly assisted Lundy in Baltimore. Former political abolitionist Austin Willey of Maine claimed that Lundy favored "Universal Immediate Emancipation" in the 1820s and called him the "morning star of Liberty." A less passionate Holst described Lundy as the "immediate precursor, and, in a certain sense, the father of the abolitionists."[8]

The tradition that the antebellum northern antislavery movement rested on southern foundations attracted considerable support among professional historians in the twentieth century. As the century began Hart and, especially, his student Alice Dana Adams embraced the theme. Hart contended that Rankin, Lundy, and other southern abolitionists prior to 1831 used "substantially the same arguments" as "later abolitionists." Adams argued that an active antislavery movement, distinct from the ACS, existed in the upper South during decades when antislavery sentiment in New England was dormant. She contended that between 1821 and 1831 southern antislavery advocates were so "aggressive" and "uncompromising" that the beginning of the great struggle over slavery "might be dated a decade earlier than it is usually reckoned."[9]

More recently Dwight L. Dumond, James Brewer Stewart, and Merton L. Dillon recognized a positive relationship between southern abolitionism before 1831 and northern immediatism thereafter. In books published in 1939 and 1961 Dumond—the leading historian of the antislavery movement of his era—traced the northern abolitionists' immediatism to "the pioneering efforts of three Southern Presbyterian clergymen," Charles Osborn, Elihu Embree, and Rankin. Stewart in 1973 supported those historians who, he said, "have argued, correctly, for the continuity which existed between antislavery thought of the upper South in the 1820s and the doctrines of northern abolitionists after 1830." Relying on extensive primary research in pamphlet literature, Stewart said that southern evangelicals formulated abolitionist arguments based on Christian and republican precepts that were later adopted by northerners. But the most complete statement of the southern origins thesis appeared in Dillon's 1966 biography of Lundy. Dillon contended that Lundy's abolitionism derived from natives of Virginia, Kentucky, and especially Tennessee, and that Lundy in 1828 initiated an effort to spread their ideas to New England, directly influencing Garrison in the process. The abolitionists of the upper South, Dillon argued, laid the foundations of northern immediatism by breaking with the racist colonizationists, developing "various techniques of antislavery propaganda," and establishing organizations. As recently as 1989 Herbert Aptheker endorsed the tradition that there was "a direct line" from Tennessee abolitionists Osborn and Embree to Lundy to Garrison.[10]

There were, however, from the start serious flaws in the southern origins thesis. Abolitionists who wrote histories of their movement contradicted themselves concerning its origins, and such contradictions persisted among later historians. While Goodell, May, Wilson, and others mentioned southern beginnings of abolitionism, they put more emphasis on its exclusively northern roots. Goodell anticipated Barnes in linking the movement to northern benevolent institutions and northern evangelicalism. May and Wilson raised questions concerning the relevance of their discussion of southern origins by insisting that there was no *real* American antislavery movement before Garrison began publishing the *Liberator*. A generation later Hart recognized southern pioneers of abolitionism while simultaneously insisting that "Garrisonian Abolitionism" of the 1830s was fundamentally different from what came before.[11]

In fact Goodell, May, Wilson, and Hart were aware that southern antislavery advocates prior to 1831 were conservatives. The southerners were not immediatists. Instead, they advocated gradual reform and the expatriation of free blacks. In contrast, northern immediatists demanded radical change and racial justice for blacks in the United States.[12] That southern gradualism could engender immediatism in the North is a dubious proposition, and it may be that Hart and his predecessors' exaggerated portrayals of southern abolitionists as immediatists constituted an effort to bridge the differences.

That very little evidence exists to substantiate such portrayals has been clear since 1882 when there was a scholarly confrontation between George W. Julian, a former Radical Republican from Indiana, and Oliver Johnson, formerly a Garrisonian journalist. Julian, in a weakly argued and poorly documented article published in the *International Review*, maintained that Osborn began immediate abolitionism in the United States in Tennessee in the 1810s. Johnson, acting out of loyalty to his old leader, responded that there was no evidence that Osborn had embraced immediatism prior to the mid-1830s—a number of years after Garrison and more than a decade after Osborn had left the South. In the process of demolishing Julian's argument, Johnson relegated Osborn, Lundy, and others who had acted against slavery in the South before 1831 to a generation of ineffective gradualists. They had been superseded, he argued, when Garrison was "raised up by Providence" to unilaterally initiate the radical immediatist campaign against slavery from the North.[13]

There were also problems in characterizing Lundy as a southern abolitionist. Unlike other contemporary historians, who emphasized Lundy's debt to southern antislavery advocates, Goodell and Radical Republican journalist Horace Greeley considered him to be a northern figure. Greeley, for example, said that a tract Lundy wrote in Ohio several years *before* he began his antislavery work in the South contained "the germ of the entire anti-Slavery movement." In addition several early historians of the movement contended that it was the shock to Lundy's *northern* sensibilities when as a young man he first witnessed the slave trade in Wheeling, Virginia, not the enlightenment of southern dissenters, that led to his antislavery career.[14]

When in 1908 Alice Dana Adams continued the tradition of investigating southern antecedents of northern abolitionism, her work demonstrated an ambivalence similar to that of her predecessors. While her main thesis was that southerners in the 1820s pioneered the northern antislavery movement, near the end of her book she recognized that the southerners were profoundly different from their successors. Unlike earlier writers, however, she denied that the northern movement was an improvement. Rather she unearthed an old southern myth that a native, well-mannered, gradual, southern antislavery effort with great potential for eventual, peaceful success had been overwhelmed in the 1830s by a justifiable southern white reaction to fanatical and unrealistic northern immediatists.[15]

Adams's reservations concerning her main thesis were in accord with the views of the great southern historian Ulrich B. Phillips, who by 1904 had revived antebellum southern portrayals of slavery as a benevolent institution that was gradually civilizing barbaric Africans. More forthrightly than Adams, Phillips contended that southern whites would have peacefully ended slavery during the nineteenth century had fanatical northerners not instigated a needless war. This view, of course, implicitly denied the possibility of continuity between southern gradualists and northern immediatists.[16]

Phillips directly influenced studies of antislavery efforts in Georgia, Virginia, and Missouri. These studies, undertaken in the 1930s, suggested that very conservative southern campaigns for amelioration and colonization would have eventually brought a peaceful extinction of slavery if northerners had not intervened. The Missouri study went so far as to claim that southern gradualists became defenders of perpetual slavery in response to northern immediatism.[17] But far more important than Phillips's impact on these state-level studies was the similarity of his perspective to that of the major school of Revisionist and Consensus historians who dominated American historiography from the 1930s through the 1950s.

Influenced by the horrors of World War I, by the theory that irrationality rather than fundamental interests led nations into war, and by the assumption that agreement rather than conflict marked American history, Avery O. Craven, James G. Randall, and others argued that the Civil War was an avoidable tragedy. It came, they contended, because fanatical northern abolitionists and their political allies undermined a bisectional consensus that would have allowed the South to work out the problem of slavery on its own. In Craven and Randall's analysis irresponsible northern abolitionists could have little to do with a southern antislavery movement that Adams, Phillips, and others described as conservative and responsible. Instead, in order to explain the origins of northern abolitionism, the Revisionists relied on the work of Phillips's student Barnes, who traced immediatism to northern evangelicalism. Subsequently, historians who were more friendly to the immediatists agreed.[18]

Although Barnes's associate Dumond clung to an old theory that a northward diaspora of southern abolitionists helped shape the northern antislavery movement, most of the movement's historians from the 1930s through the 1950s were silent concerning early nineteenth-century opposition to slavery in the South. In his sympathetic synthesis of antislavery studies published in 1960, Louis Filler concluded that while there had been antislavery spokespeople in the South before 1831, they were not immediatists and there was "little evidence that the South was building an efficient antislavery movement."[19]

Therefore, when Dillon in 1966 described Lundy as a conduit of southern antislavery thought to the North and Stewart in 1973 saw continuity between southern evangelical abolitionists of the 1820s and northern immediatists of the 1830s, they were—as Stewart acknowledged in his article—going against considerable accumulated opinion. Even as they wrote, each conceded that the southerners they treated were—judged by their gradualism, their distaste for blacks, and their inability to organize effectively—unlikely role models for northern immediatists. Both quickly repudiated their arguments—Dillon in 1969 and Stewart in 1976—and Stewart probably spoke for Dillon as well when he said that while "there were a few militant antislavery spokesmen in the upper South in the 1820s . . . their influence on young New Englanders [who became immediatists] was negligible."[20]

With these words, Stewart put an end to a long tradition of historical inquiry into southern white origins of northern abolitionism. Never uncontested, the tradition remains important for two reasons. It preserves what abolitionists liked to believe about the southern orientation of their efforts, and it demonstrates a persistent belief among historians that antislavery action in the South warrants investigation. In fact, if the issue of *white* southern origins of northern abolitionism has been decided in the negative, the issue of *black* southern origins may be opening. Although African-American historians and others have noted the role of free blacks in the beginnings of immediate abolitionism in the United States, historians almost universally have treated the slaves themselves as passive entities to be

freed. Recently, however, Herbert Aptheker—briefly—and Dillon—
at length—have argued that slaves, by resisting their masters, inspired
the beginnings of organized abolitionism in the North and profoundly
influenced its development. The subject of the impact of slave actions
on northern abolitionism will attract the attention of others, and this
study of northern abolitionism and the South includes a chapter as-
sessing what abolitionists believed slaves had done and would do in
behalf of their own liberation.[21]

Very closely related to the question of southern antecedents of
northern abolitionism is the issue of the strength and significance of
pre-1831 southern opposition to slavery in the context of the South
itself. Dillon, Stewart, and others turned away from exploring southern roots of immediatism primarily because by the late 1960s it was
clear that causes deeply rooted in New England culture were sufficient to explain northern abolitionist commitment.[22] But they were
also influenced by a forceful questioning of the very existence of a
southern antislavery movement.

Benjamin Lundy's estimate in 1827 that there were over one hundred antislavery societies in the South and only a fourth as many in
the North convinced many historians that not only was there a southern antislavery movement in the 1820s but a vital one. In 1890, William Birney, a son of abolitionist leader James G. Birney, added to
traditional regard for Rankin, Embree, and Osborn by writing a de-
tailed chronicle of antislavery activity in Tennessee and Maryland in
the 1820s, and Adams's study, published the following decade, provided apparently irrefutable evidence of extensive abolitionist organization throughout the upper South. As late as the 1960s Dillon
argued that "stronger and more persistent antislavery effort could
be found after 1815 in parts of the nonslaveholding upland South"
than in New England. Antislavery societies in Tennessee and North
Carolina, he said, were among the strongest in the country in the
mid-1820s. Many historians have assumed that a southern reaction
to Nat Turner's rebellion of 1831 and to the rise of militant abolitionism in the North destroyed this vigorous indigenous southern antislavery effort.[23]

But others have contended that even before 1831 the South was
too inhospitable to dissent to allow a real antislavery movement to
exist within its bounds. Also—just as was the case with arguments
for southern antecedents of northern abolitionism—several propo-

nents of the existence of a strong southern antislavery movement in the 1820s displayed considerable ambivalence. Some early historians of the movement, such as May and Wendell P. and Francis J. Garrison, who recognized contributions by southern abolitionists, portrayed southern antislavery societies as weak and in decline by the 1820s. John Bach McMaster in 1902 questioned the relative strength of the pre-1831 southern abolitionists by noting that there were twice as many northern antislavery newspapers in the late 1820s as there were southern. Adams and Phillips, who claimed southern whites would have peacefully abolished slavery if northerners had not interfered, paradoxically described southern abolitionism as extremely weak. Adams actually concluded that the southern movement prior to 1831 was timid and ineffectual. Its "conciliation and persuasion . . . in twenty years accomplished practically nothing," she observed. Similarly, in 1966 Dillon combined remarks on the strength of southern abolitionism in the 1820s with others on its weakness.[24]

This long story of discrepancy climaxed in 1969 with the publication of an article by Gordon E. Finnie that settled the issue and helped quell interest in post-1831 southern abolitionism as well. Finnie, who taught at West Georgia College, demonstrated the extreme weakness of antislavery organization in each of the states of the upper South. What had sometimes been described as a single pre-1831 southern antislavery movement, Finnie indicated, was an amalgamation of a tiny number of immediatists, a slightly larger group who advocated gradual emancipation combined with expatriation, and a much larger group associated with the ACS who desired to eliminate free blacks as a means of *strengthening* slavery. Because racist, proslavery sentiment was so pervasive among these groups, Finnie warned, "historians need to be extremely cautious when making generalizations about the extent to which *antislavery* sentiment actually existed in the upper South." The tiny minority that desired to end slavery was—unlike its northern counterpart—cut off from centers of power and even the colonizationists were few, their organizations ephemeral.[25]

Finnie concluded that since there was no real southern antislavery movement in the 1820s there could be no "Great Reaction" against such a movement in the 1830s. Finnie hoped to destroy the myth that the rise of northern immediatism in the 1830s had precipitated an understandable southern white reaction against a promising native gradualist movement. He achieved this goal, but, while there was no strong antislavery movement in the South to attack, there was a southern reaction against dissent, free blacks, and what many whites regarded as too lenient treatment of slaves. Rooted in long-standing insecurities in the southern-white psyche and developing *before* the rise of northern immediatism, reactionary efforts to silence dissent grew more pervasive in the 1830s following Nat Turner's revolt. Although the weak criticism of slavery that existed in the upper South constituted no real threat to the institution, it became more difficult to discuss the issue and some dissidents left the region for the North.[26]

What then of antislavery activity in the South after 1831? Kenneth M. Stampp established in 1943 that, in spite of a reaction involving physical force, oppressive legislation, and proslavery propaganda, slavery's defenders failed to entirely destroy such activity. Stampp exaggerated in claiming that "substantial groups" of antislavery activists continued to exist in the South, but organized abolitionist sentiment did indeed exist there until the eve of the Civil War.[27] This sentiment should not be confused with the continuation of weak, essentially proslavery colonizationism that Finnie described. Rather the more resolute southern abolitionists of the period from 1831 to 1861 had ties closer to Garrison, Theodore Weld, Lewis Tappan, and Gerrit Smith than to Embree, Rankin, or Osborn, and they were taken seriously by northerners and southerners alike.

In a pattern at odds with their exaggeration of the importance of pre-1831 southern abolitionists, historians of the sectional conflict have been slow to recognize the stature of these later southern advocates of emancipation. Throughout the nineteenth century, historians rarely mentioned antislavery activity in the border region during the three decades prior to the Civil War. There were several reasons for this. One was that claims that dissent had been eradicated in the South during the 1830s supported the northern view of an aggressive slaveocracy. Another was that northern-based historians with limited access to unpublished southern materials tended to focus on antislavery political organization in the North from 1840 through 1860, neglecting continued antislavery agitation and the South. Most significantly, the failure of southern abolitionists in the 1840s and 1850s to make tangible progress in their section prior to the violent destruction of slavery in the Civil War made them appear quixotic. Such disdain for southerners who worked in their section to promote emancipation has continued throughout the twentieth century, despite a greater appreciation of social and cultural history, despite much wider access to southern abolitionist materials, and despite an awareness that our knowledge of the Civil War distorts our appreciation of antebellum perspectives.[28]

Historians as different in outlook as Ulrich B. Phillips and James Brewer Stewart have stressed the marginality of abolitionism in the South after 1831. According to Stewart southern abolitionists of that period were simply "anomalies." It was, however, Carl N. Degler in 1973 who provided the most extensive application of Finnie's description of an extremely weak southern antislavery movement to the post-1831 years. Degler described antislavery efforts in the upper South in the decades following Nat Turner's revolt as "peripheral" and "minuscule." Southern opinion, he observed, tolerated them only when there was no perceived threat to slavery. Although he acknowledged that this later southern antislavery movement had its intellectual origins in the North, he emphasized the alienation of southern abolitionists from their northern counterparts. Most of the southerners, he contended, expressed "doubts and reservations" about slavery, not firm opposition. Assuming that all northern abolitionists shared a common view, he argued that the southerners generally differed from them in emphasizing economics not morality, white not black advancement, and perpetuating racism not ending it.[29]

Even historians who have been more sympathetic to post-1831 southern abolitionists as committed reformers have portrayed them chiefly as victims of southern intolerance, not as serious threats to the slave system. From Henry Wilson and Wendell and Francis Garrison through Alice Felt Tyler, Clement Eaton, and Dwight L. Dumond, scholars have balanced the bravery of slavery's southern opponents against their "folly."[30]

It is not surprising that twentieth-century historians have devoted more attention to those who left the South during those decades to become abolitionists in the North than to those who stood their ground. Such antislavery figures as Angelina and Sarah Grimké from South Carolina, James G. Birney from Kentucky, Moncure D. Conway from Virginia, and Hinton R. Helper from North Carolina have been the subjects of biographies that define them as southerners while emphasizing their work in the North. Helper in particular is frequently cited as a representative of a viciously racist form of southern abolitionism. This is at least mildly ironic in that, although Helper's Negrophobia was a product of his southern background, he did not begin to write against slavery until he moved to New York City and had minimal contacts with abolitionists who remained in the South. Meanwhile, racially enlightened individuals such as John G. Fee, Joseph Evans Snodgrass, Samuel M. Janney, and Daniel Worth, who either remained in or returned to their native South to oppose slavery, have received little notice.[31]

The major apparent exception to the rule that historians have not given post-1831 southern abolitionists their due is Cassius M. Clay, Kentucky's leading abolitionist from 1841 to 1861. Clay has served historians as the quintessential southern abolitionist ever since Holst devoted several pages of his multivolume history to him. The subject of numerous articles, Clay's career has also been analyzed in an biography published by David L. Smiley in 1962, and in a biographical sketch by Jane H. and William H. Pease published in 1972.[32]

But the best of this recent scholarship has made Clay a symbol of the futility, isolation, and insignificance of border slave state abolitionism from 1840 to 1861. While Holst portrayed Clay sympathetically as a significant antislavery force in the South, Smiley and the Peases emphasize his alienation from northern abolitionism, his lack of moral commitment, his racism, and his inconsistency. They have attributed his antislavery efforts to a vain and foolish ambition for political advancement.[33]

In contrast, a few historians have perceived more than folly in the actions of Clay and other southern abolitionists of the late antebellum era. Probing deeply into the culture of the border region, such historians portray post-1831 southern antislavery advocates as bridges carrying abolitionism into the South—a process that encouraged northern opponents of slavery and frightened slaveholders. Among these historians in the late twentieth century are Ira Berlin, who has written on southern free blacks, and Freehling, who has explored the roots of the secession movement. A century earlier Holst anticipated their most significant insights. Holst and Freehling, for example, describe Clay as a figure who frightened slaveholders throughout the South. Holst says Clay was "the best hated man in the South" of the 1840s because in 1845 he briefly demonstrated that nonslaveholding southern whites would respond to strong antislavery leadership. They did so, according to Freehling, because economic conditions, political culture, and the establishment of "a somewhat open society" had led most Kentuckians and other inhabitants of the border region to oppose slavery. Earlier Berlin stressed a moral factor, tracing changes not to politics and economics but to the persistence of antislavery sentiments associated with religious revivalism from the 1820s through the 1840s.

Several historians have portrayed the 1849 campaign, led by Clay, Fee, and Robert J. Breckinridge, to place a gradual emancipation provision in Kentucky's constitution as a dismal failure. Holst, Berlin, and Freehling, however, regard the campaign, which elected no more than two delegates to the state constitutional convention, as a sign of antislavery progress. Berlin calls it one of the "major assaults on slavery," and Freehling maintains that it ended in a compromise that left slavery weaker in Kentucky. In all, Freehling persuasively describes a border region well on its way to emancipation by the late 1840s. This, he says, brought excited warnings from proslavery advocates and encouraged secessionist strategies to block further antislavery progress.[34]

Although Berlin and Freehling, among twentieth-century historians, are exceptional in the importance they perceive in southern abolitionism, they accept the common wisdom that slavery's southern opponents were alienated from their northern counterparts. Freehling, for example, emphasizes—in rather old-fashioned terms—that Clay was "no fanatic seeking martyrdom," that he and his associates were economically rather than morally motivated, and that they were racists committed to expelling blacks from the border region.[35]

It is possible to carry such distinctions too far. Birney, Clay, Fee, Worth, and other southern abolitionists had close ties to northern abolitionist reform culture. Samuel May recalled that Garrison and the Lane Seminary debates influenced Birney and that northern abolitionist leader Theodore Weld converted Birney to immediatism. Weld also inspired Tennessee-born David Nelson, who preached abolition and served as an agent of the AASS in Missouri in 1835-36. Clay credited Garrison with awakening his moral sense and never ceased to praise the Bostonian as the beacon of the antislavery cause. Similarly, Maryland abolitionist Joseph Evans Snodgrass attributed his efforts on behalf of abolition and black rights in part to the influence of northern abolitionists James and Lucretia Mott. The Motts also influenced Quaker abolitionist Samuel M. Janney of Virginia, and two decidedly moralistic southern abolitionists—Fee of Kentucky and Worth of North Carolina—acted as agents of the northern-based American Missionary Association (AMA) and endorsed the radical abolitionist politics of Gerrit Smith. Thomas Garrett of Delaware was friendly with Garrison as well as an active participant in underground railroad activities with northern black abolitionists.[36]

Moreover, the southerners' racism and emphasis on white economic interests in opposition to slavery did not alienate them from the northern antislavery movement. All northern abolitionists appealed to white self-interest, and racism permeated all sections of antebellum white society. It influenced northern as well as southern abolitionists, and delineating the role of racial bias within the antislavery movement was a major occupation among American historians in the 1970s. One might assume that racism was stronger among southern abolitionists than northern, but Fee and Snodgrass were racially enlightened by the standards of their time, and Clay does not deserve his ranking with Hinton R. Helper as an extreme Negrophobe.[37]

If historians have mistakenly portrayed antebellum southern abolitionists as estranged from their northern counterparts, the same historians have nevertheless recognized that the post-1831 southerners positively influenced the northerners. From Samuel May to the present, students of the antislavery movement have noted the encouragement the simple existence of southern abolitionists gave antislavery northerners. Immediatists found tangible evidence that their efforts were succeeding in the conversion of slaveholders like Birney and Clay. The appearance of southern opponents of slavery in the upper South confirmed Free Soiler and Republican assumptions concerning the superiority of free labor over slave labor and the inevitable southward march of free institutions.

Beginning with Louis Filler in 1960, however, historians have stressed the irony of northern antislavery activists reliance on such evidence for encouragement. The irony is clear in Birney's frequently quoted remark that northerners did not understand the "tenacity" of slaveholders. Filler, Smiley, Degler, and the Peases argue that Birney, Clay, and the others were not typical slaveholders, that very few southerners followed them, and that they were therefore insignificant. In addition, such historians contend, those who like Clay remained in the South were not real abolitionists. They produced unfounded optimism among their northern admirers and inevitably disappointed them.[38]

But were veteran propagandists like the northern abolitionists really naive about cultural differences between southern opponents of slavery and themselves? Were they not able to use southern abolitionists to the advantage of their cause? Chapter 2 of this book discusses how the northerners developed a complex image of a southern emancipator, which they manipulated to serve a variety of promotional purposes. Also one can no longer assume that the border slave state abolitionists were powerless at home. As Dillon pointed out in 1974 and Freehling established convincingly in 1990, it was "not unthinkable" during the antebellum years that general emancipation would occur in each of the border slave states in the near future. Certainly Freehling establishes that forces for change in the upper South were powerful enough to make Clay a significant figure in the minds of slavery's staunch defenders.[39]

Change in the border region also encouraged several forms of direct northern intervention in southern affairs during the 1840s and 1850s, which constitute another category of southern antislavery action. Such efforts, including missionary activities, plans to colonize portions of the South with northern settlers, and plots to go south to help slaves escape are discussed in their relationship to northern abolitionist reform culture in several chapters of this book. Missionary activities, which from the 1830s to 1861 attempted to spread antislavery sentiment in South by word-of-mouth and the distribution of printed material, constituted an important continuation of abolitionist belief in an accessible South. Abolitionist involvement in slave escapes reflected the contrary belief that the South could not be reached by appeals to morality or reason. And the schemes to establish northern colonies contained elements of each point of view as they involved efforts to influence the South by example and to aggressively change the South by physically importing northern culture.

Portrayals of early nineteenth-century southern abolitionists as the pioneers of northern immediatism and of the pre-1831 southern antislavery movement as a significant threat to slavery were always weak and have been correctly discarded. They too often distracted historians from the more subtle and pervasive forces in New England culture that led to the first determined efforts in the North to oppose black bondage. But by centering so intensely for so long on abolitionism as a function of northern religious, economic, cultural, and behavioral developments, scholars have lost touch with the movement's real concern with slavery in the South. Well after the termination of their postal campaign in the mid-1830s, northern abolitionists encouraged native southern whites to become emancipators and promoted direct action by northerners against slavery in the South. To northern abolitionists, none of whom perceived civil war to be inevitable, the often overlooked and disparaged southern abolitionists of the late antebellum decades offered considerable hope. That hope shaped the development of the antislavery movement in the North, and, in turn, northern abolitionist support for aggressive antislavery efforts in the South directly influenced a defensive reaction among southern whites.

Chapter Two

AN IMAGE OF A SOUTHERN WHITE EMANCIPATOR

In 1857 Hiram Foote was a twenty-five-year veteran in the antislavery cause. He had lectured against slavery in New York, Ohio, Illinois, and Wisconsin. But to his mind none of his efforts measured up to those of William S. Bailey, an obscure opponent of slavery who, with the aid of his family, published an abolitionist newspaper in the slaveholding commonwealth of Kentucky. Foote pictured the Baileys, "father, mother and children, even the little ones, toiling amid obloquy, reproach, and savage foes, to redeem their noble State from the dreadful sin and curse of slavery! Mortgaging the homestead, working till midnight . . . making . . . [their] house a citadel where the weapons of truth must be defended by the weapons of death; and that not for the sake of praise, but to honor God, to save the slaves and slaveholders, and wipe from Kentucky its foulest blot of shame."[1] The product of a sentimental age, Foote's image of one southern advocate of emancipation was not unlike the image northern abolitionists held of southern emancipationists in general, including Foote's belief that they "must triumph" in the end.

As chapter 1 indicates, historians of the antislavery movement have not shared Foote's estimation of the importance of William S. Bailey and other southern advocates of emancipation. The antislavery movement that existed in the upper South was a pale reflection of northern abolitionism. Southern antislavery advocates were generally more conservative than their free state counterparts and were even less successful in convincing their white neighbors to actively oppose slavery than northern abolitionists were in convincing theirs. That southern abolitionists were insignificant in the sectional struggle over slavery is the consensus among historians.[2]

Yet the image, reflected in Hiram Foote's portrait of the Bailey family, of previously indifferent or hostile southern whites carrying the antislavery cause into the South, played a crucial role in abolitionist reform culture. As the northern abolitionists created an image of a southern white emancipator, they revealed much concerning how they hoped to reach their goal, how highly they valued southern antislavery heroes, how their cultural insularity led them to patronize those same heroes, how sophisticated was their rhetoric, and how faith in a southern emancipator supported their commitment to peaceful means.

Most important, the image substantiates the thesis that—despite the fiercely negative southern reaction to their efforts to propagandize the South in the mid-1830s—northern abolitionists remained focused on and involved in the South during the following two decades. It is impossible to read northern abolitionist newspapers from this period without noticing the frequent coverage of southern antislavery developments. While abolitionists worked to create a northern majority in favor of immediate abolition, they never forgot that the success of their effort depended on progress in the South. They lavished praise, criticism, and money on southern advocates of emancipation because they regarded them as crucial to such progress.[3]

Between 1834, when the first white southern antislavery hero emerged, and 1860, when hope for peaceful antislavery progress in the South ended, representatives of the various abolitionist factions shared nearly identical perceptions of southern white emancipators. Garrisonians such as Sydney Howard Gay and Garrison himself, church-oriented abolitionists such as Lewis Tappan and Joshua Leavitt, radical political abolitionists such as William Goodell and Gerrit Smith, and abolitionists such as Gamaliel Bailey, who came to advocate broad-based political action against slavery, all held similar views. Their image of a southern emancipator also remained remarkably stable throughout the period.

All of these abolitionists were quite selective of the individuals they drew upon to develop the image. They derived it not from the broad spectrum of antislavery opinion in the South but from a few persons whom they believed represented the thrust of abolitionism in that region. Most prominent among them were James G. Birney, Cassius M. Clay, Joseph Evans Snodgrass, John C. Vaughan, John G. Fee, and William S. Bailey. Northern abolitionist comments on these

individuals constitute the main source for the image of a southern
emancipator as it is reconstructed here.

A number of individuals who have been identified with antislavery opinion in the South are excluded for several reasons. Robert J.
Breckinridge of Kentucky and other adherents of the ACS were so
conservative that northern abolitionists regarded them as enemies
rather than friends of emancipation. Others, such as Sarah and
Angelina Grimké of South Carolina, left the South before northern
abolitionists became aware of them, and a few, such as Samuel M.
Janney of Virginia, never aroused significant interest in the North.
There were also those such as Thomas Garrett, Benjamin Lundy, and
Gamaliel Bailey who were actually northern abolitionists working in
the South.[4]

Finally, there were no African Americans whom abolitionists identified as southern leaders for peaceful emancipation. Of course, the
major reason for this was that southern communities did not tolerate
black antislavery spokespeople. In addition, northern abolitionists
imagined that black leaders in the South would follow the pattern of
Haiti's Toussaint L'Ouverture and Virginia's Nat Turner by attempting to liberate their people by force rather than by peaceful means.[5]

Of the six individuals whose activities in the slave states drew
extended comment from northern abolitionists, three—James G.
Birney, Cassius M. Clay, and John G. Fee—are relatively well-known
figures. All three were prominent for their activities in Kentucky, and
Birney had also been active against slavery in Alabama. Although
Birney, who was born in 1792, was considerably older than Clay, who
was born in 1810, and Fee, who was born in 1816, they had much in
common. All three came from slaveholding families, and Birney and
Clay had inherited large numbers of slaves. All were educated in the
North—Birney at Princeton, Clay at Yale, and Fee at Miami University and the Lane Theological Seminary in Ohio. Each of them based
his opposition to slavery on Christian precepts, although Fee's religious commitment was the strongest and Clay's has been obscured
by his biographer. Birney and Clay were aristocratic, and they both
began their careers as slaveholders who criticized slavery in their
state legislatures.

But there were significant differences among them as well. Birney served as an agent of the ACS in 1832 and 1833 before rejecting it, while Clay only flirted with the organization in the mid-1840s, and Fee always opposed it. Also, while both Birney and Clay freed their slaves and Fee repudiated his slaveholding inheritance, only Birney and Fee became immediatists.

Birney was unsuccessful in an attempt to establish an antislavery newspaper in Kentucky in 1835. Thereafter he resided in the North, where he served as the Liberty party presidential candidate in 1840 and 1844. Clay succeeded in publishing his weekly *True American* in 1845 and weathered a mob effort to suppress it in August of that year. He and Fee remained active in the antislavery cause in Kentucky until the eve of the Civil War. By the 1850s Clay was a leading national advocate of the Republican party, while Fee concentrated on preaching an antislavery gospel, distributing antislavery materials to whites, and providing Bibles to slaves. Fee also became increasingly radical in his political views. In the mid-1850s he adopted the position that statutes that supported slavery should not be observed. This cost him the support of Clay and the Kentucky Republicans, and in late 1859 proslavery forces drove him from the state.[6]

The remaining individuals—Joseph Evans Snodgrass, John C. Vaughan, and William S. Bailey—who made major contributions to the northern abolitionists' image of a southern white emancipator, are now obscure figures. In their time they were best known as journalists. Virginia-born Snodgrass and Vaughan of South Carolina were former slaveholders who became advocates of gradual emancipation as a result of their strong religious convictions and the influence of northern abolitionists. As the editor of the *Baltimore Saturday Visiter* *[sic]* from 1842 to 1847, Snodgrass spoke out mildly but persistently against slavery and in favor of the rights of free blacks. He survived an effort in the Maryland legislature to declare his paper incendiary before he sold out to Gamaliel Bailey's Washington weekly, the *National Era*. In succeeding years Snodgrass made antislavery speeches in Maryland, Virginia, and Delaware. Vaughan, who was an advocate of colonization in 1839, became assistant editor of Clay's *True American* in 1846. When Clay enlisted in the Mexican War later in 1846, Vaughan edited the paper until its suspension in September. The following June he began publishing the *Examiner* in Louisville, Kentucky, as an advocate of gradual, compensated emancipation. He left the *Examiner* and the South the following year to become editor of the *Cleveland True Democrat* and a Free Soil politician.[7]

Unlike the others who served as prototypes for the abolitionist image of a southern emancipator, William S. Bailey was not born into a slaveholding family nor even in a slave state. He was from Ohio and moved to Newport, Kentucky, in 1839. An "infidel" in religion, a Democrat in politics, and a "cotton machinist, and a steam engine builder by trade," he had been a southerner for over a decade before he became an abolitionist in 1850. As editor and proprietor of the *Newport Daily News*—renamed the *Free South* in 1858—he appealed to Kentucky's white laborers to vote to abolish slavery in order to secure better wages for themselves, as well as to help blacks. An active supporter of the Republican party, Bailey also had ties to the Garrisonians and radical political abolitionists. He successfully resisted arson, mob assaults, and an attempt to drive him from the state in 1860.[8]

While these individuals had various backgrounds, motivation, and tactics, they nevertheless cast a coherent image on the minds of northern abolitionists, and Birney was the archetype of that image. Emerging in the public eye in 1834 as a slaveholder who freed his slaves and opposed the ACS's scheme of expatriating free blacks, he had a profound impact. Birney reinforced early abolitionist optimism that slavery could be speedily eradicated. He symbolized the ability of a northern antislavery movement to encourage the rise of southern emancipators, while his southern birth and mild tone undercut slave state arguments that the South faced outside interference by fanatics.[9]

In 1834 and 1835 Birney's image lacked the focus it would later gain. This was because several factors initially prevented abolitionists from perceiving him as a peculiarly *southern* figure. Abolitionists in the early 1830s were so concerned with destroying the credibility of the ACS as an antislavery organization that they frequently stressed Birney's opposition to it rather than his geographic location. Also, in 1834 and 1835 when there was plenty of anti-abolitionist violence in the North, abolitionists were less impressed by Birney's bravery in the face of southern violence than they would be later. Because he left the South before northern abolitionists were fully aware of the degree of southern intransigence, he seemed less exceptional than he would in retrospect. Nevertheless, the main facets of Birney's brief career as an advocate of abolition on slave soil became essential components of the image of a southern emancipator as it developed over the next quarter century.[10]

The most significant component of the image was that southern advocates of emancipation represented progress for the antislavery cause in the South. Enthused with the justice of their cause, northern abolitionists believed that the advance of Christianity and western civilization foreordained the death of slavery. They also believed that pervasive latent antislavery sentiment existed among southern whites, which could be activated by the efforts of determined leaders. Just as Andrew Jackson's supporters portrayed him as a divinely inspired heroic force in establishing democracy, abolitionists assumed God would raise up heroes to implement a providential plan to destroy slavery in the South. Consequently, they persistently viewed southern antislavery advocates as harbingers of total emancipation. New York City abolitionist Lewis Tappan, for example, said of Clay that "Divine Providence is awakening the patriotism of the slaveholders on behalf of the true interests of the nation, and the poor slaves," and Hiram Foote declared that William S. Bailey's cause was God's "and must triumph."[11]

Despite fierce southern white resistance in the 1830s to their efforts to send antislavery literature into the South, northern abolitionists remained persistently optimistic that Birney and those who followed him could carry the movement into that section. But, because each southern emancipator also faced determined opposition, the image of progress against slavery they encouraged among the northerners was a paradoxically static one. Birney was certainly a pioneer in 1834 when Theodore Weld, who had himself initiated abolitionist organization in the West, told him that it was only necessary "for some one to *give the lead*" and scores of southern clergy "would *rally to his standard.*"[12] Yet northern abolitionists of all persuasions made similar assumptions concerning southern emancipators who emerged years after Birney. The northerners greeted them all as pioneers who would achieve rapid success.

In 1845 Sydney Howard Gay of the *National Anti-Slavery Standard* called Cassius M. Clay a "pioneer in this work in the slave States."

Even following the forceful attempt to suppress Clay's *True American* later that year, Gay's fellow-Garrisonians Benjamin and Elizabeth Jones of the *Anti-Slavery Bugle* in Salem, Ohio remained optimistic for rapid antislavery advancement in the border slave states. The Joneses declared it was only necessary to unfurl "the Royal standard of abolitionism" in order to arouse an emancipationist spirit in the South. Similarly, in 1848 the annual report of the AFASS declared that the initiation of John C. Vaughan's *Examiner* gave "new proofs of the rapid spread of anti-slavery views" in Kentucky, and in 1851 the same organization contended that Fee's abolitionist gospel could rapidly transform the slaveholding community. The society asserted that as a result of Fee's efforts "slaveholders will renounce the sin, and endorse a religion that affords no countenance to chattel slavery." Nevertheless, northern abolitionists, as late as 1857, still portrayed Fee as a pioneer, carrying "the torch of freedom into the strongholds of despotism."[13]

On occasion, an abolitionist pointed out that hopes for rapid antislavery progress in the border slave states were ill-founded. Garrison noted in 1835 that the inability of Birney to establish his paper in Kentucky "is strong evidence of the delusion of those who say Kentucky is ripe for emancipation." In 1844 Stephen Pearl Andrews, a Massachusetts abolitionist who had spent years in the deep South, made the essential point that the latent antislavery feeling in the South that northern abolitionists hoped to stir was "cowardly" and "enslaved" to the slaveholding interests that controlled public sentiment in that section.[14]

Even Garrison and Andrews, however, agreed with the essential abolitionist insight that if antislavery progress in the slave states was not bound to be rapid, it would be relentless. In January 1835 the New England Anti-Slavery Society had declared that the existence of southern emancipators demonstrated that "a spirit" was at work in the slave states "which will never rest till it has purified and enlightened the great mass of society, and destroyed every vestige of the system of private despotism within their limits." A decade later, the *Bugle* noted Samuel M. Janney's antislavery efforts in Virginia and predicted that this state's "bold hearted abolitionists" would not cease their agitation until slavery ended.

Therefore, when Clay momentarily disappointed abolitionists by volunteering for what they regarded as a proslavery war against Mexico, they did not despair. Because they believed God and human progress were on their side, they remained optimistic. Edmund Quincy of the Massachusetts Anti-Slavery Society (MASS) spoke for many others when he reacted to Clay's apparent apostasy by predicting that "another and greater deliverer yet to arise in the heart of Slavery . . . [would] cooperate with the besieging hosts that are enclosing it on every side." Even when Kentucky emancipationists suffered a decisive defeat in the election for a state constitutional convention in 1849, abolitionists joined Gamaliel Bailey in the observation that while the progress of truth might be slow, it was certain because the moral strength of the North and Europe invigorated the friends of freedom in the South.[15]

Abolitionist contentions that God and civilization were on their side reflected northern assumptions of cultural and economic superiority over the South. The evident economic infirmity of slavery in the border slave states bolstered such assumptions. But other factors contributed to persistent abolitionist optimism concerning the role of southern emancipators. Northern immediatists considered the emancipators to be peculiarly well suited to carry abolitionism into the South by virtue of their personal relationship to slavery, their knowledge of southern culture, their heroic stature, and their ability to appeal to the interests of white southerners. Northern abolitionists also recognized that agitation in the South—even without tangible results in legislation—placed slaveholders on the defensive. The *Bugle* in 1845 rejoiced that agitation existed in the slave states and equated it with progress toward true antislavery principles. In 1849 Gamaliel Bailey maintained that "free discussion now established [in Kentucky] would rock slavery in a few years," and abolitionists took heart because individuals like Fee, Clay, and William S. Bailey caused periodic excitement.[16]

Antislavery activists, like other people of their time, realized that the key to agitation was a partisan newspaper. Weld was aghast when Birney suggested that he might not start an antislavery paper in Kentucky in 1835. "That paper edited by yourself would give impulse incalculable to our cause," Weld insisted. When Clay announced his intention to publish the *True American* a decade later, Gay's reaction echoed Weld's. "This is the most encouraging sign that has yet greeted us," he said. "An Anti-Slavery paper in a Slave State! Thank God for that." The battle, he predicted was half over when someone established such a paper. Lewis Tappan, Gamaliel Bailey, and Benjamin and Elizabeth Jones all expected Snodgrass's *Visiter* to make the discussion of slavery more acceptable in the Chesapeake region. Following the establishment of Vaughan's *Examiner*, Edmund Quincy, an aristocratic Garrisonian, declared that the paper was a symptom of the breaking of slavery's spell. "A newspaper," he said, "is a more fatal enemy to a false institution than an army."[17]

That southern-born abolitionists were better suited than northerners to carry the movement into the South, and perhaps throughout much of the North as well, was a widely held belief. Slavery's defenders argued persuasively that the South had a right to be let alone to deal with its peculiar institution free from the ignorant meddling of northern fanatics. Colonizationists and other conservative gradualists claimed that northern interference with slavery actually retarded progress toward emancipation. They charged that, except for northern fanaticism, gradual abolition might be underway in the South.[18]

But northern abolitionists believed such charges of fanaticism could not be effectively used against native southerners who advocated emancipation. Slaveholders of high social standing, making economic sacrifices to free their slaves, seemed to the northerners destined to create an image that would belie charges of meddling radicalism. Such an image of responsible, concerned southerners acting for the benefit of their section, they hoped, would attract thousands to the antislavery cause.

When Birney embraced immediatism, William Goodell of the *Emancipator* predicted that "the opinion of one who has been for years a slaveholder, who possesses such knowledge of the whole subject of slavery . . . whose standing in the south-west is so high . . . [must have] a great effect on *southern* minds." One of Birney's correspondents told him that his situation and knowledge precluded charges of "fanaticism" and gave him "great advantages over a northern man." The *New York Tribune* observed in 1845 that "ere long" slavery would be "swept away" by the work of men like Clay, whose "right to interfere with the institution could not be disputed, and whose residence in the Slave States peculiarly qualified them for the work." Abolitionists stressed that the slaveholders' violent reaction to such mild, southern-born emancipationists as Birney, Clay, Snodgrass, and Fee revealed that it was not the abolitionists who were fanatics but the slaveholders themselves.[19]

In a similar manner, Sydney Howard Gay observed that because John C. Vaughan was a southerner he could "command the respect of his countrymen." Gay said that Vaughan knew the character of the southern people, and northern abolitionists understood this to mean that Vaughan and other southern antislavery advocates could address the economic grievances of the section's nonslaveholding whites. Although Garrison and his associates, in particular, discountenanced blatant appeals to white selfishness, they joined other abolitionists in believing an economic emphasis was a legitimate part of the character of a southern emancipator. They had no quarrel with Joshua Leavitt's praise of Clay's appeal to "the free laborers of Kentucky." Clay's "thunder tones" on the issue of Kentucky's failures in the areas of commerce, industry, and education, Leavitt said, would "wake up even the besotted and subjugated 'red-shanks' and 'corn-crackers,' with which slavery peoples the mountains and barrens of the South."[20]

But northern abolitionists did not visualize a southern emancipator as one who neglected blacks while seeking benefits for whites. Although there was much in what Birney said that appealed to white interests, in early 1836 the MASS described him as "pre-eminently the servant of slaves, laboring with untiring assiduity . . . to procure their liberation, and advance their welfare." Garrison, Gay, and Gamaliel Bailey gave especial praise to Snodgrass for his commitment to black rights. In 1846 Bailey said Snodgrass's "anti-slavery feelings comprehend the interests of the colored as well as the white population, and he has never been guilty of pandering to the corrupt sentiment of the community, by affecting that his hatred of slavery springs alone from a consideration of its effects upon the *whites*."[21]

On some occasions, their perception that southern emancipators were advocates of black interests led northern abolitionists astray concerning other white southerners who opposed slavery. Sometimes the immediatists assumed that "moral abhorrence of Slavery and a desire to do justice to the Slaves" underlay blatantly racist appeals to southern white self-interest. But more often, northern abolitionists excluded southern antislavery advocates, such as John H. Pleasants of Virginia and Robert J. Breckinridge of Kentucky, who persistently

disparaged black rights, from the ranks of those the abolitionists regarded as southern emancipators. Even Cassius M. Clay, who frequently expressed sympathy for the sufferings of blacks in slavery,
experienced close scrutiny from northern abolitionists concerning
his racial views. In reaction to abolitionist criticism in 1846, he quickly
repudiated a remark he made that appeared to disparage "Africans"
and "maudlin philanthropy." By 1853 he had redeemed himself to the
extent that when he visited a black church in Boston he received a
resounding welcome. In the presence of an overflowing congregation, black abolitionist William C. Nell declared "that we, the nominally free colored Americans . . . pour forth our libation of gratitude
to the honored and distinguished guest . . . Cassius M. Clay . . . for
practically applying the Golden Rule."[22]

So potent did this image of slaveholder turned antislavery leader
appear to be to northern abolitionists that they expected to reap benefits from it in the North as well as the South. Goodell said in 1834 that
when Birney's "high standing, commanding . . . influence, and disinterested sacrifice . . . shall be fully understood at the north . . . a great
additional . . . importance will be attached" to his actions. Garrisonian
journalist Oliver Johnson was particularly impressed   with Clay's ability to influence a northern audience at New York City's Broadway Tabernacle in 1846. Johnson told Maria Weston Chapman that "Clay's
reception here would have given you high satisfaction. . . .The people
received him from the heart, and it was a pleasure I cannot describe to
see them applauding, as they fell from *his* lips, sentiments for which all
faithful abolitionists have suffered reproach and persecution." It is not
surprising that northern abolitionists as different in outlook as Gerrit
Smith and Gamaliel Bailey joined in favoring Clay as an antislavery candidate for the vice presidency in 1852.[23]

As this suggests, northern abolitionists imagined southern emancipationists to be great leaders for the nation. In 1834, an Ohioan hoped
Birney "may prove to be a second Moses." Gay recalled that he had
believed Clay "a leader raised up to guide the oppressed nation . . .
out of the house of bondage." Goodell said, "We doubt whether, among
all the Southern heroes and heroines of freedom imagined by Mrs.
[Harriet Beecher] Stowe, there are any whose doings . . . are more
deserving of immortal remembrance than those of 'the Bailey family
of Kentucky.'"[24] But, if northern abolitionists frequently imaged the

southern emancipator to represent a heroic quest for antislavery progress in the South, they also portrayed him as one who faced tremendous obstacles in reaching antislavery goals. In other words, the image of a southern emancipator served as a harbinger of progress *and* as a symbol of southern intransigence. This dichotomy grew out of abolitionist hopes for success in the South on the one hand and their perceptions of slaveholder obdurateness on the other. It reflected a realization among abolitionists that an image of a persecuted southern emancipator offered them a useful rhetorical means to arouse northern popular opinion against the South.

As northern abolitionists came to suspect that slaveholders could not reason correctly on slavery, as they realized it was extremely difficult for southern whites to transcend their cultural biases, they perceived that southern emancipators had to be exceptional beings. "It requires far more than ordinary strength of mind, a more than common spiritual discernment, and a high degree of moral excellence, to break the strong network of prejudice which education and the daily circumstance of life weave around us," Gay said when he reflected upon racial bias among southern whites in 1846. Therefore, for individuals such as Birney, Clay, and Vaughan to overcome sectional pride and prejudice—along with personal, economic, and social self-interest—in order to favor abolition, was extraordinary. The contrary example of Robert J. Breckinridge underlined this in northern abolitionist minds. Breckinridge's early promise as a southern opponent of slavery, Gay argued, had been transformed into proslavery apology by his inability to break away from "social, political and religious fellowship with slaveholders."[25]

Because the ability to break away from southern evils was so rare and because the southern reaction to individuals who did so was so negative, the image of the exceptional southern emancipator served to focus the abolitionist belief that the South was out of step with Christianity and the principles of civil liberty. The often violent southern efforts to suppress dissent provided abolitionists with opportunities to use the image of a rejected and persecuted southern emancipator to arouse northern hostility to the proslavery regime.[26]

Before the *True American* began publication, Garrison doubted that it would be tolerated unless it became an apologist for slavery. When a mob temporarily suppressed the paper in August 1845, Gay joined Leavitt in declaring that "persecution, reviling, mobs and lynching must be the lot of those who are pioneers in this work." Five months later Gay described Snodgrass as a "marked man," who "must be silenced or submit to be silenced," and in 1860, following the destruction of William S. Bailey's press, Garrison contended that Bailey's life "is now seriously threatened." Fee and his followers made their biggest contribution to the image of a southern emancipator when they were driven from Kentucky. The sympathy of many in the North could be won by the picture, as influential black abolitionist Frederick Douglass painted it, "of quiet unobtrusive ministers in the Southern States having been driven from home under threats of personal violence for no other offense than that of being opposed to slavery."[27]

Abolitionists used these accounts of persecution and violence to justify their demands for aggressive northern action to accomplish immediate abolition. Garrisonians, for example, noted that Clay was no "fanatical abolitionist." He was, they maintained, too accommodating to slaveholding interests, but accommodation had "availed him nothing" in protecting his press from a proslavery mob. What better evidence was there than this, the Garrisonians asked, that halfway measures were useless and that the radical doctrine of no union with slaveholders must be implemented? Similarly, in March 1858 when anti-abolitionist violence in the South had increased, radical political abolitionist William Goodell insisted that the only thing that could help southern abolitionists in their battle against slavery was federal intervention.[28]

Paradoxically, violent threats to southern advocates of emancipation also encouraged northern abolitionists in their assertions that there was indeed progress in the South. Just as they had during episodes of anti-abolitionist violence in the North, abolitionists argued that fierce resistance to antislavery efforts was a portent of success. They assumed that southern whites resorted to force in desperation as abolitionism spread and that persecution suffered by southern emancipators brought new converts to the antislavery cause. Speaking of the South in 1848, Garrisonian leader Francis Jackson declared that "the violence of the antagonism we have aroused, is an evidence to us of the strength of our position, and the telling effect of our fire." Ten years later Harriet Beecher Stowe said of Fee that "afflictions, distress, only make him stronger. Antislavery churches are rising around him . . . and every inch which Christianity seems to gain under such auspices, she really does gain." So even when southern advocates of emancipation faced determined opposition, their northern friends imagined them to be pushing forward the cause.[29]

Because of the dangers they perceived southern abolitionists faced, it is not surprising that northern abolitionists made personal bravery a prominent part of the image of a southern emancipator. It is true that Garrisonians in particular often endorsed what they regarded as feminine virtues of love, forgiveness, and submissiveness in opposition to masculine aggressiveness and obstinacy. But, almost universally, abolitionists responded positively to manifestations of forceful masculinity in behalf of their cause in the South. In 1836 the MASS praised Birney for his "unshrinking fortitude." Over a decade later Edmund Quincy commended Clay's "indomitable energy and intrepid resolution." Gamaliel Bailey described Snodgrass as a "fearless editor . . . much respected for his frank and manly bearing." The *Anti-Slavery Bugle* called Fee a "moral hero," and Garrison said William S. Bailey was "indomitable," a man who stood his ground "with heroic courage, martyr-like endurance, and noble self sacrifice."[30] These comments and many similar ones suggest the high regard in which northern abolitionists held these individuals. Yet there was much in the image of a southern emancipator that patronized them.

The most extreme example of condescension by a northern abolitionist toward a southern coadjutor was Maria Weston Chapman's angry letter to Clay following his enlistment in the Mexican War. "I have always felt that your anti-slavery was, so to speak, provincial, in comparison with that sublime and magnificent cause, to which I have bound myself," Chapman told Clay.[31] Usually the northern expression of superiority was not so blatant. It appeared in gentle efforts to instruct the southerners in correct antislavery principles, to mix praise with criticism, and to adjust principles to meet the requirements of encouraging antislavery activity in the border slave states. The impression was that it would take time for the southern emancipator to rise to northern standards, and in the meantime his deplorable shortcomings could be excused.

Of the six southerners under consideration, Birney, Fee, and by 1856 William S. Bailey unequivocally embraced the cardinal northern abolitionist doctrine of immediate, uncompensated emancipation without expatriation. That left Clay, Snodgrass, and Vaughan to be publicly instructed, criticized, or excused. It was the Clay of the mid-1840s, however, who received most of the instruction. This was because he was furthest from the northern ideal when he embraced the cause and because abolitionists believed he had the greatest potential. For example, in 1844 Garrison said that Clay had the "great elements of character, which, if directed aright, may make him a blessing to millions."[32]

Northern abolitionists insisted that Clay must free his slaves in order to become a creditable antislavery leader, and by early 1844 he had emancipated the bondspeople he owned. He was slower to comply with abolitionist requests that he withdraw from the Whig party and embrace immediatism. In addition, nonviolent northern abolitionists objected to his frequently violent behavior, including his warnings that he would defend the *True American* office with "cold steel and ball." When Clay responded positively to such criticism, the abolitionists universally agreed he was a "truth-seeking man" and "progressing." So disappointed were they when his Mexican War service seemed to frustrate their hopes, more than one of them wished him dead. Northern abolitionists also condemned Clay's 1849 engagement in an election campaign brawl in which he fatally eviscerated a proslavery antagonist, but by then they had begun to realize that he would have to pursue his own course against slavery.[33]

Far more common than efforts to instruct were northern abolitionist juxtapositions of criticism of southern emancipationists with praise and excuses for the southerners' failure to adopt basic immediatist principles. That Elizur Wright Jr. of the *Emancipator* could ridicule Clay's recognition of the legally binding nature of slave codes as a "monstrous absurdity" while conceding that Clay's statements had "redeeming qualities, and very glorious ones" was typical and stemmed from conscious policy. Beginning in the early 1830s, northern abolitionists distinguished between slave state advocates of gradual emancipation who supported the ACS and aimed at "the *continuation* of slavery by means of deception" and gradualists such as Clay, Snodgrass, and Vaughan, who aimed at "*abolition.*" While the former could be unequivocally condemned, the latter had to be commended as well as criticized.

Political abolitionists Joshua Leavitt and Gamaliel Bailey acted in this tradition when they described Clay's gradual emancipation plan as "crude and impracticable" but hesitated to condemn it. Leavitt said, "We wait for further developments before we judge a man like him." More radical abolitionists took the same position. The Garrisonian Joneses of the *Bugle* denied that Clay and Snodgrass were abolitionists "in the high meaning of the word" but hastened to add, "When we see the Clays and Snodgrasses of the South agitating the public mind ... our heart leaps for joy, for we know that good must result." Similarly when Snodgrass resisted pressure from the Maryland legislature to back away from his vague commitment to "ultimate freedom" for the slaves "by some process at once lawful and peaceable, as well as just to their masters," Gay described Snodgrass as "manly."[34]

These statements reflect the pervasive belief among northern abolitionists that a border slave state location mitigated normally inexcusable lapses. But willingness among northern abolitionists to excuse their southern colleagues' shortcomings reached its apogee in relation to Vaughan and the *Examiner*. Unlike Clay before him and William S. Bailey after him, Vaughan launched his newspaper parroting the anti-abolitionist argument that the reason for the slow pace of antislavery progress in the South was northern interference. Garrison said Vaughan was too cautious. But Gay spoke for other prominent northern abolitionists when he said that, while Vaughan was wrong to "deprecate" northern interference with slavery, a southern editor could not always speak as northerners thought best "in the infancy of the cause" in his section. Even after Vaughan had left the paper and Fee began to complain that it had lapsed into colonizationism, Gamaliel Bailey insisted that, in view of its location, no other newspaper did so much for freedom, and the Garrisonian-dominated MASS regretted its termination in 1851.[35]

This northern abolitionist perception of the southern emancipator as one who could be instructed in correct antislavery principles or excused for failure to live up to those principles had roots deep in Yankee assumptions of superiority.[36] It suggests that similar abolitionist perceptions of their black coadjutors were products of cultural rather than racial prejudice. More directly, such paternalistic attitudes toward southern abolitionists sprang from the northerners' contention that they were responsible for the existence of such southerners, in whom they believed they had a vested interest.

From the early years of their movement, northern abolitionists confronted taunts based on their opponents' assumption that while their activities were pointless in the North, where there were no slaves, they were afraid to "go where the slaves are." As early as 1834, abolitionists responded that northern appeals to "justice and humanity" could engender antislavery sentiment in the South. They claimed the emergence of Birney and later Clay, Snodgrass, Vaughan, and William S. Bailey as proof "of the efficiency of our doctrines to which we refer those of our opponents who ask, 'Why do you not preach immediate emancipation in the South?'" It was, abolitionists argued, their faithful and uncompromising testimony that created the public sentiment in the North that provided the foundation for pioneering antislavery efforts in the slave states.[37] So defense of their own tactics led northern abolitionists both to instruct their southern colleagues and to excuse them when they proved to be less than perfect pupils.

If northern abolitionists perceived the southern emancipator to be a product of their tactics and proof of their effectiveness, they also saw him as a product of their financial support. They could patronize southern antislavery advocates because they were literally the southerners' patrons. Birney, for example, became a paid agent of the AASS in 1834, and the abolitionist AMA employed Fee beginning in 1848.[38]

It was newspaper publishers Snodgrass, Clay, Vaughan, and William S. Bailey, nevertheless, whose dependence on northern financial support was most striking. Snodgrass received contributions for his *Saturday Visiter* from the AFASS and individual northern abolitionists. Northerners helped Clay raise subscriptions, and may have donated funds as well. In October 1845 he reported that the *True American* had twenty-seven hundred subscribers. Of these, seven hundred were in Kentucky, no more than eight hundred were in other slave states, and the rest were in the North. When Clay's enlistment in the Mexican War led large numbers of northerners to end their subscriptions, Vaughan, who had succeeded Clay as editor, warned "the friends of freedom in the free States" that the paper could not survive "unless they stand by it." Following the suspension of the *True American*, Vaughan traveled to the Northeast seeking financial support among abolitionists for his *Examiner* and raised at least five thousand dollars.[39]

During the 1850s William S. Bailey made similar trips and, by playing upon abolitionist and Republican sympathies, was very effective in procuring funds for the relief of his family as well as his publishing enterprise. The message from Clay, Vaughan, and William S. Bailey was that the southern emancipator needed not only the tolerance of northern abolitionists but their financial support to survive. Gamaliel Bailey echoed Vaughan in 1847 when he said "no Anti-Slavery paper can thrive in a slave State, unless the few who are inclined to support it, be encouraged by those in the other sections who sympathize with them."[40]

Northern abolitionist funding of southern antislavery efforts from the 1830s through the 1850s underlines the high regard the northerners had for southern advocates of emancipation, although there was negligible support for such advocates among southern whites. Optimism for indigenous southern antislavery action is usually ascribed to Liberty, Free Soil, and Republican politicians. But the use of southern emancipationists as symbols of progress, as antislavery heroes, as proof of the effectiveness of northern abolitionist tactics, and as illustrations of the oppressiveness of slaveholders was characteristic of the entire antislavery movement.[41] The termination of the great abolitionist postal campaign to convert slaveholders to abolitionism did not destroy but actually enhanced the movement's need for southern antislavery heroes. If northerners faced obstacles in carrying their message to the South, said the abolitionists, converted southerners would do it more effectively, and, if such individuals were rare, the more damned was the slave system that made them so.

It would be a mistake, however, to suggest that the image of a southern emancipator was a concept completely divorced from southern realities. Northern abolitionist enthusiasm for indigenous white southern antislavery action peaked in the 1840s. It was sustained in part by adverse economic conditions that encouraged widespread nonabolitionist dissatisfaction with slavery in the upper South. It gradually declined following the failure in 1849 of Kentucky emancipationists to add a gradual abolition clause to that state's constitution and as the southern economy rebounded in the 1850s. Even so, northern abolitionist expressions of optimism for the prospects of Clay, Fee, and William S. Bailey remained common in antislavery newspapers through most of the 1850s. Gamaliel Bailey and others who supported the program of the Free Soil and Republican parties continued to expect rapid antislavery progress in the South based on southward expansion of the free labor economy. In the late 1850s radical political abolitionists and Garrisonians promoted William S. Bailey as a determined southern abolitionist who criticized the Republican party for merely opposing slavery in the territories.[42]

Nevertheless, northern abolitionist interest in the activities of their southern counterparts declined, and, as violent opposition to southern antislavery advocates intensified after 1856, the northerners began to lose hope for peaceful emancipation in the South.[43] That they continued to nurture dreams of a nonviolent end to slavery as long as they did owed much to their image of southern antislavery activists carrying their cause into the South. But on the eve of the Civil War the image of a southern emancipator as rejected prophet had finally prevailed over the image of a southern emancipator as herald of progress.

Chapter Three

AN IMAGE OF A SOUTHERN BLACK LIBERATOR

"Slaveholders have but one alternative, either to emancipate their slaves voluntarily, and thus escape the danger they dread, or have the slaves emancipate themselves by force," said the Reverend Amos A. Phelps of Massachusetts in 1834. Phelps, who had a year earlier helped organize the AASS, observed that "the colored population of the South is rapidly increasing" and predicted that "half a century will not pass, before they will have become a great mighty people. . . . a mass of physical strength that will not always sleep."[1] Phelps's prediction was blunt. The South had to free the slaves, or the slaves would take their freedom. Blacks would liberate themselves in the most direct form of antislavery action.

Organized slave revolts, such as the one led by Nat Turner in Virginia, which inspired Phelps's warning, were rare in the antebellum South. But the specter of such revolts had an undeniable impact on American culture. The resistance of the enslaved to their condition and the reality of southern white fear of slave violence have been common themes for American historians for years.[2] Far less frequent have been efforts to understand the role northern abolitionists assigned to southern slaves in destroying black bondage. The purpose of this chapter is to present such an understanding and to indicate how abolitionist perceptions of slave liberators shaped antislavery reform culture from the 1830s through the 1850s.

Phelps and other immediatists were hardly the first to regard slaves as active participants in the antislavery struggle. Gradual abolitionists had, since the successful Haitian slave revolt of the early 1800s, played on white fears that a similar uprising could occur in the South in lieu of peaceful emancipation. The northern immediatists simply elaborated the theme. Nearly all of them believed that the slaves could achieve self-liberation, and reports of slave revolts served as catalysts for confrontational antislavery rhetoric in the North.[3] Yet, for several reasons, historians of the sectional conflict have tended to portray abolitionism as a movement of northern blacks and whites in behalf of an amorphous body of passive slaves.

Of primary importance among these reasons is that the abolitionists themselves were ambivalent concerning the role slaves were to play in abolishing slavery. This is evident in Phelps's assumption in 1834 that the slaves were currently asleep. Secondly, for the past three decades most historians of the antislavery movement have sought to understand that movement by placing it in an exclusively northern cultural context. This approach, while providing important insights, has tended to isolate the slaves from the abolitionists in all but a distant, inert, and symbolic sense.[4]

In addition, studies of racism among slavery's white opponents have emphasized their alienation from, rather than their commonality of goals with, the slaves. Finally, most of those who have studied the growing tendency of abolitionists to advocate violent means have also focused on developments in the North—such as violent resistance to enforcement of the Fugitive Slave Act of 1850 and the role of northern blacks—rather than on the actions of slaves in the South.[5] Just as historians of the sectional conflict have neglected the role of southern white emancipators in sustaining a northern abolitionist orientation toward the South, historians have generally overlooked a continuing abolitionist focus on the efforts of enslaved blacks to free themselves.

Nevertheless, there are four important studies dealing with the issue. Three have narrowly defined goals. The first is Robert H. Abzug's 1970 essay, which argues that fear of slave revolt shaped immediate abolitionism in the early 1830s. Northern abolitionists, according to Abzug, were so frightened by the prospect of a southern holocaust that they advocated immediate emancipation to prevent one. The second is a chapter in Jane H. Pease and William H. Pease's 1974 book on black abolitionists. The chapter deals specifically with northern black advocacy of slave revolt in the 1840s and 1850s and suggests that white abolitionists lagged behind blacks in recognizing that slaves could help achieve their own liberation. In the third study— published in 1982—Jeffery S. Rossbach analyzes the struggle of a

small group of John Brown's white supporters to overcome their belief that African Americans were too submissive to follow Brown in
rebellion. None of these studies attempts to cover the entire antebellum period nor the breadth of the abolitionist movement.[6]

A more extensive treatment is Merton L. Dillon's insightful 1990
analysis of the relationship between southern black resistance to slavery and northern abolitionism. Like Abzug, Dillon portrays the threat
of slave revolt as a key factor in the development of immediatism in
the North. The abolitionists' commitment to nonviolence in the 1830s,
he argues, was in part a tactical response to charges that they encouraged Nat Turner's rebellion. He contends that the abolitionists,
in a related pragmatic maneuver to avoid public condemnation, contradicted their earlier portrayals of the enslaved as able warriors by
describing them as passively awaiting peaceful emancipation. In
Dillon's assessment, it took an increase in slave escapes and two dramatic slave uprisings around 1840 to convince white abolitionists to
change their tactics and embrace the slaves as allies in the antislavery struggle. In the process, he says, abolitionists began to abandon
moral suasion and imitate the slaves by advocating violent direct action.[7]

All of these fine studies have limitations, if only in regard to understanding the abolitionist image of a black liberator. In his short
article, Abzug does not explore the implicit threat to the South in the
abolitionists' fearful warnings of slave rebellion. Dillon does not account for the continued distrust after 1840 among white abolitionists
of the slaves' ability to fight for their freedom that the Peases and
Rossbach note. In addition, by attributing contradictory abolitionist
statements concerning black character to tactical decisions in the
1830s, Dillon undervalues studies that indicate such contradictions
pervaded white American assumptions about race throughout the
antebellum years. The Peases neglect early white militancy in behalf
of slave resistance as well as black abolitionist expressions of caution
regarding slave revolt, and Rossbach isolates only one element in
white abolitionist perceptions of slave character.

This chapter argues for greater continuity in abolitionist depictions of the role of slaves in the antislavery movement and for closer
agreement among black and white abolitionists concerning that role.
Nevertheless, it has benefited from each of these studies. Dillon, in

particular, by forcefully demonstrating a relationship between acts of self-liberation among southern blacks and the development of northern abolitionism, has profoundly shaped this chapter's spirit. From the beginning of immediate abolitionism, a southern black liberator appeared to all abolitionists to be an alternative to northern initiatives as a potential disrupter and destroyer of slavery. Yet ambivalence on the issue continued to exist, and abolitionists had to be frequently reminded by slave action of this alternative.

The persistence of doubts among *both* black and white abolitionists concerning the efficacy of slave rebellion as a means of abolition reflects the force of racism and sexism in antebellum America. Black and white abolitionists were part of a culture that held African Americans to be incapable of the initiative required for gaining and exercising freedom. The abolitionists struggled against this racism, but they never escaped it.

Proslavery arguments that blacks were naturally submissive and content to be slaves, as well as the conflicting claim that freed blacks would retrogress into unmanageable brutes, influenced abolitionist perceptions. So did American scientists who assigned blacks to a separate, intellectually inferior species. It is, therefore, not surprising that the abolitionists compromised by embracing a racial doctrine that recognized inborn differences of character between the races while ostensibly denying black inferiority. Indirectly derived from the notion of *volksgeist* in German romanticism and called "romantic racialism" by historian George M. Fredrickson, this doctrine held that each race had special attributes.

The doctrine was sexist as well as racist because, while it focused on white and black males as representatives of their races, it held that African males had more feminine or Christlike qualities than Anglo-Saxon males, whom it portrayed as extremely masculine. Accordingly, the African male was emotional, sedentary, submissive, generous, and peaceful—the perfect Christian ready to forgive his oppressors rather than take vengeance upon them. The Anglo-Saxon male was intellectual, adventuresome, aggressive, exploitative, and militaristic—less suited for Christianity than the African but much more able to dominate in the rough nineteenth century. While predicting a glorious future for Africans and African Americans as founders of a truly Christian civilization, romantic racialism justified whites in assuming a paternalistic, condescending attitude toward slaves who were unlikely to struggle to free themselves.[8]

Romantic racialism reached its apogee in Harriet Beecher Stowe's character Uncle Tom in 1851. Stowe portrayed as heroic Tom's Christlike ability to transcend slavery and white brutality by meekly submitting and forgiving. But more radical abolitionists—both black and white—were always bitter about what they perceived to be black docility. In his famous *Appeal . . . to the Colored Citizens of the World*, published in 1829, David Walker, a North Carolina free black who had migrated to Boston a year earlier, lamented that blacks "all over the world, have a mean, servile spirit. They yielded," he wrote, "in a moment to the whites, let them be right or wrong—the reason they are able to keep their feet on our throats." Fourteen years later black Liberty abolitionist Henry Highland Garnet of Troy, New York, rhetorically complained to male slaves, "You are a patient people. You act as though your daughters were born to pamper the lusts of your master and overseers. . . . You tamely submit while your lords tear your wives from your embrace, and defile them before your eyes. In the name of god we ask, are you men?"[9]

Militant white abolitionists like John Brown and Bostonian minister Theodore Parker agreed. In an article Brown published in a black abolitionist newspaper in the late 1840s, he pretended to be black and sarcastically admitted, "I have always expected to receive the favor of whites by tamely submitting to every species of indignity, contempt and wrong, instead of nobly resisting their brutal aggressions." Parker charged in 1858 that it was because "the black man would not strike"—that he had "so little ferocity"—that whites were able to enslave him.[10]

Such perceptions led abolitionists to occasionally assume that theirs was an essentially northern effort in which the slaves could do little more than cry for help. Printed images of manacled, kneeling slaves supplicating aid "from a distant quarter" were familiar to abolitionists of all persuasions. Frederick Douglass voiced a common sentiment when at an abolitionist meeting in Boston's Faneuil Hall in 1842 he said of the slaves, "They are goods and chattels, not men. It is to save them from all this that you are called."[11]

But striking as these images are, they never defined abolitionist attitudes toward slaves. Rather they represent an extreme in a broad spectrum of opinion, the bulk of which placed considerably more confidence in the ability of slaves to assist in their liberation. In fact, slave initiatives and rumors of them periodically disrupted theories of black passivity. The armed struggle for freedom by the enslaved black people of Haiti, which ended successfully in 1803, and Turner's bloody but hopeless insurrection in Southampton County, Virginia, in August 1831 stood as profound refutations of claims that African Americans would not act to free themselves. As if to drive home this point, William Lloyd Garrison in the decades following the Southampton revolt published numerous credulous accounts of minor slave plots and rumored revolts.[12]

Much more influential, however, as reminders to abolitionists that blacks were not always helpless victims of slavery were two maritime uprisings that occurred in 1839 and 1841 and rumors of a massive insurrectionary plot in the wake of the national election of 1856. The first of these incidents involved fifty-three West Africans who escaped enslavement by forcefully taking command of the Spanish schooner *Amistad*. Although these individuals were not American slaves, they became symbols among black and white abolitionists of aggressive black resistance to slavery. Their leader, Joseph Cinque, joined Haiti's Toussaint L'Ouverture and Southampton's Nat Turner as heroes of black liberation.

The same may be said of Madison Washington, who in November 1841 led a successful revolt of 135 slaves in transit from Virginia to New Orleans aboard the brig *Creole*. Washington, a fugitive slave who had been reenslaved when he returned to Virginia for his wife, sailed the *Creole* to the British Bahamas and freedom. Fifteen years later, the widespread rumors of slave revolt in late 1856 stimulated a revival of abolitionist discussion of slave rebellion. Coming at a time when Democratic and Know-Nothing party campaign rhetoric had linked the new Republican party to servile insurrections, isolated cases of slave unrest in the upper South frightened southern whites and encouraged abolitionists.[13]

Other factors also counteracted racialist notions among abolitionists concerning slave passivity. The increasing number of slave escapes beginning in the late 1830s, noted by Dillon, and subsequent northern black resistance to the fugitive slave acts bolstered the image of African Americans as active opponents of slavery. European revolutions in 1830 and 1848 suggested that similar forces were at work in the South. By the 1850s the transfiguration of the image of a white southern emancipator from hero to victim and the apparent ineffectiveness of peaceful antislavery tactics placed a premium in the minds of abolitionists on forceful actions by the slaves themselves. But it is extremely important to emphasize that abolitionist receptivity to arguments for slave violence in the 1850s was rooted in a process that began much earlier. Actions by slaves created a widespread acceptance of them as a major factor in the antislavery movement *throughout* the antebellum years.[14]

From early in the nineteenth century to the Civil War, abolitionists frequently argued that slaves were capable of general revolt. There were difficulties, however, because despite evidence of isolated uprisings, the American intellectual climate continued to support perceptions of black docility. Even a fading Enlightenment belief that the environment, rather than fundamental nature, caused differences among peoples suggested that enslavement handicapped blacks. Therefore, abolitionists relied on the Bible's assertion that God had created all peoples of one blood and on a contention—derived from Scottish moral sense philosophy—that degraded blacks retained the same inherent desire for liberty as whites.[15]

In the 1830s and 1840s abolitionists contended that because blacks shared a common humanity with whites and an innate desire for liberty, slaves would fight for freedom. "Slaves are like other men," Garrison warned the South a month before Nat Turner's uprising. After that revolt had been crushed, Garrison added, "Why should one wonder at his [Turner's] determined efforts to revenge his wrongs and obtain his liberty?" Shortly after the *Creole* mutiny, Joshua Leavitt of the Liberty party responded to charges that abolitionists had brought unrest to formerly happy slaves by noting that slave rebellions had long predated immediate abolitionism. "Something besides modern abolitionism has a 'tendency to excite discontent' in the bosoms of enslaved men," he wrote. "It is THEIR MANHOOD, GOD-GIVEN, that stirs their pulses more rapidly at the thought of the wrongs the oppressor heaps upon them. Slavery cannot utterly destroy their manhood."[16]

If slavery could not destroy its victims' innate spirit, abolitionists also argued that it could not entirely control the slaves' environment.

A correspondent of the *Liberator* contended in May 1831 that no law could stop "the rudiments of learning" from reaching the slaves and that it was "impossible that they can be prevented from discussing their wrongs." He reported that slaves had knowledge of *Walker's Appeal* and the Haitian revolution and said he would "rejoice" if that knowledge led to revolt. While abolitionists generally assumed that southern white efforts to keep slaves illiterate and ignorant were partially successful in limiting unrest, they also assumed that slaves, in the border region at least, could not be shielded from notions of liberty, which would lead them to actively resist oppression.[17]

By the late 1850s some abolitionists had also begun to attack the foundations of romantic racialism or to use that doctrine as a means of praising, rather than dismissing, slave initiatives for freedom. An instance of the former strategy came during Wendell Phillips's March 1858 speech at a commemoration of the Boston Massacre. Theodore Parker, who preceded Phillips at the podium, had suggested that, unlike Anglo-Saxons, blacks lacked the courage to fight for their freedom. Phillips responded with a variation on a common abolitionist argument. He contended that Anglo-Saxons and other Europeans were no braver than blacks because they had been held in bondage as serfs in the Middle Ages and had not rebelled. In fact, he maintained, "If you go to the catalogues of races that have actually abolished slavery by the sword, the colored race is the only one that has ever yet afforded an instance, and that is St. Domingo [Haiti]."[18]

Later that same year, second-generation immediatist Thomas Wentworth Higginson of Cambridge, Massachusetts, provided an illustration of the second tactic. Fascinated by the conduct of blacks on the underground railroad, Higginson wrote an essay entitled "Physical Courage" in which he used a racialist assumption that black men belonged to a "feminine" race to assert that they were capable of the noblest form of courage—"the courage created by desperate emergencies." It was the type of courage, he said, that brought women and slaves "at one bound . . . from cowering pusillanimity to the topmost height of daring." Fugitive slaves displayed this physical courage when, having risked death to save themselves, they went "voluntarily back to risk it over again, for the sake of wife or child." Higginson asked, "What are we pale faces that we should claim a rival capacity with them for heroic deeds?"[19]

Were heroic deeds enough? Could desire and courage alone permit slaves to overthrow oppression? At times, a variety of abolitionists doubted they could—doubted that successful slave revolt was possible. Abolitionists with ties to the border region, such as Gamaliel Bailey of Cincinnati and John C. Underwood of Virginia, and black abolitionists such as Garnet, Douglass, and John S. Rock—a Boston lawyer—were most likely to describe revolt as "inexpedient." But white New Englanders, including Garrison, Nathaniel P. Rogers, and Wendell Phillips, on occasion expressed similar practical reservations. It was not, Douglass and Rock insisted, a question of bravery but numbers. Although Douglass at times made warlike statements, as late as 1857 he spoke against slave revolt because, he said, it was "certain to result in the extermination of the colored race."[20]

Confronted with this horrible specter and influenced by their commitment to peaceful means, black and white abolitionists occasionally suggested that slaves might better act to achieve their freedom through a general strike or that the cumulative effect of individual slave escapes would cause the destruction of slavery. But they were more likely to believe slaves could indeed free themselves by force. Shortly after the Southampton insurrection Garrison mixed metaphors in declaring that it was "the first step of the earthquake, which is ultimately to shake down the fabric of oppression," and New York judge William Jay, one of the more conservative immediatists, predicted that "the slaves will either receive their freedom as a boon, or they will wrest it by force from their masters."[21] Other abolitionists made similar remarks throughout the antebellum years.

The *Creole* mutiny certainly had a lasting impact. While insisting that he himself was a "peace man," Douglass in 1849 mentioned Madison Washington and declared that "those who have trampled upon us for the past two hundred years, who have used their utmost to crush every noble sentiment in our bosom . . . may expect their turn will come one day." In the 1850s Gerrit Smith, John Brown, Wendell Phillips, Thomas Wentworth Higginson, and others increasingly expressed both fear that the slaves would have to free themselves by violent means and confidence that the slaves had the ability to do so.[22]

Abolitionists gave a variety of reasons for their belief that a rebellion could produce freedom for the slaves. Most often they asserted that blacks were far better warriors than whites believed. Based on the showing of black Haitians against European troops, on African-American service in the American War for Independence and the War of 1812, on Indian influences on slaves, on the physically hardening impact of slavery, and on genetic mixture with Anglo-Saxons, such arguments were common from the late 1840s until the Civil War changed the issue from black rebellion to enlistment in the Union armies.[23] An alternative scenario, popular among militant abolitionists in the late 1850s, held that rebellious slaves might lose on the field of battle but still win emancipation by encouraging the North to take action in their behalf or by frightening southern whites into freeing them. Douglass argued in 1857 that "one manly movement of the slave of the South might rouse [the North]" and that "Virginia was never nearer emancipation than when General Turner kindled the fires of insurrection at Southampton."[24]

Believing that a massive slave revolt could take place and succeed was different from claiming that slaves had a moral right to revolt. It was even further removed from forthright advocacy of servile insurrection, and in the 1830s abolitionists mixed expressions of admiration for Nat Turner and predictions of future uprisings with denials that they approved or desired them. Genuinely repulsed by bloodshed and acutely aware that their most abstract approval of slave insurrection could unleash a violent popular backlash, the founders of the AASS in December 1833 disassociated themselves from slave violence. "The society will never," they declared, "in any way, countenance the oppressed in vindicating their rights by resorting to physical force."[25]

Yet, as historian John Demos notes, there was from the start of immediate abolitionism in the United States a barely concealed threat in the rejections of slave violence. The threat reflected an abolitionist recognition of a role for slaves in the antislavery movement, which persisted throughout the antebellum period. Again and again abolitionists declared that while slave rebellion was a horrible thing, it would come unless slaveholders immediately emancipated their bondsmen. "The slaves must soon receive a gratuitous freedom, or they will take it by force. . . .The dreadful tragedy of Southampton is but a prelude to a more dreadful slaughter," Garrison warned in 1832. Eight years later, New York Liberty abolitionist Alvan Stewart declared that either political action would destroy slavery "or else it will be accomplished by the slaves *rising*. As to their rising & by one bold & mighty effort overthrowing their bloody masters, god grant that way, if no other mode can be found out." In 1854 a northerner who claimed to have interviewed slaves reported that those in bonds were ready to act. The choice was, he said, "proclaim emancipation, or ere long be prepared for servile war!"[26]

By the 1840s abolitionist demands that the North refuse to aid the South in suppressing servile insurrection had become closely associated with these threats. A fundamental assumption of immediatism was that northerners shared the guilt for slavery because northern power guaranteed black bondage in the South. Without "the dread of the northern bayonet," Wendell Phillips commented in 1842, " . . . the whole South were but the deck of a larger Creole, and the physical strength of the bondsman would, as on board that vessel, sweep the oppressor from his presence." Such logic contributed to the AASS's adoption of a disunion resolution the following year. An independent North would not have to fulfill constitutional obligations to help put down insurrection in the South. Some Liberty abolitionists assumed a similar position at about the same time by maintaining that the Constitution, properly interpreted in favor of freedom, did not require northern militia or the central government to suppress slave uprisings.[27]

Abolitionists, by making such threats and by adopting such positions, had from the start of their campaign compromised their commitment to peaceful tactics. They began to believe not only that the slaves had the ability to use force effectively but also a right to use it to gain freedom. Those like Garrison and his friend Henry C. Wright, who embraced the nonresistant doctrine that even defensive violence was morally wrong, were careful to qualify their recognition of the justice of slave rebellion. In 1837 Garrison declared that the Declaration of Independence and the spirit of the American people "authorize and urge" slaves to "'cut their masters' throats,'" while noting that he personally denied "the right of any man to fight for liberty." Two decades later Wright took the same position. But abolitionists who were not nonresistants need not make such distinctions. They could flatly declare, as William Jay did in 1840, that the *Amistad* captives had committed "'justifiable homicide'" because they fought for "'the recovery of personal liberty.'"[28]

Abolitionists justified slave revolts in a variety of ways. Assertions that slave rebels acted as agents of divine retribution against those who practiced the sin of slaveholding were very common. Abolitionists from the 1830s through the 1850s were fond of recalling Thomas Jefferson's warning that as God was just, the divinity would not side with oppressors in a race war. But aside from equating black liberators with Moses and noting that scripture sanctioned violence in self-defense, specific Bible references were surprisingly rare. More frequently abolitionists compared insurrectionary slaves to European revolutionaries of 1830 and 1848 or maintained that the explicit violence of enslavement itself legitimized forceful resistance.[29]

It was, however, the legacy of the American Revolution that was foremost in the minds of abolitionists when they considered the justice of slave revolt. The practice of linking slave uprising to the Declaration of Independence and the War for Independence was as old as immediatism. In the 1830s AASS leaders Samuel J. May, John Greenleaf Whittier, and James G. Birney recognized that a "noble spirit of liberty" animated slave rebels as well as America's revolutionary generation. The black mutineers on the *Amistad* and the *Creole*, several abolitionists insisted, had simply "imitated the example of our fathers in fighting for liberty," and in 1857 Henry C. Wright contended that the slaves of George Washington would have had as much right to kill the general as he did to fight the British. Although remarks like Wright's have been used as evidence of increased willingness of abolitionists to contemplate the use of force in the 1850s, his words reflected a long tradition of antislavery rhetoric.[30]

America's racially determined concept of manhood usually slighted individuals of African descent, but, just as southern white emancipators did, slave rebels had an extended history as abolitionist heroes. The image of a noble southern black revolutionary already existed in abolitionist reform culture in the 1830s. A month after the Southampton uprising, the *Liberator* published an account of Gabriel, a Virginia slave rebel of thirty years earlier. The account portrayed Gabriel declaring heroically at his trial, "'I love my [black] nation— We have as good a right to be free from oppression as you had to be free from the tyranny of the king of England. I know my fate—you will take my life. I offer it willingly as a martyr to liberty. My example will raise up a Gabriel, who will, Washington-like, lead the Africans to freedom.'" This heroic image was especially attractive to blacks, but white abolitionists employed it with a surprising lack of ambivalence. Slave rebels achieved mythic stature among all abolitionists as representatives of black intelligence and bravery—as heroes comparable not only to George Washington but to Garibaldi, William Tell, Leonidas, and Moses.[31]

It was the relatively conservative *Evangelist* of New York City which, in its 1842 description of Madison Washington, most clearly related the positive abolitionist perception of slave insurrectionists. Washington, the *Evangelist* maintained, "manifested astounding presence of mind and decision of character. . . .His commanding attitude, and daring orders, when he stood a free man on the slaver's deck, and his perfect preparation for the grand alternative of liberty or death, which stood before him, are splendid exemplifications of the true heroic." Seven years later Douglass singled out Washington as a symbol of slave revolt, and, following the reports of slave unrest in late 1856, Douglass took bitter pride in asserting that every such instance of rebelliousness counteracted the image of blacks "as a nation of Uncle Toms, good at psalm-singing, but not caring enough for liberty to fight for it."[32]

Black and white abolitionists also agreed in portraying slave rebels as individuals driven to take bloody action by terrible suffering, who were vilified for their deeds because of their race, although an objective evaluator would rate them as high or higher than white heroes. Garrison said of Turner in October 1831, "Why should one wonder at his determined efforts to revenge his wrongs and obtain his liberty? Such treatment as he received at the hands of his tyrannical owner was calculated to feed his wrath and bring a dreadful retaliation." It was only because Turner was black, Garrison continued, that he would not receive "a portion of the applause which has been so prodigally heaped upon Washington, Bolivar, and other *heroes*, for the same rebellious though more successful conduct." Instead, he would "be torn to pieces and his memory cursed!" Similarly, black Garrisonian Charles Lenox Remond complained in 1844 that, although "*Nathaniel*" Turner was "a nobler soul" than all other heroes, "the Union does not even preserve his name . . . in history he is only Nat Turner, the miserable negro. Sir," Remond continued, "I will never contemptuously call him *Nat* Turner, for had he been a white man, Massachusetts and

Virginia would have united to glorify his name and to build his monument."[33]

Racialist stereotypes and attempts to refute proslavery claims that blacks would revert to savagery in freedom led white abolitionists to describe southern black liberators as gentle revolutionaries, reluctant to spill blood. The *Evangelist,* for example, praised Washington for his "generous leniency towards his prisoners, his oppressors" on the *Creole.* "All of his movements," said the *Evangelist,* "show that malice and revenge formed no part of his motives." In 1861 Higginson went so far as to argue that Turner's slaughter of white women and children was aimed at saving lives in the long run and that the Southampton rebels were more humane than whites and Indians because they did not rape the women.[34]

By 1842 some abolitionists had gone beyond praising slaves for their self-liberating efforts and began to demand such action. Events in the South, not in the North, led to these explicit calls for slave resistance. The *Amistad* and the *Creole* mutinies, the increasing number of slave escapes, and the imprisonment of three young white northerners in Missouri for attempting to encourage such escapes inspired the rhetoric.[35] Nowhere was it more prevalent than among the black and white leaders of the New York Liberty party, although Garrison and some of his associates joined in.

The most prominent example of early abolitionist advocacy of slave action against slavery was Gerrit Smith's "Address to the Slaves of the United States," which he delivered at a New York Liberty convention in January 1842. A year and a half later, first Garrison and then black Liberty activist Henry Highland Garnet made similar speeches with the same title. Garrison presented his at a Boston antislavery meeting in May 1843, and Garnet addressed a convention of African Americans in Buffalo that August. All three built on the tradition of abolitionist recognition of the ability of slaves to act against slavery in the South.[36]

Although some abolitionists applauded Smith's boldness and others were shocked by his willingness to offend southern whites by claiming to communicate with their slaves, the idea of addressing slaves was not new. Smith had made a similar, though less well publicized, speech in 1839, and, as early as 1835, his friend William Goodell affirmed that "in respect to slaves there is no earthly power that can possibly have a right to forbid our intercourse with them for Christian and moral purposes. . . . Whatever the Bible teaches respecting oppression, or any other subject, we have a right to teach to every one, and of course to the slave." Some abolitionists denied communication with the slaves was possible. But, throughout the antebellum era, others disagreed, and by the late 1840s abolitionist missionary organizations had actively engaged a slave audience.[37]

What made Smith and the others' addresses remarkable was their *explicit* advocacy of active resistance by slaves. Smith and Garrison rhetorically advised slaves to escape, and Garnet suggested that they refuse to work in order to force masters to either free them or initiate a violent confrontation. Smith, in particular, stretched abolitionist morality by justifying fugitive slaves in stealing in the North as well as the South in order to effect their escapes. He also expressed a common belief among New York Liberty abolitionists that a northerner had a right to go south "and use his intelligence to promote the escape of ignorant and imbruted slaves from the prison-house."[38]

Yet all three addresses followed an old abolitionist pattern of mixing admiration for slave courage and predictions of slave violence with invocations of pacifism—designed, perhaps, to avoid legal prosecution. Garnet, for example, linked a rhetorical call to slaves that "you had better all die . . . than live slaves. . . . There is not much hope of redemption without the shedding of blood" with the warning, "We do not advise you to attempt a revolution with the sword, because it would be INEXPEDIENT. You are too small, and moreover the rising spirit of the age, and the spirit of the gospel, are opposed to war and bloodshed."[39]

Others in the early 1840s were not so cautious in asserting solidarity with slaves. Even before Smith delivered his address, less prominent New York abolitionists made forthright endorsements of slave violence. In resolutions condemned by Lydia Maria Child and the executive committee of the AASS, a Liberty convention, meeting in December 1841 at Williamsburg, Long Island, declared without qualification "that the slaves of the brig *Creole*, who rose and took possession of said vessel, thereby regaining their natural rights and liberty, acted in accordance with the principles of the Declaration of Independence . . . and we trust that their noble example will be imitated by all in similar circumstances." Also, just prior to Garrison's address, a correspondent of the *Liberty Press* of Utica, New York, asserted that "it is our duty to encourage and aid slaves to *rise* and take their liberty; and if the master attempts to shoot or kill the slave for taking his liberty, then that master must take the consequences of his folly; and if he loses his life, 'he dies as a fool dieth.'"[40]

Such explicit calls for slave violence were rare in the 1840s, confined to New York Liberty advocates and approved only by a few outside that group. Well into the 1850s, even the more radical abolitionists usually assumed that oppression, God, and perhaps disunion would lead slaves to act without encouragement from the North. It is worth repeating, too, that because the addresses to the slaves were *responses* to reports of slave revolts and escapes, the abolitionists who wrote them were actually registering their approval of antislavery actions in the South among slaves, rather than exerting any real leadership over slaves.

A similar pattern of reported slave action and abolitionist response occurred in the 1850s. Certainly, the increasingly violent nature of the sectional struggle in that decade, with bloody clashes over the enforcement of the Fugitive Slave Act in the North and guerrilla warfare in Kansas over the introduction of slavery into that territory, encouraged hyperbolic references to physical force. So did perceptions that years of antislavery struggle had not lessened the power of slaveholders over the country.[41] But in the 1850s, as earlier, it usually took reports of slave action to elicit explicit abolitionist calls for such action.

In August 1850 there occurred a dramatic slave escape attempt from Washington, D.C., in which two fugitives fired pistols at pursuing police while New York Liberty leader William L. Chaplin drove the fugitives' carriage. Within a month of the escape attempt, a Cazenovia, New York, convention of fugitive slaves and their white friends endorsed black Liberty advocate Jermain Wesley Loguen's "letter to the slaves." Loguen urged slaves to escape by violent means if necessary, predicted insurrection in lieu of "voluntary emancipation," and pledged that northern blacks would then join slaves "with death-dealing weapons in their hands." Like others before him, Loguen denied that he actually meant to "encourage, or justify" slave violence. But by mid-1852, even such qualified calls for servile insurrection had disappeared from abolitionist rhetoric, despite continued violence associated with resistance to the Fugitive Slave Act in the North.[42]

It was not until the reports of widespread slave unrest following the national election of 1856 reached the North that there was another outburst of abolitionist calls for rebellion. This time Garrisonians took the lead. Although black and white supporters of the AASS had always used the possibility of slave violence to bolster their ostensibly peaceful campaign, they had generally avoided explicit calls for slave rebellion. But the rumors of incipient slave revolt that swept the South in late 1856 and the frightened southern white response unleashed Garrisonian demands for rebellion at least as intense as those of their Liberty rivals in the 1840s.[43]

"I wish to call your attention to the present excitement at the South respecting slave insurrection," Henry C. Wright told the annual meeting of the Massachusetts Anti-Slavery Society in 1857. "We owe it as our duty to ourselves and to humanity, to excite every slave to *rebellion* against his master . . . .An insurrection against slaveholders!" Wright continued the paradoxical practice of denying that he favored a violent solution to the problem of slavery. But other Garrisonians no longer quibbled. Eight months later, the Cleveland "Disunion Convention" resolved without qualification "that it is the duty of the slaves to strike down their tyrant master by force of arms" whenever there was a chance of success. Black Garrisonian Charles L. Remond explicitly linked abolitionist calls for revolt with the rise of a black liberator in the South. "If we recommend to the slaves of South Carolina to rise in rebellion, it would work greater things than we imagine," Remond remarked. "If some black Archimedes does not soon arise with his lever, there will spring up some black William Wallace with his claymore, for the freedom of the colored race."[44]

Several historians have noted the abstract quality of such rhetoric, its function as "dramatic gesture." Yet such *gestures* seemed threatening enough that a significant number of prominent abolitionists were never entirely comfortable with open calls for slave insurrection. White abolitionists such as Garrison, Goodell, and Lewis Tappan and black abolitionists such as Douglass, Garnet, and Josiah Henson, who admired southern black liberators and acknowledged the right and ability of slaves to revolt, held back from endorsing or actively opposed the calls on practical and moral grounds.[45]

Others reacted negatively to any abolitionist encouragement of slave resistance. In the early 1840s, black and white Garrisonians condemned Smith and Garnet's addresses to the slaves as unchristian and reckless. Such nonresistants as Lydia Maria Child and Maria Weston Chapman were especially outspoken in this regard. Throughout the antebellum period, abolitionists of the border region, including Gamaliel Bailey, William Henry Brisbane, Samuel M. Janney, John G. Fee, and Cassius M. Clay, emphatically discouraged discussion of slave resistance and revolt for fear of southern white retaliation against the slaves and themselves.[46] But a few abolitionists such as Gerrit Smith's friend New York judge Jabez D. Hammond, Boston lawyer and constitutional theorist Lysander Spooner, enthusiastic journalist James Redpath, and especially John Brown desired to go beyond revolutionary rhetoric to actively instigate a slave revolt. They also represented the persistence among white abolitionists of the belief that blacks would not fight for their freedom without white leadership.[47]

Only Brown put such a plan into operation. In the process he transcended the abolitionist image of a southern black liberator and diminished it by placing himself—a white northerner—in the role of a Turner, Cinque, or Madison Washington. Following his successful 1858 rescue of slaves from Missouri and in response to knowledge of his wider plans, abolitionists most strongly inclined to forceful measures in the South thought in terms of a white, northern initiatives to which they hoped slaves would respond. The failure of slaves to rise following Brown's Harpers Ferry raid brought renewed questioning of the willingness of bondsmen to fight for their liberty. Yet Brown was himself a product of thirty years of abolitionist assertions that the slaves were indeed willing and able to rise against the system that oppressed them.[48] Brown's attempt to spark a slave rebellion in October 1859 was a result not only of the increasing violence that marked the sectional struggle in the 1850s but, more important, of an abolitionist vision of southern black antislavery action that had existed for decades.

The image of a southern black liberator ready to fight to free his people also foreshadowed the struggle of black and white abolitionists to allow blacks to enlist in the Union army during the Civil War. But the aim of this chapter has been to demonstrate that just as northern abolitionists looked on the appearance of southern white emancipators as progress toward their goal, northern abolitionists of nearly all persuasions always regarded the appearance of black liberators in the South to be a viable means of promoting general emancipation. The abolitionists' most explicit calls for slave action against slavery were always sparked by dramatic reports of revolt or escape, and as their hopes for emancipation initiated by southern whites declined in the late 1850s, such explicit calls became more common and less qualified. While abolitionists were ambivalent about black character, while they consciously portrayed blacks in a variety of ways to achieve different rhetorical effects, they had always seen southern black self-liberation as a likely terminus for slavery. With significant exceptions in the border region, they never left much doubt concerning whom they would favor in such a struggle.

Chapter Four

JOHN BROWN'S FORERUNNERS

"Seven of our citizens are now in southern prisons," the abolitionist editor of the *Green Mountain Freeman* observed in December 1844.[1] The seven included two students and a carpenter from a school for missionaries in Illinois, two ministers from New York, a Cape Cod seaman, and a schoolteacher from Vermont. They were only the better known of scores of people from the North who had ventured into the slave states to undertake what the *Freeman's* editor believed was a holy mission to help slaves escape from bondage. During the next six years there would be other well-publicized cases in which northerners risked their lives and freedom to rescue blacks from slavery. These individuals were not typical of most of those who went south to aid slaves to escape. They nevertheless enjoyed acclaim and financial support among abolitionists, who generally regarded them as significant actors in the antislavery drama.

Such high regard has not persisted. Just as the imagery associated with slavery's black and white opponents in the South has not been integrated into an understanding of abolitionism, the role of those who ventured into that section to help slaves escape has been generally ignored by historians of the sectional struggle. A significant amount of what has been written about the slave rescuers is negative, and there has been no serious evaluation of their role in the antislavery movement.

In the 1890s, Wilbur H. Siebert gave the slave rescuers their due in his study of northern efforts to help fugitive slaves on their way from the South to secure freedom in Canada. But, in his chronicle of what contemporaries called the underground railroad, Siebert concentrated on those who aided slaves who had already reached the free states. More recently, Larry Gara has argued that the activities of those who went south to help slaves escape had little relevance to organized abolitionism. Most studies of John Brown—the most famous northerner who entered the South to free slaves—do not mention his predecessors. Only Brown biographer Richard O. Boyer links Brown's efforts to the example set by these individuals, and only Herbert Aptheker suggests that they were an important part of a much more physically aggressive antislavery movement than is generally described.[2]

The tendency to ignore the northerners who went south to rescue blacks from slavery or to disparage their significance in the antislavery struggle is consistent with recent trends in abolitionist studies. As the introduction to this book suggests, historians have during recent years become less likely to characterize abolitionists as radicals challenging racial oppression in the South. The process that resulted in this climate of opinion began in the 1960s as liberal historians sought to counteract earlier Revisionist portrayals of the abolitionists as neurotic fanatics on the ideological fringe of northern society. The process continued in the 1970s and 1980s as studies of the abolitionists stressed what they held in common with other white northerners, including racial prejudice.

These studies, which investigated the roots of northern immediatism in the interrelated forces of religious revivalism and an emerging northern market economy, greatly improved understanding of what caused some white northerners to oppose strongly an institution that had little impact on their daily lives. According to this interpretation, individuals who embraced evangelicalism and economic change regarded slavery in the South not so much as an act of oppression against black people but as a symbol of immorality and inefficiency that prevailed among less enlightened portions of the northern population. In other words, by emphasizing the abolitionists' cultural environment in the North, such studies created a portrait of white abolitionists as middle-class reformers who rhetorically opposed slavery in reaction to conditions in the North rather than as radicals who aggressively sought to end slavery in the South. Often the abolitionists are portrayed as inwardly directed individuals essentially concerned with their own moral purity and salvation. Contentions that the abolitionists had minimal relevance to the sectional struggle follow logically from this portrait.[3]

The role historians have assigned to the intensely negative southern white reaction to the antislavery postal campaign of the mid-1830s is just as important in current portrayals of abolitionists as exclusively northern in orientation. The assumption is that this southern reaction forced the abolitionists to concentrate thereafter on influencing popular opinion in the North rather than acting directly against slavery in the South. Historians contend that it took a general northern perception of southern aggressiveness in the 1850s to finally lead abolitionists to seek the kind of direct physical confrontation with slavery that culminated in John Brown's raid on the federal arsenal at Harpers Ferry, Virginia, in 1859.[4]

The previous two chapters discussing the northern abolitionist images of the South's black and white opponents of slavery are designed to modify these prevailing interpretations. But a more formidable challenge to such interpretations arises from abolitionist engagement in, and support for, northern-based direct action against slavery in the South. If those who went into the South in the 1840s to help slaves escape were closely associated with organized abolitionism, it would indicate that the immediatists were indeed focused on slavery in that section. It would prove that confrontation with slaveholders was much closer to the heart of the movement than has recently been supposed. In that case, John Brown's raid and the overwhelmingly positive abolitionist response to it were not mere products of increasingly strained sectional relations in the 1850s but of a tactically radical reform culture that emerged in the 1840s. In addition, a close association of slave rescuers with organized abolitionism supports a contention that the abolitionists were as aware as their proslavery antagonists that slavery was vulnerable in the upper South. By physically challenging slavery in that region, abolitionists were not bystanders in the sectional conflict but were active participants in driving the South to secession.[5]

This chapter investigates the characteristics of the most prominent of the slave rescuers and evaluates their role in abolitionist reform culture. Gara argues that the slave rescuers were on the periphery of this culture and that other abolitionists held their risky ventures into the South to be counterproductive. The contention here is that abolitionists generally embraced slave rescuers—as they did southern white emancipators and southern black liberators—as integral parts of a movement designed to transcend northern concerns and directly impact slavery in the South.

The overwhelming majority of fugitive slaves who reached the North and Canada during the decades prior to the Civil War escaped from the South on their own or with the help of other blacks. Today, the most famous of these black slave rescuers is Harriet Tubman, a fugitive slave from Maryland who undertook over a dozen rescue missions from the North into the slave states in the 1850s. Yet, in the 1840s and 1850s, Tubman and other blacks who engaged in such efforts did not become celebrities among either white or black abolitionists as the result of their exploits. Latent racism among white abolitionists and the impact of the dominant culture on black abolitionists played a role in this. But other forces were at work as well. Slave rescue attempts were clandestine operations, so it was necessary for their perpetrators to be caught and given a public trial if they were to be renowned. Because Tubman and several other black and white slave rescuers were never apprehended by southern authorities, they remained unknown to most of their contemporaries, as did those predominantly black slave rescuers who, though captured, never received a public trial.[6]

There were also those such as Thomas Garrett, a Quaker businessman of Wilmington, Delaware, who made no attempts to rescue slaves from their masters but helped fugitive slaves on their way out of the South. A member of the Abolition Society of Pennsylvania before moving to Wilmington in 1822, Garrett claimed to have helped 2,245 slaves on their way to freedom by 1860. He was heavily fined in 1848 for helping one slave family. But, while he enjoyed the respect of black and white abolitionists, he never in his long career attracted the acclaim attached to those who directly intervened between masters and slaves.[7]

Consequently, the handful of whites who were caught helping slaves escape received far greater attention from abolitionists than did their black counterparts or steady underground railroad agents of the border region such as Garrett. It is the extensive testimony regarding these prominent white slave rescuers that provides a means for judging what motivated such individuals to take extreme risks on behalf of southern slaves. That testimony also provides a means to judge the role of such confrontational tactics in abolitionist reform

culture. Before making such judgments, however, it is necessary to
introduce the prominent slave rescuers. They may be divided into
three cohorts based upon chronology, geography, and association.

In the first cohort were Alanson Work, James E. Burr, and George
Thompson. These young men were the first to gain renown for entering a slave state to attempt to conduct blacks to freedom. Burr and
Thompson were students at the Mission Institute at Quincy, Illinois,
just across the Mississippi River from the slaveholding state of Missouri, and the institute employed Work to build houses. Inspired by
David Nelson, the institute's president and a former Missouri abolitionist, faculty and students at the institute had since the late 1830s
helped fugitive slaves reach Canada. Acting in that tradition, the three
men crossed the Mississippi in July 1841 to try to entice five slaves to
escape. The slaves told their masters, who trapped the would-be liberators and took them to the nearby Palmyra town jail. In September,
a jury found them guilty of slave-stealing, and a judge sentenced them
to twelve years in the state penitentiary, although all three gained
pardons by 1846.[8]

The second cohort of slave rescuers gained prominence in three
unrelated incidents during the summer and early autumn of 1844. In
the first incident, Maryland authorities arrested Charles T. Torrey in
June for helping several slaves escape. Torrey had become an abolitionist in 1835 and by the late 1830s was a major Massachusetts antagonist of William Lloyd Garrison in a bitter struggle over the
direction of the antislavery movement. The struggle led Torrey out
of Massachusetts, into the abolitionist Liberty party, and into the
South. He was jailed briefly in 1842 for attempting to report on a
slaveholders' convention in Annapolis for several Liberty newspapers.
In 1843 he was serving as editor and Washington correspondent of
the *Albany Patriot* on behalf of the radical wing of the Liberty party
when he began to respond to requests from fugitive slaves to help
their families join them in the North. He moved to Baltimore in early
1844 to help slaves escape on a regular basis, and his activities in
Virginia and Maryland led to his arrest in that city. Prevented by a
technicality from posting bond, he stood trial in December, was convicted, and began serving a six-year sentence in the Maryland penitentiary in 1845. He died there of tuberculosis in May 1846.[9]

In the next incident, in July 1844 two sloops overtook an open boat piloted by Jonathan Walker, who was attempting to sail seven slaves to the Bahamas and freedom. Walker, a Cape Cod seaman and shipwright, had become an abolitionist in 1831. In 1836 he, his wife, and several children moved to Pensacola, Florida Territory, where Walker hired, boarded, and befriended slaves, whom he treated "on terms of perfect equality with his family." Distrusted by his white neighbors and fearful of the influence of slaveholding institutions on his children, Walker brought his family back to Massachusetts in 1841. In June 1844, he returned alone to Pensacola and set out in the boat with his former slave employees. They traveled seven hundred miles along the Florida coast before the sloops captured them and towed them to Key West. In November, a territorial court convicted Walker on charges of slave-stealing and aiding slaves to escape. His punishment included having the letters *SS*—for "slave stealer"—branded into his hand and imprisonment until June 1845, when abolitionists paid his fine and costs totaling six hundred dollars.[10]

The final incident in 1844 occurred in September when a Kentucky posse apprehended Calvin Fairbank and Delia A. Webster, who had just carried future black leader Lewis Hayden and his family across the Ohio River to the North. Fairbank was a Methodist minister from western New York who, operating out of Cincinnati in the early 1840s, made numerous trips into the South to guide slaves to freedom. At Oberlin, Ohio, in 1844, he agreed to go to Lexington, Kentucky, to rescue the wife and children of a fugitive slave named Gilson Berry. At Lexington, Fairbank met Webster, an unmarried school teacher from Vermont who was principal of the Lexington Female Academy. When Fairbank's plan to help Berry's family collapsed, he enlisted Webster in the Hayden escape, which led to their arrest. During their separate trials in December, Webster steadfastly maintained her innocence while Fairbank admitted his guilt in helping slaves escape. Juries found both of them guilty, but Webster served only two months of a two-year sentence before public opinion forced Governor William Owsley to pardon her. Fairbank, who received a sentence of fifteen years at hard labor, served until 1849 when a campaign initiated by Hayden in Massachusetts led Governor John J. Crittenden to pardon him as well.

Neither Fairbank nor Webster, however, could resist returning to Kentucky. In November 1851 Kentucky marshals arrested Fairbank in Indiana for "abducting" a slave woman. He was convicted and again sentenced to fifteen years in the state penitentiary, where he remained until 1864. More surprising, Webster, who had tenuous connections with organized abolitionism, purchased a tract of land in Kentucky in 1852 to establish a free labor colony. Local slaveholders claimed she was aiding slaves to escape, had her repeatedly arrested, and drove her from the state in 1854.[11]

The third cohort of slave rescuers gained wide recognition between 1848 and 1851 as a result of their interrelated activities in and around Washington, D.C. One of the three was William L. Chaplin, a dedicated New York abolitionist very much in the mold of Torrey. The other two, Daniel Drayton and Edward Sayres, were soldiers of fortune without deep abolitionist sympathies. Chaplin was born and raised in Massachusetts, where he practiced law and became involved in benevolent reform in the 1820s. Preceding Torrey by several years, he moved to New York in 1837 and joined the Gerrit Smith circle of abolitionists. When Torrey was arrested Chaplin succeeded him as the Washington correspondent of the *Albany Patriot* and later became editor of the paper. While in Washington in early 1848 Chaplin made arrangements through abolitionists in Philadelphia to hire coastal trader Drayton to transport a large group of slaves by sea to the North. Drayton then chartered Sayres's schooner *Pearl* to carry out the mission. In April, the *Pearl* departed Washington with about seventy-seven slaves crowded below its deck, only to be overtaken and captured by a steamer. Angry masters sold most of the *Pearl* fugitives south, and Drayton and Sayres, convicted of transporting slaves for the purpose of escape, were sent to Washington Jail until they paid fines totaling twenty thousand dollars—a life sentence for poor men.[12]

Southerners in Washington suspected that Chaplin was responsible for the *Pearl* escape attempt. But Drayton refused to implicate him, and Chaplin remained free to become a participant in another attempt two years later. In August 1850 he undertook to drive a carriage containing two escaped slaves north from Washington through Maryland to Pennsylvania. Washington police captured the trio after a violent confrontation just across the Maryland line from the capital. Washington prosecutors charged Chaplin with "larceny of slaves" and Maryland indicted him for assault with intent to kill. Fearing that Chaplin would become another Torrey, New York abolitionists persuaded Gerrit Smith and northern-born Washingtonian David A. Hall to post bail for Chaplin's release. He never stood trial, but his active involvement in the antislavery cause soon ended.[13]

What were the characteristics and motives of these individuals whose exploits in the South have been briefly chronicled? Did their attributes and actions place them on the periphery of abolitionism or in its mainstream? If Drayton and Sayres, who were primarily driven by desire for monetary gain, are excepted, the slave rescuers' backgrounds and their motivations are very similar to those of other advocates of the immediate abolition of slavery. Like most opponents of slavery, they shared a New England heritage, having been raised there or in an outpost of Yankee culture in western New York or Ohio.[14] More important, they shared motives for their actions in the South that reflected in accentuated form the motives of other abolitionists. These motives included a religious impulse, concern for blacks, and a desire to resolve personal dilemmas.

Like other abolitionists, the prominent slave rescuers came to maturity during the evangelical revivalism that swept the North during the early decades of the nineteenth century. The revival's impulse was especially strong among them, but, while they were deeply concerned for their personal salvation, they can not be described as inwardly directed or essentially concerned with northern social issues. Torrey was a Congregationalist minister who preached the doctrine of active benevolence associated with the great revivalist Charles G. Finney. The religious excitement of New York's Burned-over district shaped the personality of Methodist preacher Fairbank. Burr and Thompson studied to be missionaries, and their friend Work's letters testify to his strong religious commitment. Chaplin was the devout son of a Congregationalist minister, northerners and southerners alike alluded to Walker's Christian character, and even Webster—whose commitment was the weakest of this group—was reputed to be a very pious woman.[15] Each of them believed that slaveholding was an unmitigated sin and that Christianity required them to free those they found in bonds.

Stimulated by an increase in slave escapes in the late 1830s and by southern state laws prohibiting speaking and writing against slavery within their bounds, the slave rescuers resolved to take direct action to fulfill God's commandments. They attempted physically to apply the Golden Rule and such other biblical injunctions as "rid them out of the hand of the oppressor" and "remember those in bonds as bound with them." They saw the hand of God in their actions and aspired to be militantly Christlike. Work said, "We looked up to Him, who came to preach 'deliverance to the captives, and the opening of prison doors to them that are bound.'" Chaplin revealed his own motivation in December 1846 when he asked, "Was not poor Torrey, in his dauntless efforts to burst the prison door and plunge into the deepest cell for the rescue of the forlorn captive, more Christ-like than any of us? . . . He *felt* and acted . . . .He laid his all on the alter of the great cause." That such individuals believed they were obeying a higher law when they disobeyed state, territorial, and federal laws in order to help slaves escape followed from their deeply religious outlook.[16]

Concomitant to the slave rescuers' religious impulse was their intense identification with the suffering of blacks. There can be no doubt that these individuals had a deep-set need to help slaves and attempted to treat them as brothers and sisters. In 1838 Chaplin alluded to "fellow-men & fellow citizens crushed & dumb—of husbands torn & mangled by the brutality & lust of the lawless despot—of wives more than widows—mothers more than childless, and orphans more than motherless, made so by the infernal spirit of slavery." Thompson, Torrey, Walker, and Fairbank spoke similarly of their sympathy for suffering slaves. Desirous of ending that suffering and encouraged by their own religious aspirations, they began by cultivating personal relationships with blacks. Torrey served in 1841 as the secretary of the biracial Boston Vigilance Committee, which aided local fugitive slaves. He was active in the black community in Philadelphia and when in Washington he attended only black churches. Walker was notorious in Pensacola for his good relations with blacks, and Fairbank preached in black churches and lived with blacks at various times in his life. Chaplin went out of his way to help fugitive slaves in the North and among abolitionists had a reputation for his "strong sympathy with slaves." Even Webster, who told Kentuckians she wished the slaves were back in Africa, pledged to go there to teach them.[17]

So strong was their empathy that when they came into proximity to slavery they were easily tempted to take direct action against it.

Thompson imagined he could hear the cries of whipped slaves from across the Mississippi River. The dehumanizing character of the domestic slave trade, in particular, deeply disturbed Walker, Torrey, and Chaplin. Fairbank and Chaplin acted as agents of northern abolitionists in efforts to purchase the freedom of individual slaves before they were sold to slavetraders. They entered, along with Torrey, the milieu of slave and free black communities of the border region. All three came to share the perspective of black families attempting to preserve themselves and protect the virtue of daughters and sisters threatened by sale into prostitution. Torrey spoke for the others when he said his experience in slave regions made him more "deeply impressed with the horrors of slavery than ever." Such conditions enhanced their identification with the slaves, made them willing to help in escapes when legal measures failed, and stimulated their desire to emulate Christ. Even in prison they persisted in slave escape schemes. As Chaplin told an anti–Fugitive Slave Law convention in January 1851, "Imprisonment is a great, but not the greatest calamity. Worse than death was the withering, killing consciousness that you have left the poor to perish, when they have stretched their hands out to you for mercy and deliverance."[18]

While intense religious commitment and identification with blacks underlay the efforts of these individuals to help slaves escape, a disposition to take dramatic risks in attempts to resolve personal difficulties also contributed. Historian Peter Walker has shown that a search for personal identity played a role in difficult decisions to embrace abolitionism. More desperate searches led to engagement in extremely dangerous rescue efforts. In Torrey's case, financial embarrassments connected with his proprietorship of the *Albany Patriot* in 1843 and fears that he had alienated other abolitionists precipitated his efforts to rescue slaves and thereby regain stature. "*Private* causes of personal misery render me—perhaps *reckless*," he told Gerrit Smith. "In toil and excitement the misery one cannot relieve, may be forgotten." Like Torrey, Chaplin suffered financial distress as editor of the *Patriot*, and a break-up of the Gerrit Smith cluster of abolitionist leaders set him adrift. Deeply impressed by Torrey's example and, like Torrey, seeking a meaningful antislavery role, Chaplin too believed he could resolve his own difficulties by taking direct action against slavery. "We believe the man is not yet born, who has failed of a rich return in any endeavor he may put forth, at whatever expense, to storm the castle of tyranny and rescue from its cruel grasp its bruised and peeled victims," he wrote in December 1848.[19]

Torrey, Chaplin, and other slave rescuers paid a high emotional price for their undertakings. While in prison and suffering from terminal tuberculosis, Torrey feared he was losing his mind and lashed out uncontrollably at his closest friends. In jail Chaplin experienced "the intensest mental agony" and became obsessed with his physical safety. Following his release he perplexed his admirers by withdrawing from the cause. In the early 1850s Thompson, as director of the AMA's Mendi Mission in Africa, experienced considerable difficulty relating to his subordinates, one of whom characterized him as "deranged." Imprisonment caused these problems, but on occasion even friends of the slave rescuers questioned the sanity of the enormous risks they took. Thompson in 1841, for instance, had to advise a correspondent, "Lest you may feel that I am disturbed in my mind, you may be assured that it is fixed on God," and ten years later Gerrit Smith described Fairbank as "an insane person." It is important to note, however, that questions of sanity arose *after* these slave rescuers were arrested, and Smith's remark came in the context of an attempt to save Fairbank from further imprisonment.[20]

Such expressions of concern for the rescuers' well-being in fact underline the high regard abolitionists had for individuals who faced grave dangers to confront slavery. None of the rescuers acted in isolation from abolitionist reform culture. The great majority of them had strong ties to organized abolitionism, and the three who did not— Webster, Drayton, and Sayres—were associates of persons who did.

The closest ties were to the New York or radical political abolitionist wing of the Liberty party. Chaplin was one of the faction's leaders, and Torrey, after years of leadership at the highest levels of abolitionism, also affiliated with the New York Liberty organization. More locally, Chaplin and Torrey were by the early 1840s active members of the Albany Vigilance Committee. Dedicated, like its Boston counterpart, to protecting fugitive slaves from recapture in the North, this committee also openly supported individuals who promoted slave escapes in Maryland, the District of Columbia, and Virginia. Therefore, although historians have portrayed Torrey in particular as an eccentric, his and Chaplin's actions in the South were direct products of their local immediatist environment in eastern New York.[21]

Work, Burr, Thompson emerged from a similar but smaller institutional framework at Quincy, Illinois. Later, they and Fairbank joined Torrey and Chaplin in identifying with the radical political abolitionist faction. The trio from the Missionary Institute maintained close ties to Gerrit Smith and, instead of embracing the Free Soil and Republican parties in the 1850s, remained "True Liberty Party" advocates. Fairbank, during his months of freedom between 1849 and 1851, attended antislavery meetings, served as an abolitionist organizer, and expressed views compatible with Smith's. Of the prominent slave rescuers, only Walker had institutional ties to the Garrisonians. For several years after his return to New England from prison in Florida, he traveled as a lecturer for the Garrisonian-dominated MASS. But he also joined in Liberty functions.[22]

The strong institutional affiliations of these individuals contradict the assumption that they were mere adventurers on the periphery of organized abolitionism. Just as important, the preponderance of radical political abolitionists among them suggests the aggressiveness of that group compared to other political abolitionists, Garrisonians, and church-oriented abolitionists. This aggressiveness involved more than participation in isolated escape attempts. It included related efforts to destroy slavery through judicial action and to create a climate of fear that would destabilize slavery in the border South.

Garrisonians were committed to a proslavery interpretation of the United States Constitution. They maintained that because the country's organic law protected slavery, the only recourse of concerned northerners was to dissolve the Union. Most political abolitionists believed the Constitution left slavery in the states to local jurisdiction. Therefore they advocated Congressional action against slavery in the national domain but conceded that the peculiar institution was legally inviolable in the South. Only the Gerrit Smith cadre of radical political abolitionists held that the Constitution, interpreted in compliance with natural law, outlawed slavery throughout the country.[23]

This radical interpretation of the Constitution allowed slave rescuers to assume they acted in accordance with human as well as divine law. As Fairbank put it, when he learned at Oberlin that the Constitution was antislavery and that slavery was therefore against the law, "I was no longer under obligation to respect the evil institution as protected by Government, but was free . . . to follow the promptings of duty." This interpretation also raised the expectation among abolitionists generally that trials of slave rescuers in southern courts could serve as test cases to win federal court rulings against slavery in southern states, the Florida Territory, or the District of Columbia. Torrey saw the main issue in his case to be, "Has SLAVERY any constitutional or legal existence in Maryland or Virginia?" If not, what legal recourse had slaveholders to protect their vested interests against slave escapes and aggressive abolitionists? Although they were outmaneuvered by local prosecutors and judges in each instance, the northern abolitionist supporters of slave rescuers—from the time of Work, Burr, and Thompson onward—vigorously pursued legal action. They solicited the services of prominent constitutional lawyers, raised legal defense funds, and honed their constitutional arguments in anticipation of striking a judicial blow against slavery.[24]

While these legal maneuvers created widespread interest among northern antislavery activists, abolitionists also believed that slave rescue attempts could by themselves help undermine the institution of slavery in the border region. Beginning in 1841 when Work reported from the Palmyra jail that his actions had encouraged more slave escapes from Missouri, abolitionists linked wholesale slave exodus to rescue attempts. They also assumed that such attempts would stimulate antislavery agitation in the slave states. Together these phenomena, they predicted, would make slaveholding hazardous in the border region and quickly "topple down the whole crazy fabric of slavery." For example, when Kentucky emancipator Cassius M. Clay noted an increase in slave escapes from that state's northern counties in 1845, Elizur Wright Jr. of the *Emancipator* attributed the increase to Fairbank's and Webster's activities. Wright exclaimed, "Success, we say, to 'slave-stealing.' It is doing more to make Cassius M. Clays in Kentucky, than any other cause." That same year James C. Jackson declared in the *Patriot*, "One hundred like Torrey would do more to deliver the slaves speedily than all paper resolutions, speeches, presses, and votes." There may not have been a "deep-laid scheme," but Wright and Jackson, and others believed that helping slaves to escape had an important role to play in the attack on slavery.[25]

Proslavery southern whites agreed. From their perspective, slave rescue attempts constituted violent northern aggression against the South. By the 1840s the border slave states experienced heightened racial tensions as increasing reliance on free black labor disrupted their slave-labor economies. Those tensions created the despair among black families to which slave rescuers responded and inspired the rescuers to believe that their actions might help destroy a weakened slave system. Such tensions also insured that southern whites would react strongly to direct interference from the North. Spectacular slave rescue attempts made Thompson, Fairbank, Torrey, and the others typical abolitionists in southern minds, and southern whites attributed the schemes of slave rescuers to the major abolitionist leaders of the North. Proslavery advocates characterized northerners who invaded the slave states to help slaves escape as "vile fiends," "emissaries of mischief," and "worse than thieves, robbers, or murderers."[26]

Such individuals reinforced decades-old rumors that abolitionists sent agents into the South to work among slaves in order to encourage escape and rebellion. Invariably following the capture of slave rescuers in southern communities, extremely agitated mobs arose to insist that the rescuers be severely punished under or, if necessary, beyond the law. Southern leaders contended that if northerners continued to interfere in the South there would be bloodshed and desolation. It was, therefore, not just secondhand accounts of abolitionist activities in the North but fear of direct abolitionist assaults in a region where slavery was vulnerable that heightened southern sectionalism.[27]

There was considerable support in the North for southern outrage against direct abolitionist interference with slavery. But there was considerably less opposition to such attempts among abolitionists—especially among black abolitionists, radical political abolitionists, Garrisonians, and church-oriented abolitionists—than has been suggested by Gara and other historians.[28] The impact of slave rescuers and the adamant southern response to them was to push abolitionists into a more confrontational stance toward the South.

Initially there was some sentiment among abolitionists that those who went south to help slaves get away from their masters acted impetuously and foolishly. But once a slave rescue had been undertaken and the perpetuators arrested, abolitionists and their organizations consistently provided strong verbal, moral, and financial support for such individuals. William Lloyd Garrison called aiding slaves to escape "an act of mercy worthy of all praise . . . but treated in this Christian land as the most flagrant crime that can be committed," and the MASS and AASS consistently echoed this position. The church-oriented AFASS raised funds for the defense of Torrey, Walker, Drayton, and Sayres and took a keen interest in the constitutional issues raised by efforts to help slaves escape from the South.[29]

Political abolitionists took similar positions. In 1850 radical political abolitionist leader Gerrit Smith told United States Senator William H. Seward, "For many years I have regarded the helping of slaves to liberty, especially at the great peril of the helper, as among the most beautiful expressions and among the most decisive evidences of disinterested benevolence and genuine piety." The less militant New England Liberty advocates hardly fell short of Smith's standard. Speaking for Joseph C. Lovejoy, Joshua Leavitt, and Henry B. Stanton, John Greenleaf Whittier said of Torrey, "His work among the poor and helpless was well and nobly done. . . . He gave his life for those who had no claim on his life save that of human brotherhood. How poor, how pitiful and paltry seem our own labors!"[30]

Torrey also gained great renown among blacks as an intrepid friend of humanity, and black groups honored Walker, Drayton, and Chaplin. Black abolitionist spokesperson Jermain Wesley Loguen, himself a fugitive slave, told Chaplin, "Sir, the black man has many friends—but they are not all of that kind who are ready to go down and meet us at the spot where American tyranny has placed us, and there . . . to offer themselves as our deliverers. . . . Sir, your name will dwell on the lips of the colored man forever."[31]

As these comments indicate, abolitionists perceived slave rescue attempts to be important and legitimate steps toward the destruction of what they believed to be an inherently illegal and violent slave system. However, abolitionists were always ambivalent concerning the use of violent means against slavery. Just as abolitionists usually qualified their recognition of the justice of slave revolt, they were reluctant to characterize slave rescues as forceful endeavors. In contrast to southern and proslavery northern spokespeople, abolitionists usually played down the violent implications—and in some cases actual violence—of slave rescue attempts in order to portray them as properly peaceful antislavery tactics. Frederick Douglass, Henry B. Stanton, William Lloyd Garrison, and Gerrit Smith, representing a variety of abolitionist persuasions, stressed, in Garrison's words, that slave rescuers endeavored to save people from oppression "not . . . by any act of violence, but in the spirit of good will to the oppressed, and without injury to the oppressor." Garrison and a group of black leaders expressed a core precept of northern immediatism when they resolved in 1844 "that to assist those who are pining in slavery to break their chains, and obtain their freedom by flight, instead of being a criminal act, is one that must be pleasing in the sight of God, and applauded by all who remember those in bonds as bound with them."[32]

And the slave rescuers received applause. In a manner identical to their response to the appearance of southern white emancipators, northern abolitionists eagerly claimed the rescuers as their own. The MASS, for example, declared in 1846 that abolitionism had produced the conditions that favored attempts to help slaves escape. "If that movement never accomplishes any thing else," the society's annual report asserted, "it has already been the means of the deliverance of thousands from the house of bondage, by opening the way for their escape, and raising up willing friends to assist them." When Walker, Chaplin, Drayton, and Fairbank returned from southern prisons, each received more than one hero's welcome from abolitionist meetings called in their behalf. Although Garrisonians questioned Webster's commitment to immediatism, Liberty abolitionists invited her to their meetings, lavished praise upon her, and defended her stature as an abolitionist. In terms similar to those that would be applied to John Brown a decade later, a correspondent of the *Boston Courier* pictured Drayton as "bold, stern, determined, ready to do battle unto death in the cause of right."[33] Certainly slave rescuers were antislavery heroes. More significant yet, they were martyrs to the cause and symbols of antislavery progress.

Abolitionists were thoroughly convinced of the truthfulness of the early Christian adage that a cause thrives on the blood of its martyrs. They persistently assumed that to suffer in behalf of the slave was a means of creating more abolitionists and hastening the destruc-

tion of slavery. Most of the slave rescuers thought of themselves this
way, and immediatists agreed. Loring Moody of the MASS spoke
for numerous Garrisonian and black abolitionists in 1844 when he
said that the punishment of individuals who followed Christian principles by aiding slaves to escape would force the issue of slavery on
the North. Abolitionists, Moody declared, could afford to "sacrifice
some of our brave spirits" to raise a "great cloud of witnesses" in their
place. Garrison described Chaplin's arrest as a nail in slavery's coffin.[34]

Not all abolitionists agreed that slave rescue attempts were positive developments in the antislavery cause. But Gara has exaggerated the prominence of dissenters, at least among radical political,
church-oriented, and Garrisonian abolitionists. Instead, the strongest
opposition among abolitionists to slave rescuing came from Gamaliel
Bailey, Cassius M. Clay, and other antislavery advocates who resided
in the border region. Bailey and Clay sought a bisectional consensus
against slavery and feared passions aroused by northern physical
interference in the South would undermine their efforts.[35]

Otherwise, abolitionist criticism of slave rescuers was weak, in-
consistent, and in some cases designed to mollify southern authorities who made repentance a condition for leniency toward or pardon
of slave rescuers. The most common abolitionist criticism of failed
slave rescue attempts was that the would-be liberators had acted im-
prudently or indiscreetly not that they had acted illegally or incor-
rectly. Garrison, for example, said Fairbank had "acted benevolently,
if not wisely." Other abolitionists quickly established that to act im-
pulsively on one's emotions in a romantic age was hardly to be condemned. In 1845 black abolitionist David Ruggles complained, "Some
soi-desant friends of Mr. Torrey have said he was rash and impru-
dent. This charge is ever made against the faithful and true in the
cause of humanity." Torrey and the others, Ruggles believed, were
simply braver than other abolitionists.[36]

In no other instance was the abolitionist identification with slave
rescuers clearer than in their response to Gamaliel Bailey's consistent opposition to efforts to help slaves escape. Bailey was the abolitionist editor of the *Philanthropist* in Cincinnati from 1836 through
1846 and the *National Era* in Washington from 1847 until his death in
1859. His location near or on slave soil, his persistent optimism that

the South could be peacefully converted to abolitionism, and the similarity of his views to those of Free Soil and Republican politicians separated him from other major abolitionist spokespeople. Like the southerners among whom Bailey lived, he believed slave rescue attempts encouraged violence. He also argued that such necessarily deceitful undertakings brought the antislavery movement into disrepute and hampered progress toward general emancipation. In this regard, he spoke for such leading antislavery politicians as Joshua R. Giddings and John P. Hale, who would emerge as leaders of the radical wing of the Republican party in the 1850s.[37] But to most prominent immediatists, Bailey's refusal to support helping slaves to escape made him a traitor to the cause.

Elizur Wright Jr. spoke for Massachusetts's political abolitionists when he criticized Bailey for failing to praise "the heroic conduct" of Drayton and Sayres and for casting "an imputation upon them" by boasting of his own refusal to break the law. Even stronger condemnation came from Gerrit Smith and a convention of radical political abolitionists following Bailey's criticism of Chaplin's illegal actions in 1850. Smith and his associates regretted that so many minds had been influenced by Bailey's "diluted, heartless, nominal Anti-Slavery that denied the right of a man to help his brother by any means not approved by Slaveholders." That abolitionists such as Henry B. Stanton and William Elder, who defended and praised Bailey's position, were, like Bailey, on their way into mass political organizations indicates the difference in temperament as well as reform philosophies that divided radical immediatists from their more conventional coadjutors. These differences concerning the advisability of helping slaves to escape from the South anticipated the contrasting responses of abolitionists and Radical Republicans to John Brown's raid nearly a decade later.[38]

Just as significant, however, were opportunities slave rescue attempts provided for cooperation among individuals representing different abolitionist factions. Such opportunities counteracted divisive tendencies within the movement and helped to unite all opponents of slavery. Efforts to raise defense funds, to employ lawyers, and to provide for rescuers' families became important unifying antislavery rituals. Garrison, for example, pledged to put earlier animosities behind him in joining with Liberty and AFASS leaders in raising funds in a futile effort to gain Torrey's release. Fund raising efforts for the benefit of Walker, Fairbank, Drayton and Sayres, and Chaplin also transcended factional boundaries, and in several instances blacks joined actively with whites in such undertakings. It was such a combined effort that secured a presidential pardon for Drayton and Sayres in 1852. This spirit of cooperation was not perfect, but the unifying impact of such efforts far outweighed occasional vindictiveness. As strong a critic of southern slave rescue attempts as Gamaliel Bailey expressed sympathy for those who undertook them, visited Torrey in jail, and worked diligently for the release of Drayton, Sayres, and Chaplin.[39]

Even antislavery politicians, who technically were not abolitionists, implicitly sanctioned the efforts of slave rescuers in the South. Former President John Quincy Adams, United States Senators William H. Seward and John P. Hale, and Congressmen Joshua R. Giddings, Horace Mann, Charles Durkee, and George W. Julian either offered to donate their legal expertise, helped raise funds, or otherwise expressed sympathy for the accused.[40] As limited as these politicians' commitment to immediate abolition was, the direct action of a very few against slavery drew them along with more dedicated abolitionists into a confrontational stance toward the South.

By the late 1840s most abolitionist leaders had endorsed such illegal direct action against slavery. Although their own field of endeavor was in the North, they responded positively and emotionally to the efforts of colleagues to go south to free slaves. Abolitionists took the efforts seriously and deeply admired persons who undertook them. They believed slave rescuers were a vital part of the antislavery movement and contended that its moral campaign had produced these heroes and martyrs. They insisted that slave rescue attempts furthered their cause by weakening slavery in the border region and by drawing others to the movement. Support for such slave rescue attempts was already part of abolitionism in the 1840s, and it was then that John Brown formulated his plan to use illegal and violent means to free slaves in the South. Although Brown never joined an antislavery organization, he had for years immersed himself in abolitionist reform culture and deeply admired Torrey and Walker.[41]

Brown had much in common with the slave rescuers described in this chapter. He was intensely religious and aspired to be Christlike.

He had strong empathy with blacks, and he relied on direct action against slavery as a means of resolving personal dilemmas. Brown's emphasis on arms and recruiting a band of followers set him apart from the prominent slave rescuers, as did his decision to raid a federal arsenal and the high level of violence that decision entailed. But Fairbank carried a pistol, Torrey relied on armed associates when he tried unsuccessfully to escape from Baltimore Jail, and a furious gun fight preceded the capture of Chaplin. Critics within and without the antislavery movement emphasized the inherent potential for violence in all such adventures. Most abolitionist spokespeople had, however, preferred to portray the slave rescue efforts as legal and peaceful measures against a violent system. It was not a long mental step from such prevarication to rationalizing Brown's violence in a righteous cause.

The abolitionists' reaction to Brown's capture, imprisonment, and death also echoed their response to similar events associated with earlier would-be liberators. The efforts to help his wife and children, the meetings in his honor, the portrayals of him as a hero and a martyr, the invocation of the higher law on his behalf, and the predications that his action and punishment hastened the death of slavery were all part of an old abolitionist drama. Even talk of Brown's possible insanity had a familiar ring, as did the posture of antislavery politicians within the Republican party denouncing Brown's actions while praising his courage and accepting his goals. The heightened sectional animosity of the 1850s may have made a raid such as Brown's more likely.[42] But the cultural prerequisites for one were firmly grounded in an abolitionist movement that by the 1840s had come to value direct physical confrontation with slavery in the South. While abolitionism had deep roots in northern culture and served emotional needs of its advocates, it was not a movement turned inward or on the periphery of the sectional conflict but one with a tradition of forcing the issue of slavery upon the South and the nation.

Chapter Five

PREACHING AN ABOLITIONIST GOSPEL IN THE SOUTH

As images of southern white emancipators, daring slave rescuers, and heroic slave rebels proliferated within northern abolitionist reform culture in the 1840s, evangelical and political abolitionists of diverse backgrounds began to demand a revival of a religious campaign to directly impact the South. As early as 1839 Charles T. Torrey publicly asked, "What say you to a NEW MISSIONARY SOCIETY, to 'evangelize the slaveholders' and their slaves? whose missionaries shall preach that 'the laborer is *worthy* of his hire?'. . . who shall in spite of slavery and its bloody laws, *teach the slaves to read the Bible*, and then put Bibles and tracts into their hands?" Torrey assumed that a few missionaries "might fall" in the process, but that "*pure* Christianity" would destroy slavery.[1]

Seven years later Cassius M. Clay, calling on every Christian "to bear testimony against this crime against man and God," also suggested the creation of an abolitionist missionary organization for the South. He wanted an interdenominational board of home missions established in New York City to coordinate the project. But, influenced by his own experience with proslavery violence and fearful that missionaries from the North would provoke more mob action, he proposed that the missionaries be southern-born and that they avoid a violent reaction by being "instructed never to speak of slavery in the presence of blacks and slaves."[2]

That personalities as different as Torrey and Clay endorsed an aggressive antislavery missionary effort in the South suggests the breadth of interest in such an undertaking. By the time Clay wrote, the idea had wide support, and in late 1846 Joshua Leavitt, an evangelical abolitionist and the leading spokesperson of the Massachusetts Liberty party, used Torrey's remarks and his legend in behalf of the missionary cause. Torrey, Leavitt declared, had been ahead of his time in providing "some admirable hints on the method by which the gospel is to be brought into direct action for the overthrow of slavery." In a spirit quite different from Clay's, Leavitt invoked Torrey's "hand-to-hand methods of encounter" and his martyr spirit as appropriate for antislavery missionaries in the South.[3]

Clay did well in envisioning the organizational form of the missionary undertaking in the South. When it emerged in the late 1840s as an important facet of abolitionism, the effort was, nevertheless, closer to the hearts of Torrey and Leavitt than to the Kentuckian's. At that time, the American Wesleyan Connection, the AMA, and the American Baptist Free Missionary Society (ABFMS) each initiated measures to spread antislavery religion in the South. Yet abolitionist missionaries in Kentucky, North Carolina, Virginia, Missouri, and the District of Columbia have been ignored in recent histories of the antislavery movement. More specialized studies that do consider religiously oriented abolitionists in the South tend to isolate them from northern abolitionism, or, as in the case of John R. McKivigan's excellent study of antislavery in the northern churches, devote only a few paragraphs to them.[4]

This reflects the prevalent opinion among historians of the sectional conflict that after the mid-1830s abolitionists concentrated exclusively on changing the North or themselves, that abolitionism is better understood by its northern origins than by its southern goals, and that southern antislavery activists were a breed apart from northern abolitionists. An exception to these opinions is Carlton Mabee's *Black Freedom,* published in 1970, which places antislavery missionary activity in the South in the broader context of abolitionist nonviolence. Such activity, Mabee contends, "represented in part a renewal of the effort the American Antislavery Society had begun in the 1830s and drifted away from because it seemed hopeless—the direct conversion of the South to the belief that slaveholding was sin." Mabee, however, underestimates continuity in northern abolitionist focus on impacting the South from the 1830s onward. It is also important to note that the organized abolitionist missions in the South, begun in the 1840s, constituted a more aggressive and enduring effort than the mailing of antislavery publications to prominent southerners during the great postal campaign of 1834-35.[5]

In fact, southern antislavery missionary action was deeply rooted in American abolitionism. It remained a priority among northern abolitionists throughout the antebellum era and contributed to their optimism concerning progress against slavery. Antislavery missionaries in the South were not isolated from northern abolitionist reform culture nor were they more timid than their northern counterparts. They pursued tactics in the South among slaveholders, nonslaveholding whites, free blacks, and slaves that fundamentally challenged the slaveholding status quo and elicited a strong response from leaders within the slaveholding community.

An abolitionist missionary may be defined as an individual of either northern or southern birth who, under the auspices of a northern abolitionist organization, worked in the South to build antislavery churches and spread antislavery sentiment. Prior to the late 1840s no one met all of these criteria. There was, nevertheless, a long tradition of religiously inspired and northern-supported antislavery action in the South. In 1835 Amos Dresser, former Lane Theological Seminary student and disciple of Theodore Weld, distributed antislavery "tracts and periodicals" in Kentucky and Tennessee. He also talked openly with slaves before a Nashville mob beat him severely for his efforts. Historians have frequently used the beating of Dresser to illustrate the difficulties northern abolitionists faced in the South, but Dresser also became a martyr whose conduct inspired others to go south to help the slaves.[6]

A year later, abolitionist missionary efforts of another Weld protégé, David Nelson, became the focus of confrontation between religiously oriented abolitionism and slavery in Missouri. A southerner, a Presbyterian minister, and a former slaveholder who had freed his slaves, Nelson was president of Marion College in eastern Missouri when Weld converted him to immediatism in 1835. As an agent of the AASS, Nelson contacted slaves, called on slaveholders in his congregations to free their bondspeople, and attempted to attract young northern abolitionists to his college. Driven out of Missouri by mob threats, he established the Missionary Institute in Quincy, Illinois, that produced Work, Burr, and Thompson's slave rescue attempt in 1841.[7]

Although he died in 1844, abolitionists still praised Nelson's efforts over a decade later. Less renowned but just as illustrative of the continuing northern promotion of religiously oriented antislavery efforts in the South was Samuel M. Janney of Loudon County in northeastern Virginia. A Quaker, Janney, like Joseph Evans Snodgrass, was drawn into active abolitionism by the visit of Philadelphia Quaker Garrisonians James and Lucretia Mott to Maryland and Virginia in 1842. Janney circulated northern antislavery publications in Virginia, preached against slavery, corresponded with northern abolitionists, and relied on northern abolitionist funding to publish his own antislavery essays. Although Janney was very cautious, he clearly served as an agent of northern abolitionism in Virginia in the 1840s and 1850s.[8]

It was, however, the organized efforts of the AMA, the Wesleyans, and the ABFMS starting in 1847 that best exemplify the continuing commitment of northern antislavery forces to religious abolitionism in the South. Each of these organizations was solidly immediatist with strong ties to the AFASS. Based on the "comeouter" principle of no Christian fellowship with slaveholders, they demanded secession from churches and missionary associations with ties to slaveholders. Together the three organizations demonstrate that far from giving up moral suasion in the South after the mid-1830s, a large portion of the northern abolitionist community made its greatest effort in behalf of that strategy in the last dozen years of the antebellum era.

Established by the AFASS in 1846, the AMA served as an abolitionist alternative to the major American missionary societies in supporting evangelical missions at home and abroad. It shared a New York City office and the leadership of Lewis Tappan, George Whipple, and Simeon S. Jocelyn with the AFASS. In 1852 it assumed financial responsibility for Wesleyan missionaries in the South, and in 1855 it took over some of the functions of the disbanded AFASS as well.[9]

The Wesleyans, however, were the first to support antislavery missionaries in the South. This small denomination had its origins in the failure of Methodist abolitionists to convince the Methodist Episcopal Church to denounce slaveholding as intrinsically sinful. After years of struggle, the new church organized in 1843 under the leadership of Orange Scott, La Roy Sunderland, and Luther Lee. In 1847 its Allegheny Conference, representing eastern Ohio and western Pennsylvania, received a request for help from dissident Methodists in Guilford County, North Carolina, and responded by dispatching

Adam Crooks of Ohio to become the minister of four small congregations in the Guilford region. A year later the conference sent Jarvis C.
Bacon to assume responsibility for a preaching circuit Crooks had
established in southwestern Virginia, and in 1849 Jesse McBride arrived in North Carolina from Ohio to help Crooks.[10]

Meanwhile the AMA began its southern missionary effort in late
1848 by committing itself to support John G. Fee's free church movement in Kentucky. Fee's effort became the largest southern missionary enterprise, employing a cumulative total of fifteen missionaries,
ten colporteurs, and numerous temporary agents between 1848 and
1861. In the 1850s, the AMA not only assumed responsibility for the
Wesleyan mission in North Carolina, it maintained other missions in
Washington, D.C., and Missouri, and encouraged antislavery action
in Maryland, Tennessee, and Virginia. The much smaller ABFMS
supported only the brief mission of Edward Mathews in Virginia and
Kentucky in 1851.[11]

The stated goal of each of these organizations was the rapid abolition of slavery through the peaceful means of establishing antislavery churches in the South, preaching an antislavery gospel,
distributing Bibles and antislavery literature, and opening a dialogue
with masters and slaves. The aim, said Luther Lee in November 1846,
was "to send anti-slavery missionaries to the south, or aid in supporting those whom God in his providence may rise up in that land of
whips and chains and gags, to preach deliverance to the captives, and
the opening of the prison door to them that are bound." Lee and the
others were well aware that such tactics, while ostensibly peaceful,
were highly threatening to slaveholders and were bound to engender confrontation. They, nevertheless, remained optimistic throughout the 1850s that their efforts in the South would end in the abolition
of slavery.[12]

It was Fee who was chiefly responsible for initiating this spirit of
confidence. In 1845 as the pastor of a small New School Presbyterian
church in northern Kentucky, he was one of a handful of southern
antislavery ministers supported by the conservative American Home
Missionary Society (AHMS). Increasingly dissatisfied with the willingness of his denomination and the AHMS to tolerate slaveholders,
he broke with both in 1848 and embraced nonsectarianism and the
AMA. Thereafter his ability to form additional antislavery congrega-

tions in Kentucky created in the minds of many northern abolitionists a belief that his experience could be replicated elsewhere in the
South. "The success of Rev. John G. Fee of Kentucky in forming an
anti-slavery church in that State," the AFASS declared in 1850, "shows
that the Gospel can be thus preached in slave States."[13]

This image of success, combined with demands from Fee and
others in the South for northern financial assistance, played a crucial
role in a growing abolitionist commitment to southern missions. But
other factors were important as well. Reflecting a common belief that
slavery marred America's moral leadership in the world, Wesleyans
and AMA leaders contended that missions to convert foreign nations
could not succeed so long as missionary associations failed to confront the great sin of slaveholding in the South and neglected the
spiritual needs of the slaves. The persistent hope of separating
nonslaveholding whites from slaveholders was also important in sustaining the commitment.

Just as important, advocates of antislavery missions were very
conscious that missionary work in the South could be used—along
with the efforts of southern white emancipators and the exploits of
slave rescuers—to further the antislavery cause in the North. Following well-publicized convictions of Wesleyan missionaries on charges
of inciting slave revolt in 1850, the *True Wesleyan* declared, "If the
North need anything further to bring out their Anti-Slavery sentiment
. . . and produce determined opposition to it, until it shall be over-
thrown, a few such convictions will do the work. Such developments
do more to awaken attention and rouse the conscience against slavery, than Northern men can do by their arguments. . . . Slavery can
not survive long after such trials and convictions become common."[14]

The willingness of the AMA to commit significant portions of its
limited financial resources to southern antislavery missions reflects
the stress church-oriented abolitionists placed on action in the South.
Although the AMA received almost all of its contributions in the North,
the ratio of its southern missionaries to its total domestic missionaries rose from one in seventeen in 1849 to one in ten a decade later.
The AMA created a special fund to support colporteurs in Kentucky,
and individual southern missionaries were always among those with
the higher stipends. As the country headed into recession in late 1856,
the association pledged to cut other home missions before those in

the slave states and the Kansas Territory, arguing that "a few thousands of dollars more, expended in maintaining missions in these fields, would give impetus to our entire Home enterprise." On the eve of the Civil War the AMA had begun an expansion of its southern effort, increasing the number of its full-time southern agents from four missionaries and one colporteur in 1857 to eleven missionaries and three colporteurs in 1859.[15]

Antislavery missionary efforts in the South extended over three decades and a considerable territory. They represented the initiatives of a variety of individuals and organizations. Nevertheless, the approximately three dozen missionaries were in several respects a homogeneous group. They were with a few exceptions quite young. They were also, except for Janney, orthodox evangelical comeouters, many of whom had been directly influenced by the millennial theology of Charles G. Finney. Although two of the missionaries were from England and a large portion from New England or the South, the nucleus of their activities was the antebellum West—western New York, and the states of the Old Northwest Territory, especially Ohio. New York's revivalistic Burned-over district was the birthplace of AMA missionaries George Candee and Otis B. Waters, and Wesleyan missionaries Crooks, Bacon, and McBride were all born in Ohio. Antislavery missionaries born elsewhere migrated to the West, and often the attraction was Oberlin College. Founded in the antislavery heartland of northeastern Ohio in 1833, Oberlin became a center of abolitionism following the expulsion of Weld and other abolitionist students from Lane Theological Seminary in 1834. Closely associated with Finney, who taught theology at the college and later served as its president, Oberlin—rather than Boston or even the New York City headquarters of the AMA—became the intellectual and spiritual home of the missionary effort.[16]

James Scott Davis, who was born in Virginia and raised in Illinois, was at Oberlin in the early 1850s prior to becoming a missionary in Kentucky. John A.R. Rogers, who helped Fee in central Kentucky, was born in Connecticut and attended college and seminary at Oberlin in the late 1840s and early 1850s. Candee and Waters were enrolled at Oberlin while serving as missionaries in Kentucky in the late 1850s, as was London-born William E. Lincoln. In addition, John W. White, John M. McLain, and Obed Marshall, who served temporarily in Kentucky, were Oberlin graduates. Students from the college spent winters teaching in missionary schools in Kentucky, and AMA agents in Missouri, G.H. Pool and William Kendrick, had ties to the college as well.[17]

Even those missionaries who did not attend Oberlin traced their conversion to abolitionism to stays in the Burned-over district or the Old Northwest. Edward Mathews, the only Free Baptist missionary to the South, was born in England and came under the influence of abolitionists Beriah Green, James G. Birney, and Gerrit Smith as a student at a theological institute near Utica, New York in 1838. Francis Hawley, who was born in Connecticut and spent years in North and South Carolina, developed a very close relationship with Smith prior to becoming a missionary in Kentucky in the mid-1850s. Daniel Worth, who served as a Wesleyan missionary with AMA support in Kentucky and North Carolina, also became an abolitionist in the West. Born in North Carolina to Quaker parents, he migrated to Indiana as a young man, became a Methodist, served as president of the Indiana Anti-Slavery Society in 1840, and helped establish the Wesleyan Connection in 1843. George Clarke, who served briefly as an antislavery minister in Kentucky and Washington, D.C., was, like Dresser and Nelson, converted to immediatism by Weld, the leading western abolitionist of the 1830s, and Fee traced his abolitionism to his years as a student at Lane Seminary in the early 1840s.[18]

If one were to concentrate exclusively on the abolitionist missionaries, one might conclude that historian Gilbert H. Barnes was correct when in the 1930s he located the "antislavery impulse" in western evangelicalism and the activities of Weld. There were no Garrisonians among the missionaries, no true nonresistants, no disunionists. Their eastern ties were to the evangelical Tappan circle, the AFASS, and, of course, the AMA. In the 1840s those who were of age identified with the Liberty party. In the late 1840s and 1850s the more conservative of them supported the Free Soil and Republican parties.[19]

Other missionaries were similar to the slave rescuers in their identification as radical political abolitionists. They adopted the views of Gerrit Smith and William Goodell and carried them into the South. Worth, for example, declared in North Carolina in 1858 that he was "an abolitionist of the Gerrit Smith type." In Kentucky, Fee, Davis, Hawley, Candee, Lincoln, and Virginia-born colporteur Peter H. West were all radical political abolitionists and joined Smith and Goodell in declaring that slavery could never be legalized. Hawley's service as a vice president of the Cazenovia Fugitive Slave Convention, which so lavishly praised William L. Chaplin, Fee's willingness to sacrifice his relationship with Cassius M. Clay rather than admit that he would recognize proslavery laws as binding, and Lincoln's arrest in Ohio in 1859 for his role in the famous Oberlin-Wellington fugitive slave rescue case illustrate their commitment on the point.[20]

The missionaries' ties to Oberlin, to the Liberty party, to the Smith-Goodell circle of New York abolitionists underline the fact that—regardless of their birthplace—they functioned as representatives of northern abolitionism in the South. There were very few gradualists or colonizationists among them. They were also acutely aware that, as Fee put it in 1856, the work of reform in the South must be for years sustained by northern contributions. He and Worth had to request additional AMA funding to expand their missionary enterprises, and the individual missionaries relied on AMA stipends to supplement the meager salaries they received as ministers to poor churches.[21]

Of them all only Fee had the stature that allowed him consistently to shape as well as carry out abolitionist policy. He played a prominent role at AMA annual meetings, was a leader at the Christian Anti-Slavery Convention at Cincinnati in 1850, conducted speaking tours across the North, and was intimate with leading northern abolitionists. But other missionaries maintained contacts with northern abolitionism as well. Mathews served as a secretary at the Christian Anti-Slavery Convention; Davis, Worth, and Rogers functioned effectively at AMA meetings; and even Daniel Wilson, a relatively insular North Carolinian who served as the Wesleyan/AMA missionary in his home state in the mid-1850s, regularly traveled to Ohio to attend Wesleyan conference gatherings.[22]

At the heart of the organized antislavery missions to the South was a belief deeply rooted in the reform culture of evangelical abolitionism. It was the conviction that the gospel would "'burst the bonds of the slaves.'" This was not the gospel preached regularly in the South or in much of the North. From the 1830s onward, abolitionists denounced what they called a proslavery gospel that either ignored the issue of slavery or actively denied that Christian principles favored emancipation. In contrast, they preached what they called a "whole," "pure," or "free," gospel, emphasizing Bible precepts that non-abolitionists avoided.[23]

It was a gospel that abolitionists insisted on preaching to slaves and free blacks as well as to whites. In 1835 Goodell linked the Biblical injunction to preach "the whole counsel of God" to every creature with his assertion of the right of abolitionists to address slaves. Seven years later, Leavitt denounced southern plans to send missionaries to slaves because such missionaries were likely to expurgate Bible passages favorable to emancipation from their sermons and emphasize those passages calling on servants to obey their masters. Abolitionists, Leavitt insisted, could join in such missionary efforts only "provided they could be permitted to preach the *whole* gospel." The South knew that would be dangerous, Alvan Stewart noted in 1845, because it involved informing slaves of their political rights. But this is exactly what antislavery missionaries intended to do.[24] The concept of preaching a whole gospel in the South was a radically aggressive departure from the postal campaign of 1835, when northern abolitionists scrupulously aimed their propaganda exclusively at slaveholders.

Adam Crooks on his way to North Carolina in 1847 perceived it to be his task "to go to the far South, to pronounce that Gospel which proclaims *liberty* to the captive, and the *opening* of the prison to them that are bound." In 1852 Daniel Wilson of North Carolina requested continued AMA support so that he might "be enabled to proclaim a Free and Full Gospel in this land of whips & chains & mobs." But Lewis Tappan best summarized the meaning of a whole gospel in the AMA annual report for 1858. Tappan wrote that "among the slaves and slaveholders, the Gospel, as it came from its divine founder, is to be preached without concealment or compromise. . . . whether human enactments authorize or forbid it." It was the duty of antislavery missionaries, he continued, "to preach a free, an evangelical, an antislavery Gospel . . . that had no complicity with caste, polygamy, or slaveholding; that would fearlessly and perseveringly . . . proclaim freedom, peace, temperance, holiness, the equality of man before the law, and the impartial love of God."[25]

Tappan's statement reflected what antislavery missionaries had been preaching regularly for years to southern audiences. Although these sermons were rarely published or preserved, there is enough evidence to indicate that they faithfully inculcated major precepts of northern abolitionism. Among their aims was to challenge proslavery Bible arguments and to emphasize that slaveholding was intrinsically sinful. Like abolitionists in the North, antislavery missionaries contended that slaveholders usurped God's authority by controlling the lives of the enslaved and denying them their God-given rights. Therefore, the missionaries insisted, all slaveholders, regardless of how they treated their slaves, were bound for hell.

Moreover, they warned that nonslaveholders who remained in churches that tolerated slaveholders were emersed in sin as well. Southerners, McBride charged, had to clearly tell slaveholders that they could not be Christians nor gain salvation. Horse thieves, he said, were angels compared to them. The missionaries also pleaded for recognition of the humanity of the "'bleeding, bound, and dumb'" slaves and frequently argued that Christ suffered from the brutalities inflicted on slaves by their masters. They cited the Bible passage: "'In as much as ye have done it to one of the least of these my brethren, ye have done it unto me.'" An individual who engaged in the slave trade, the missionaries argued, "sold [Christ] in the person of 'one of his little ones.'" They preached against "inequality and cruelty, oppression and degradation, injustice and inhumanity," as well as against negative impact of slavery on southern morality.[26]

Fee, Worth, and the other missionaries knew that their efforts depended on agitation for success. They designed their churches in Kentucky, North Carolina, Virginia, and Washington, D.C., to provoke dissention in neighboring congregations and to develop a corps of comeouters. Although persecution succeeded in blocking the establishment of lasting antislavery churches in Virginia and the Washington church floundered for lack of local support, the number of antislavery churches in Kentucky grew from one in 1846 to twelve in 1858 and in North Carolina from one in 1845 to ten in 1859. In Kentucky there were also missionary schools. The missionaries took pride that these institutions were not isolated, that slaveholders attended services and sent their children to schools taught by abolitionists.[27] But the churches and schools were small and their influence limited. The missionaries had a broader impact as itinerant preachers visiting congregations in their own and neighboring southern states. They and AMA colporteurs also talked informally with slaveholders, nonslaveholding whites, and slaves, and distributed large amounts of antislavery publications to whites.[28]

In the 1830s each of the slave states enacted laws designed to block the circulation of such publications, and historians have assumed that there was no significant effort to distribute printed abolitionist propaganda in the South after 1835. Yet in the 1840s and 1850s abolitionist organizations responded enthusiastically to requests from southern missionaries for antislavery books and tracts. In 1843, with the help of J. Miller McKim of the *Pennsylvania Freeman*, Janney established a network for the circulation of northern antislavery publications in Virginia. In 1845 Fee offered to distribute similar publications in Kentucky as a traveling agent of the Ohio Anti-Slavery Society, and he began to circulate AFASS materials over a year before he affiliated with the AMA. Between 1849 and 1851 Crooks, Bacon, and McBride handed out antislavery publications in North Carolina and Virginia, and in 1850 Edward Mathews "distributed a large number of Anti-slavery tracts . . . furnished by the [Baptist] Free Missions Society" in Virginia and Kentucky. Daniel Worth reported similar activities in North Carolina in 1859 as did AMA missionary Stephen Blanchard in Missouri in 1860-61. AMA agents in the 1850s provided antislavery publications to Marylanders and Virginians as well.[29]

But it was Fee who kept the best records, established the most efficient network of distribution, and convinced the leaders of the AFASS and AMA that publication of antislavery propaganda for southern audiences was worthwhile. Fee argued that the circulation of antislavery literature was the most effective means of counteracting proslavery forces in the South. Printed material, he believed, could reach thousands in areas where antislavery preachers dared not venture and pave the way for the establishment of free churches. He reinforced these claims by constantly requesting more publications to circulate and by demanding that AMA colporteurs in Kentucky meticulously record their activities. One colporteur, for instance, reported that in one month in 1853 he visited 340 families, sold eighty-seven volumes, and distributed "a large amount of religious and anti-slavery tracts." By 1859 Fee claimed that "'twenty millions of tracts'" could be distributed in the South.[30]

Many of the books and tracts Fee and others handled were designed for northern audiences. They included letters of Amos A.

Phelps, Goodell on comeouterism, and the fugitive slave narratives of Frederick Douglass and Henry Bibb. "There are some hear [*sic*] that can bear 'strong meat,'" Fee told Whipple in 1849. But Fee preferred antislavery materials specifically designed for southern audiences, and the publication in 1843 of the AFASS *Address to the Nonslaveholders of the South* indicated that its leaders would be receptive to his desires. By the early 1850s the society was publishing pamphlets, written by him, repudiating the proslavery Bible argument, denouncing colonization, rejecting Christian fellowship with slaveholders, and delineating the sinfulness of slaveholding.[31] Fee preferred such moral appeals to economic arguments, but given the missionaries' preference for publications addressed to southerners it is not surprising that in the late 1850s they circulated in North Carolina, Kentucky, and Missouri copies of North Carolina native Hinton R. Helper's *Impending Crisis of the South*, which called on nonslaveholding whites to strike for abolition on the basis of their economic self-interest.[32]

This circulation of antislavery publications in the upper South became the focus of a good deal of anger among slaveholders and their allies. Although the publications were invariably addressed to whites, local proslavery leaders maintained that their content was bound to reach the slaves, encouraging resistance and revolt. That such expressions of fear were not simple paranoia or demagoguery is clear in the attitudes of the missionaries toward the slaves and their willingness to directly contact slaves and free blacks. Like the slave rescuers, the missionaries developed considerable empathy for the enslaved. Adam Crooks felt "sorrow" and "indignation" in 1847 when he observed slavery in Virginia on his way to North Carolina. It amounted to "chattelizing humanity, and driving the iron chariot of oppression over her breast," he reported. Even those like Wilson of North Carolina, who had lived their entire lives in the South, recoiled at the suffering. "Truly it is verry [*sic*] desirable that our antislavery principles would advance," he told Whipple in 1853, "for it is heart sickening to see the poor slaves driven to market like brutes—parents torn from their children without mercy and compelled to drag out a miserable existence in the rice swamps or the cotton plantations."[33]

The missionaries' empathic response to the sufferings of slaves, their commitment to northern abolitionist concepts of racial equality, and their interpretation of Christ's command to "preach the gospel to every creature" led many of them to contact blacks in a manner that challenged basic assumptions of slaveholding culture. Throughout his years in North Carolina McBride preached to mixed-race congregations. In the spring of 1851 he estimated that in a large outdoor audience of six hundred, seventy five to eighty were black, many of them slaves. That same year in Kentucky a proslavery mob attacked Free Baptist missionary Mathews and drove him from the state after he preached at a black Baptist church. Worth took pride in 1857 that a group of slaves listened from outside a window to the first sermon he delivered in North Carolina, and he and his associate Alfred Vestal frequently preached to congregations that included slaves as well as slaveholders. It was, of course, no novelty in the South for whites to preach to slaves or for there to be mixed-race congregations— slaves frequently attended white churches and proslavery southern whites ministered to black churches. What was threatening to slavery was that at missionary churches slaves would hear a whole, antislavery gospel, would be treated—by the minister at least—on equal terms with whites, and would not be subjected to sermons that reinforced the morality of oppression. One slaveholder told McBride, "'You have ruined my slaves; I can't do a thing with them.'"[34]

It was Fee and other AMA missionaries in Kentucky who in the 1850s made the most sustained effort to institutionalize integrated or what they called "anti-caste" churches. Because, unlike North Carolina, Kentucky had no law against teaching slaves to read and write, the Kentucky missionaries also established a number of schools that served an entirely black or integrated clientele. The results were uneven. Fee and James Scott Davis had success in attracting slaves and free blacks to AMA churches and schools in northern Kentucky, but in the interior of the state masters discouraged slaves from attending. Fee, who advocated abolition of "the negro pews," also discovered considerable resistance to integration among white members of his churches. "'Tis harder to get men to take right ground against cast[e] than act against slavery," he told Lewis Tappan in 1851. Although Fee always succeeded in having his egalitarian policies adopted by church boards of trustees, in 1858 there was only one black member of his Berea congregation. Racism among antislavery Kentuckians and proslavery violence also restrained the progress of black and integrated schools in the state.[35]

In Kentucky the AMA's Bibles for slaves campaign more clearly succeeded in bringing abolitionists into direct contact with large numbers of slaves and, in turn, led to several anti-abolitionist reactions. Like efforts to evangelize slaves in general, abolitionist advocacy of distributing Bibles to slaves originated in the 1830s. Contemporary with the postal campaign, the AASS attempted without success to establish a fund to carry out such a project under the direction of the American Bible Society. When abolitionist interest in direct action in the South blossomed in the mid-1840s, Leavitt, invoking Torrey's spirit, revived the Bible project. The Bible Society again refused to cooperate, and in 1848 the AMA assumed responsibility by establishing a fund to support the placement of Bibles in the hands of literate slaves in Kentucky. By 1853 there were three abolitionist colporteurs active in six of the state's counties, contacting masters, identifying slaves who could read, and providing them with free Bibles.[36]

In the North the Bible effort strengthened abolitionist ties with more conservative evangelicals who might favor giving Bibles to slaves without embracing immediatism. But the principal proponents of the scheme—Leavitt and black abolitionist Henry Bibb—defined it as an abolition measure. Leavitt declared in 1846 that "a more incendiary doctrine than this . . . never appeared even in the columns of the Emancipator!" If it were implemented, he predicted, "the slave will become too big for his chains." Bibb was even more hyperbolic in 1849, claiming that "the moment the Bible got among them, they (the slaves) could not be held in bondage any longer."[37]

Critics of the plan within the antislavery movement lampooned Leavitt and Bibb's exaggerated claims. They noted that very few slaves could read and claimed that, if Bibles were a threat to slavery, masters would not allow slaves to have them. But colporteurs' reports of slaves visited and Bibles distributed contributed to a sense among abolitionists of progress against slavery in the South.[38] In addition, the abolitionist critics of the scheme failed to comprehend its potential for generating slave unrest in the border region. At the very least, slaves learned from contact with AMA colporteurs that there were whites who sympathized with their aspiration for freedom, and, occasionally, they found encouragement to escape.

In June 1850 officials in Maysville, Kentucky, arrested Pennsylvania-born colporteur William Haines for enticing slaves away from their masters. In 1853 and 1854 other colporteurs faced similar charges in the commonwealth. In the former year, there was an indictment against South Carolina native A.G.W. Parker in Rockcastle County, and in 1854 a Lewis County vigilante group forced native Kentuckian James M. West to leave the state. Haines admitted giving advice to a free black man concerning the rescue of the man's enslaved family and privately contended that Fee had encouraged him to do so. Parker was the victim of an early sting operation in which slaveholders sent a slave to his house and eavesdropped until Parker suggested escape.

Juries acquitted Haines and Parker of the specific charges against them, and West asserted that the vigilantes had failed—at least to his satisfaction—"in sustaining the charge" against him at a lynch law hearing. But two of the colporteurs had clearly demonstrated a predisposition to encourage slave escapes, and they certainly operated within a reform culture that valued such behavior. A few months after the arrest of Haines, the AMA pledged its "sympathies, prayers, and assistance" to incarcerated slave rescuers. In 1855 George Clarke privately boasted that in northern Kentucky "of thirty three Slaves to whom Bibles were given by one Bro. thirty two have escaped."[39]

Fee in the mid-1840s had joined other abolitionists of the border region in publicly criticizing slave rescue attempts. But, as Haines suggested, Fee objected to a lack of discretion on the part of Haines and others, not to their actions. In 1855, Fee complained to Jocelyn that Francis Hawley, while in Kentucky, "told a friend (*in the presence of another person*—as Haines did) how the underground Railroad was managed in slave states by dropping pieces of white paper in the road. Also that he had a talk with an overseer in the state who was helping off—Now I censure not his humanity but his *want of prudence* in talking before *others*." AMA agents in Washington, such as Edward L. Stevens and Jacob Bigelow, also helped fugitives on their way north, and Crooks, before he reached North Carolina, and McBride, after he left, spoke favorably of the underground railroad.[40]

As antislavery missionaries preached to whites and blacks, as they distributed abolitionist literature and gave Bibles and advice to slaves, they were highly conscious of the intense animosity their activities engendered among many white southerners. The missionaries realized, Hawley reported in 1854, that to act against slavery in the South was "to be constantly among enemies filled with the most deadly hate who would if they dare commit the most brutal outrage against you." Therefore the missionaries made concessions to their circumstances in order to avoid suppression. For example, they rarely raised the specter of slave revolt or divine retribution. Fee, in particular, emphasized avoiding abusive language. "A free, pure and full antislavery gospel can be preached in the South by meek, kind, prayerful, faithful and persevering men. Fiery zeal against slavery, with coarse epithets and vulgar abuse will not succeed," he said.[41]

Yet the background of the missionaries in a northern abolitionism that emphasized agitation, expressions of sympathy for the oppressed, and a willingness to suffer in their behalf, made consistent meekness difficult. Fee did not always follow his own advice, as Cassius M. Clay reminded him in 1855. "I think 'sum of villainies' is not an *expedient* term in time of excitement," Clay warned following Fee's Independence Day address that year. "In other words—we should not needlessly offend any one: as it is neither our duty, nor our interest. . . . On this question we are supposed already to be *fanatical* . . . and we must remember that those who we influence do not at once feel all of the wrong of slavery that we do, and may be rather *chilled* than *warmed* by our over heat!" Worth, however, received no rebuke from the AMA when he reported in 1858 that in North Carolina, "We tax to the utmost our knowledge of 'plain sinewy Saxon' for words to describe a crime called the 'sum of villainies': one which would disgrace an atheist, and ought to shame a devil." And the association's executive committee terminated Missouri missionary G.H. Pool when he talked of going slowly and attempting to ingratiate himself with slaveholders.[42] The result was that the missionaries, despite their awareness of their precarious situation, inevitably provoked proslavery reactions.

In the wake of John Brown's raid, threats of violence and/or legal prosecution forced AMA missionaries out of Kentucky and North Carolina. During the secession crisis of 1860-61, similar threats ended the AMA's antebellum effort in Missouri, and, for years prior to these terminal confrontations, the prospect of suffering physical harm or incarceration was a constant factor in the lives of abolitionist missionaries. The Wesleyans in North Carolina and Virginia had just begun their work when proslavery forces raised cries of racial amalgamation and slave stealing against them. By 1849, a sustained legal, propaganda, and vigilante campaign, designed to vilify, hamper, and ultimately expel the missionaries, had begun. Prosecutors gained indictments against Bacon in Virginia and Crooks and McBride in North Carolina for inciting slaves to insurrection through the circulation among whites of antislavery literature. Bacon escaped with a fine, and a jury exonerated Crooks. Only McBride was sentenced to prison, and he kept his liberty by posting bond pending appeal.

But local journalists used the trials as occasions for warning their readers of the bloody threat posed by the missionaries to a slaveholding community. By 1851 violent action against the missionaries and their coadjutors had become intense. McBride reported that he was "once stoned, poisoned once, choked twice, and mobbed a number of times," and Crooks and Bacon suffered similar treatment. As the likelihood that they would be killed increased, they returned to Ohio. In May McBride accepted a mob demand that he leave North Carolina in return for a promise to reimburse his bail bondsmen. Crooks left in August after he was stoned, and Bacon departed that same month when local authorities posted a one-thousand-dollar reward for him, dead or alive, following the murder of a white man by fugitive slaves near Bacon's church. Native North Carolinian and Virginian Wesleyans also suffered arrests and mob violence in 1851. Many of them migrated to the West or North as a result. The antislavery missionary effort in southern Virginia ended, and in North Carolina it entered an accommodationist phase lasting until the arrival of Worth in 1857.[43]

In Kentucky the missionaries endured similarly violent proslavery campaigns. From the mid-1840s onward Fee suffered verbal and physical attacks, and, although in Kentucky only colporteurs faced legal prosecution, by 1850 a pattern of extralegal action against the missionaries had been established. In that year an assailant seriously injured Fee with a blow to his head as he left Haines's jail cell, and a mob nearly drowned Free Baptist missionary Mathews. Major confrontations between Fee and large, well-armed mobs occurred in 1853,

1855, 1857, and 1858. In each instance vigilantes roughed Fee up and threatened to kill him if he continued to preach against slavery, and the violence extended well beyond Fee. The 1858 mob stripped colporteur Robert Jones and beat him with a heavy "sycamore switch." During the weeks following such confrontations, other AMA agents had their houses and churches burned, received death threats, and were assaulted. Even in periods of relative calm, there were threats of violence against missionaries. Visiting Oberlin student, John M. McLain commented in 1857 on the "pervasiveness of the advocates of oppression" in the "'Sunny South.'"[44]

The missionaries responded to proslavery legal and extralegal actions in a variety of sometimes contradictory ways. They publicly denied they desired slave rebellion. Several claimed they told slaves to be patient, and others showed a willingness to give up agitation or repudiate their efforts to contact slaves. In Missouri a threat of mob action was enough to prevent AMA missionary G.H. Pool from even raising the slavery issue. Wilson of North Carolina never recovered his zeal for controversy after he witnessed the mob violence associated with the expulsion of McBride, Crooks, and Bacon. Following imprisonment for distributing incendiary publications, Worth claimed he had never sought to influence black opinion.[45]

In most cases, however, missionaries, like northern abolitionists who faced mob violence in the 1830s, sought to "persevere" without compromise. Crooks and McBride on several occasions were able to use a nonviolent tactic of kneeling to pray aloud or sing hymns to confuse and disorganize their vigilante adversaries. But in North Carolina and Kentucky the southern tolerance of private use of force made consistent nonviolence on the part of antislavery advocates difficult. Crooks and McBride's followers in North Carolina threatened violence in their leaders' behalf on more than one occasion, and the missionaries left the state in part to avoid such an event.[46]

In Kentucky, although Fee endorsed nonviolence and never carried weapons, he and other missionaries willingly acquiesced when others used force to protect them. Nor was Fee a nonresistant. In order to show that he gave up no right willingly, he always physically resisted efforts by mobs to drag him from churches. He and his associates also ignored nonresistant principles and the wishes of AMA officials by seeking legal judgments against those who attacked them or their property. Most strikingly of all, the Kentucky missionaries reflected their close ties to the Gerrit Smith circle in their flirtation with advocacy of slave revolt. In 1855 Fee responded to vigilante charges that he encouraged slave violence by saying that if his accusers meant he had undertaken a "direct and personal effort with the slaves, then the charge was untrue." But if they meant "that our preaching indirectly excites the slaves, then we answer the preaching of Moses and Aaron excited the minds of the oppressed Hebrews. A wronged and outraged people will be aroused by every ray of light . . . which shows their wrongs." Two years later Fee's associate John C. Richardson warned slaveholders against continuing to keep blacks in bondage by claiming that "there are 40 thousand [blacks] in Canada training daily and they will come down here & *cut your throats*," and it was Fee's barely concealed admiration for John Brown that sparked the expulsion of the Kentucky missionaries in late 1859.[47]

In all of these interactions with slaveholders and their supporters the missionaries experienced great emotional stress. Fear and frustration took a toll on their confidence and self-esteem. In the case of Worth, months of imprisonment pending his trial for circulating copies of Helper's *Impending Crisis* and the prospect of at least an additional year of confinement following his conviction in March 1860 deeply depressed him. "The conflict of spirit is fast breaking me," he told Lewis Tappan. "Do something for me if possible." In other instances constant struggle against great odds was enough to dispirit missionaries. McBride, among others, lamented that persecution caused individuals to turn away from antislavery churches or to leave the South. Wilson was discouraged because even in "our little churches" the influence of slavery "is so wonderfully mixt up with things here that it is hard to keep clear of it." In Missouri, Pool complained, "What can one do among so many—one poor weak man," and Fee, who seemed so resilient, became seriously depressed in the late 1850s. Repeated mobbings, lack of progress, and poor health led him to experience what he described as a "pressure" on his brain that caused him to lose sleep and become irresolute. In March 1861 at the very end of their antebellum effort in the South, George Candee saw the missionaries' predicament with brutal clarity. "Our external evidences of success," he wrote, "are; first and principally the fact that our *stay* here is barely tolerated."[48]

But missionaries were rarely so candidly pessimistic. Despite their inner turmoil, the image they presented to northern abolitionists was an optimistic one. Conditioned by a belief that they were instruments of divine providence, by a need to justify their demands for continued northern funding, and by a focus on small victories, they usually reported that so long as they persevered they would make progress against slavery. "Public sentiment is undoubtedly changing for the better," McBride advised the *True Wesleyan* weeks before the successful effort to drive him from North Carolina began. The missionaries, like their northern supporters, also assumed that persecution advanced their cause and repeatedly expressed a willingness to be martyred. Mathews, McBride, and Fee contended that their deaths would help spread antislavery sentiments, and shortly after his arrest in 1859 Worth asserted, "God will glorify his name by my suffering for him as much as though I was at liberty & working in his vineyard."[49]

It was difficult for abolitionists in the North not to be moved by such dedication. Just as they reacted to images of black liberators and slave rescuers, northern antislavery activists perceived southern abolitionist missionaries to be heroes as well as potential martyrs. It was, of course, in the institutional interest of the Wesleyan Connection and the AMA to characterize the missionaries in this manner. Just one step removed from these organizations, the AFASS declared in 1850 that the missionaries had to be as brave as American soldiers at the bloody battle of Lundy's Lane in the War of 1812. It was also not surprising that the politically oriented *National Era*— itself located on slave soil—gave favorable coverage to the missionaries. But Garrisonians, who had no institutional or geographical ties to the missionaries, were impressed with them as well. The *Pennsylvania Freeman* portrayed Crooks and McBride as "heroic and devoted," and the *Anti-Slavery Bugle* called Fee a "moral hero."[50]

At various times such abolitionists as Harriet Beecher Stowe, William Goodell, former slave rescuer George Thompson, and Levi Coffin of underground railroad fame expressed confidence that the missionaries could change the South. Goodell joined Wesleyan and AMA leaders in predicting that the missionaries' experience would arouse the North as well. Acting in this spirit, a few prominent northern abolitionists, including Goodell in 1850 and Jonathan Blanchard in 1855, briefly visited Kentucky to join the missionaries in preaching against slavery in a slave state. There could be no stronger affirmation of their belief in the importance of antislavery missions in the South. Northern abolitionists, who supported the missionaries through their donations, who praised and visited them, and especially those who risked becoming missionaries, demonstrated the emphasis abolitionist reform culture of the 1840s and 1850s placed on aggressively challenging the morality of slavery on its own ground. It was their answer to the perennial, taunting challenge of their proslavery adversaries: "Why do you not preach immediate emancipation in the South?"[51]

Not all abolitionists agreed with them. William H. Brisbane, a South Carolina slaveholder who emancipated his slaves and moved north to advocate immediate abolition, suggested in 1846 that political action had to precede antislavery missions in the South. Others, including Garrison and his associates, went further. They contended that abolition must come before a free gospel could be promulgated in the South, and it was the Garrisonians who were the chief critics of the Bibles for slaves effort. Although they did not condemn the missionary effort itself, they perceived little chance that a northern-based abolitionist effort could succeed in peacefully confronting slavery in the South. For them, the answer to the question of why do you not go to the South was that the South was too far gone in sin and crime, too dangerous a place for peaceful abolitionists, and they used reports of persecution of antislavery missionaries to illustrate their point.[52]

The final antebellum expulsion of the missionaries, secession, and civil war indicate that the Garrisonians were in the long run correct. What is not correct is the assumption on the part of historians of the antislavery movement and sectional conflict that the Garrisonian reluctance to actively confront slavery in the South was typical of all abolitionists. In the 1840s and 1850s important shapers of abolitionist opinion continued to believe that moral suasion in the South could contribute to the abolition of slavery. Their optimism that antislavery progress was possible in the South led them to send missionaries there, and, until the eve of the Civil War, the missionaries' generally positive reports confirmed that optimism. In turn, antislavery missionary efforts in the border region, involving widespread contacts with slaves and nonslaveholding whites, provided slaveholders with additional tangible evidence of abolitionist aggression. Proslavery whites in Kentucky, North Carolina, Virginia, Missouri, and the District of Columbia need not have vicariously learned to fear abolition-ism through newspaper accounts of doings in the North. There were abolitionist agents in their midst, whom they associated with slave escapes, slave rescues, and the potentially violent destablization of their communities. As William W. Freehling suggests, slavery's stanch defenders in the deep South perceived a threat to slavery on their northern flank, which certainly played at least as important a role in their ultimate commitment to secession as issues related to slavery in the western territories.[53]

Chapter Six

ANTISLAVERY COLONIES IN THE UPPER SOUTH

In the spring of 1859 John C. Underwood wrote to Oliver Johnson of the Garrisonian *National Anti-Slavery Standard* to promote a "plan of Christian colonization of the border slave States by organized emigration." Underwood, a Republican, a former Liberty party abolitionist, and a sometimes resident of the slave state of Virginia, was the leader of the American Emigrant Aid and Homestead Company. Claiming that his experience in Virginia had convinced him "that a given amount of effort in favor of freedom in the presence of slavery will produce ten times the effect of the same effort at a distance," he challenged Johnson and other Garrisonians to become more aggressive in their antislavery work. Were Christ present, Underwood maintained, he would—unlike "some professed reformers"—go south "despite any consideration of personal peril." Underwood especially wanted wealthy abolitionists to invest in Virginian lands, build schools and churches, and introduce the "habits of industry and all the elements of enlightened free society."[1]

Johnson published Underwood's letter without comment, and no Garrisonians announced their removal to Virginia. They had little inclination to go, and the southern reaction to John Brown's raid six months later precluded any such undertaking. Underwood's letter, nevertheless, reflected an idea—organized northern colonization of the upper South—that enjoyed considerable eclat in antislavery circles in the latter half of the 1850s. The letter also indicates that there were religious and abolitionist elements in a colonization attempt that has been portrayed as a business-oriented, conservative-Republican scheme aimed at making profits and northernizing the South without confrontation over slavery.

The purpose of this chapter is to modify such portrayals by analyzing the role in abolitionist reform culture of organized efforts to
attract northern settlers to the upper South. Previously published studies have concentrated on such settlements in Virginia and on the economic motives of their proponents. But a different perspective
emerges when Underwood's abolitionism is fully considered and when
similar efforts to establish northern colonies in Kentucky are brought
into focus. Events in Kentucky lend credence to an interpretation that
stresses Underwood's abolitionism and to a contention that moral, as
well as political and economic, motives underlay these undertakings.

Linking the Virginia colonization scheme to the Republican party
and to northeastern business interests is certainly correct.
Underwood and his associate Eli Thayer of Massachusetts were
prominent Republicans when they began the effort in 1857. They
enjoyed the support of major Republican newspapers, as well as that
of the independent but radically anti-abolitionist *New York Herald*. In
an influential article published in 1945, George W. Smith established
that a dozen wealthy New York businessmen and bankers were the
principal stockholders in Underwood and Thayer's company and that
the two men were disciples of Whig political economist Henry C.
Carey. Carey argued that the introduction of mechanized farming and
manufacturing into the South would result in a very gradual disap-
pearance of slavery and the transition of blacks from slaves to free
laborers.[2]

Smith portrayed the Virginia colonization scheme as imperialism designed to extend the northern economic system into the agrar-
ian South and to enrich northern capitalists. More recently Eric Foner
and others have identified plans for organized northern emigration
into the South with Republican economic nationalism aimed at destroying a backward southern economy that supported the political
power of an anachronistic slaveholding oligarchy. In this view those
who sought to send northern settlers into the South desired to re-
make the South in the North's image not primarily because they opposed the oppression of blacks in slavery but for the sake of capitalism,
northern political interests, and free white labor.[3]

No historical figure better serves these interpretations than Eli
Thayer. An odd, egocentric educator and promoter, Thayer is best
known for his attempt beginning in 1854 to send New Englanders to

Kansas Territory in order to make it a free state under the rules of popular sovereignty. He certainly emphasized profits rather than abolitionism in many of his statements concerning the similar Virginia settlement scheme. Because of remarks he made in the 1880s, Thayer has also been portrayed as a bitter critic of abolitionists in general and the Garrisonians in particular. Like many other Republicans of the late 1850s, he professed concern for free white laborers and, unlike immediatists, demonstrated little sympathy for slaves. He made disparaging remarks about blacks and contended that northern free-labor colonization would end slavery in the upper South not through emancipation but by forcing black labor farther south.[4]

If this were all there was to it, northern colonization in the upper South would seem to have had little to do with abolitionist reform culture. But, as historian Ronald G. Walters points out, northern abolitionism had always embodied commercial, middle-class values as well as Christian morality. Decades before the birth of the Republican party, William Lloyd Garrison linked abolition of slavery with northernizing the southern economy. More important, abolitionists had ample moral reason for supporting direct action to transform the South. By establishing colonies in the South that reflected idealized versions of northern values, they could demonstrate their own purity, Christianize the South, and set an example for an increasingly corrupt North.[5] That such desires played a significant role in these efforts to intervene in the South is clear in Underwood's career and abolitionist attempts to attract northern settlers to Kentucky.

Underwood had a great deal in common with other individuals who became immediate abolitionists in the 1830s as well as with those who became Radical Republicans in the 1850s. His career illustrates the hazy line between morally directed concern for the slave and opposition to the political power of the slaveholder. Born on the eastern periphery of New York's Burned-over district in 1809 to parents who had migrated from New England, Underwood came to maturity amid the fervent revivalism that gave the region its name. Like other New York abolitionists, he engaged in a variety of reform activities in the 1830s and identified with the Whig party until the organization of the abolitionist Liberty party in 1839. An 1832 graduate of Hamilton College and a member of the bar, Underwood by 1842 had assumed leadership of the new party in his native Herkimer County.[6]

As a member of the New York Liberty party, Underwood came under the influence of Gerrit Smith. But unlike Smith he never accepted the party as a permanent force for antislavery agitation. In 1846 Underwood favored a coalition with the Whigs in order to expand black suffrage in New York. In 1848 he supported the Free Soil party, which Smith regarded as a sell-out of abolitionism. Underwood, nevertheless, remained close to Smith, and he refused to endorse an "unprincipled coalition" of New York Free Soilers and Democrats in 1849.[7]

Underwood's relative political flexibility stemmed from his involvement in the late 1840s in antislavery action in Virginia. After his graduation from college, he had spent two years in the northern portion of that state as tutor for the children of a wealthy slaveholder, converting the children to abolitionism in the process. When in 1839 Underwood married one of his former pupils, he acquired property in the upper Shenandoah Valley, and by 1846 he had determined to begin what he called a "free labor experiment" there. The experiment, which he explicitly tied to abolitionist goals, took him out of New York for extended periods of time and introduced him to a political environment where slavery's most timid critics were potential political allies.[8]

As early as 1841, groups of northerners had established farms worked by free white labor in northern Virginia. That same year, Gerrit Smith told William Ellery Channing that a southerner had suggested "the establishment of a 'free labor colony' upon the highlands of N. Carolina or E. Tennessee." In the mid-1840s Charles T. Torrey and William L. Chaplin had displayed a passing interest in such settlements. But the northerners in Virginia had no explicitly abolitionist motives, nothing came of the plans mentioned to Smith, Torrey and Chaplin acted more directly against slavery, and their fellow New York Liberty party advocate, Underwood, became the first to put an *abolitionist* free-labor colonization scheme into practice.[9]

At its peak in the early 1850s, Underwood's experiment consisted of about nineteen dairies, all but two of which were on rented land. He brought in dairymen—some of whom were abolitionists—from Herkimer County to manage the farms and told Smith that the enterprise could not "fail to be advantageous both to my pecuniary interests & to the cause of freedom." But he admitted that occasionally a

slave might be employed at one of the dairies. Smith and other abolitionists feared that such compromises indicated a probability that,
rather than transform the South, individuals like Underwood might
themselves be changed by it.[10] Despite such compromises, however,
abolitionist values continued to shape Underwood's efforts.

In his moralistic understanding of the antislavery struggle, in his
personal conduct, which made him a hero among abolitionists, and
in his goals, Underwood demonstrated his ongoing commitment to
aggressive antislavery action. Not surprisingly, when his slaveholding
mother-in-law died in 1850, he and his wife refused to accept her slaves
in inheritance. Instead Underwood tried unsuccessfully to have the
slaves freed, and throughout the 1850s he personally encouraged
other slaveholders to emancipate their chattels. Underwood also
maintained something of the militancy of the Gerrit Smith circle by
expressing admiration for "brave" Chaplin's effort to help slaves escape from Washington, D.C., and by publicly doubting in 1857 that
slavery could be peacefully abolished. He dwelt on the image of a
black liberator, who might serve as an agent of divine retribution,
openly denounced the oppression of blacks in slavery, invoked a Christian duty to help them, and cultivated friendly relations with slaves in
the vicinity of his Clarke County home—a dangerous practice for an
abolitionist in a slave state.[11]

Obviously Underwood perceived his mission in Virginia to be
more than financial investment and the demonstration of the superiority of free over slave labor. He hoped to create an island of freedom from which to confront the state's slaveholding rulers. He
reported to Gerrit Smith in 1851, "I have been in the habit of speaking boldly of you & of the cause of Freedom in Va. so much so as on
several occasions to give great offense to the powerful & have been
told on more than one occasion that I was too much of an abolitionist to be tolerated." Because of the small population of Clarke County,
Underwood hoped that "twenty abolitionists moving there[,] buy-
ing land & carrying on mechanical [trades] or manufacturing of
coarse fabric" would generate the political base to elect Smith or
Chaplin to the Virginia House of Delegates. "Land," he told Smith,
"is good & cheap & why not concentrate a colony in some such
situation with a view to agitation where agitation may be most effec-
tual[?]"[12]

A few years later, Underwood's agitation became more than his slaveholding neighbors would tolerate. His moral condemnation of slavery had isolated him, his free-labor dairies had failed by mid-decade, but the establishment of the Republican party in the North renewed his antislavery enthusiasm. Hoping to secure the nomination of William H. Seward for president, Underwood presented himself as a delegate to the Republican national convention in Philadelphia in June 1856 and made one of the more radical antislavery speeches at the gathering. He quoted Thomas Jefferson's remark that God's justice would not slumber forever and excoriated Virginia's politicians for cementing slavery's walls with the "'blood of crushed humanity.'" He opposed the expansion of slavery not so much to protect the interests of whites but because expansion would forge "'more manacles for the arms and ancles [*sic*] of Christian men and women, brothers and sisters, husbands and wives; to be separated from one another, lashed and chained in the coffle gangs of the trader, driven to the cotton fields and dreary sugar plantations of the far South.'"[13]

When reports of Underwood's speech reached Virginia, proslavery forces demanded that he not return to the state. During the next several years Underwood resided in New York City, joined only occasionally by his wife and children. His "exile" made him a hero among Republicans and abolitionists, and he was in great demand as a John C. Fremont campaign speaker. In this capacity Underwood became more typically Republican in his depictions of slavery as a threat to the interests of free white labor. He employed statistical comparisons demonstrating Virginia's lack of economic development and noted violations of his own civil liberties. Meanwhile, he sought Republican support for an expanded northern colonization effort in Virginia.[14]

In effect, Underwood was preparing himself to cooperate with Thayer in an organized emigration plan that often appealed to white selfishness. A number of factors contributed to the launching of the project in early 1857. They included the evident decline of the slave-labor economy of the upper South, a speculative business cycle rapidly reaching its peak, a mistaken belief that Thayer's New England Emigrant Aid Company had secured the northern victory in Kansas, a conservative desire to save the Union through economic consolidation, and a continuing commitment to abolitionism. Although Thayer may have suggested a free-labor colonization effort for the upper South as early as 1854, it was Underwood who took the first practical steps to organize what became the American Emigrant Aid and Homestead Company. Working in New York City, Underwood published a letter on the subject in January, located Virginia land held by New York merchants, enlisted Thayer's active cooperation in early February, and successfully lobbied the New York state legislature for the passage of a bill chartering the company in April.[15]

Once he had enlisted in the project, Thayer eclipsed Underwood as its most visible public representative. Hoping to avoid a hostile southern reaction, Thayer in late February persuaded conservative, prosouthern, and Negrophobic James Gordon Bennett of the *New York Herald* to become the foremost journalistic champion of the venture. Between 1857 and 1860, Thayer and Underwood encouraged free-labor colonization projects in Kentucky, Maryland, North Carolina, Tennessee, and Missouri, as well as in several portions of Virginia. But Thayer quickly centered on the upland region, spanning the border of western Virginia and eastern Kentucky, where there were few slaves. In May 1857, he personally chose a tract of land in northwestern Virginia on the Ohio River, near coal and timber resources. By early summer Thayer had secured the delivery of four large stationary steam engines, the construction of a lodge, and the arrival of the first settlers at the town he named Ceredo in honor of the Roman goddess of plenty. Ceredo rapidly grew to a thriving community of five hundred and remained so until John Brown's raid aroused enough local hostility to force most of the colonists to leave.[16]

Long before then, the American Emigrant Aid and Homestead Company had failed as a financial enterprise. Its failure to fill its minimum stock subscription of $200,000 and deteriorating business conditions in the summer of 1857 forced its reorganization. As the burst of energy associated with the company's establishment dissipated, Thayer concentrated on developing Ceredo. Meanwhile, Underwood maintained the company as an agency for selling southern lands to northerners, building small northern colonies in a number of Virginian counties, attempting to increase antislavery sentiment in the state, and promoting Republican party organization. He remained optimistic that the colonization plan was transforming popular opinion in Virginia and that with better funding it could free the border region of slavery.[17]

Ceredo itself was never an abolitionist enclave—it attracted entrepreneurs not antislavery activists—and Thayer and Underwood's effort there was only implicitly antislavery. To reassure whites of the upper South that free-labor colonization would benefit them, they stressed a common belief in the North and border region that slave labor had retarded economic and cultural development. They assumed that the existing drain of slaves from the border slave states to the Southwest provided an opportunity for speeding up an inevitable and peaceful replacement of inefficient black slave labor with efficient white free labor. Virginians, they argued, had no reason to fear the impetus northern colonies would give to this process. Thayer publicly denied that the Emigrant Aid and Homestead Company was aggressively abolitionist. Instead he said it was a legal, peaceful business, strictly concerned with profits. It amounted to, he said, a "friendly invasion" by a "renovating army of free laborers," whom he called "The Neighbors." Neither he nor Underwood had much to say about the slaves who were to be replaced. What Thayer did say was disparaging. Ceredo's steam engines, he noted, were superior to "negro power." The engines, he continued, "never run away. They do not steal hams and chickens." Thayer's ally Bennett declared "that free white labor, even to the utter exclusion of the niggers, would be the salvation" of the upper South, and even Underwood linked the process of free-labor colonization with the sale of slaves south.[18]

From a proslavery perspective, however, such disclaimers were mere prevarications, and Thayer was a "wily abolitionist." Several border–slave-state newspapers welcomed the colonization scheme as economically advantageous, and others anticipated twentieth-century historians by ridiculing the effort as impractical. The *Washington Star* said it was "just a scheme to rob credulous fanatics at the North." But several journals in Virginia and the deep South reacted fiercely to what they portrayed as a grave threat to slaveholding interests. The *South* of Richmond described the colonization plan as a crusade against slavery that, if permitted, would "embolden the Abolitionists." The *Southside Democrat* of Petersburg urged Virginia's governor, Henry A. Wise, to "order out the militia to put to flight this army of aliens," and the *Richmond Whig* called on the "people of Virginia" to repel the colonists "with sword in hand" and make their "carcasses . . . adorn the trees of our forests." Underlying such extreme hostility was the abiding fear among slavery's defenders that—because of its fundamental economic weakness—very little effort could end the peculiar institution in the border South.[19]

These proslavery characterizations of the free-labor colonization scheme in Virginia were essentially correct. Much of what Thayer said about it being strictly a business venture without reference to slavery was designed to quiet southern outbursts that could frighten potential investors and colonists. Underwood's new reticence concerning the plight of slaves had a similar cause. But neither Underwood, who had been an abolitionist for most of his adult life, nor Thayer, who had more in common with abolitionists than he publicly admitted, could fully mask their sympathies and objectives in 1857.

While he imagined white colonists replacing slaves sold south, Underwood simultaneously contended that an influx of organized northerners into Virginia would free the slaves "at no distant day . . . by the diffusion of knowledge and Christian charity." Both men assumed that their plan would effect the transplantation into the upper South of northern-style public schools and activist churches as well as industry and free labor. They would create, in Underwood's words, a "Christian civilization," or, in Thayer's, a "Gospel of Freedom" with which human slavery would be incompatible. "The anti-slavery of interest," Thayer told western Virginians, "is the father of the anti-slavery of principle."[20]

There was also a militancy of language. When Underwood contacted Thayer, he wrote of carrying "the war into Africa." Realizing that Thayer had for years been preoccupied with Kansas, Underwood echoed the radical political abolitionists by insisting that "it is better even for Kansas to strike at the heart of slavery than its extremities." And, of course, Thayer talked of invasions and armies, friendly and peaceful as they might be. Passages that have been used as evidence of Thayer's greedy motivation were in fact militantly sarcastic responses to southern threats. "We shall not be intimidated," he wrote in March 1857. "We are not that kind of people when good dividends are at stake." Yankees, he noted, risked their lives whaling and their souls in the Atlantic slave trade for "'filthy lucre.'" Therefore, they would "probably participate in making slave States free for the same filthy lucre. . . . If half of us were shot," he insisted, "the rest would press on towards the shining dollars."[21]

Emancipationist intent and militant expressions do not in themselves prove a direct relationship between abolitionism and northern colonization schemes in the upper South. Many conservatives in both sections advocated emancipation, and one need not be a reformer to be militant. However, Thayer and Underwood's efforts to recruit abolitionist support and the abolitionist response—along with Underwood's background—reveal the intimate relationship between abolitionism and efforts to establish northern communities in the upper South.

Thayer and Underwood relied primarily on Republicans to promote their efforts. But, because of their reputations as dedicated opponents of slavery and their personal ties to abolitionist leaders, they were also able to elicit immediatist support. Underwood was a friend of Gerrit Smith, and Garrisonians respected him for his willingness to go into the South. Thayer's effort to make Kansas a free state endeared him to Smith, John Brown, and a number of second-generation immediatists, who in the late 1850s stressed action over rhetoric.[22]

From 1857 through 1860 Underwood used his stature as an antislavery hero to encourage Garrisonian support for the establishment of northern colonies in the South. In March 1857, while soliciting New York City journalists to publicize his project, he spoke with Oliver Johnson. The following May, he attended the annual meeting of the AASS, where he met William Lloyd Garrison and succeeded in enhancing his renown as "a Virginian of high respectability" who had sacrificed a great deal for the cause. In 1859, a few months before he wrote to Johnson about Christian colonization in the South, Underwood attended a compensated emancipation convention in Albany to oppose such proposals and to promote his own ideas. Differing from his old friend Gerrit Smith, who had for years defended purchasing the freedom of slaves, Underwood argued that slaveholders would not cooperate in a compensated emancipation plan and, even if they would, it was always morally wrong to purchase slaves. Northern colonization of the South, he insisted, was a more effective means of achieving general emancipation.[23]

Thayer, meanwhile, revealed another dimension of his antislavery commitment in his contacts with Smith, Brown, and others. In his bitter old age, Thayer's ego and his disdain for the labor radicalism of the late nineteenth century led him to distort his relationship to the earlier abolition radicalism of the 1850s. He claimed that he had always abhorred Brown's use of violence and implied that he would never have cooperated with *any* abolitionists in regards to Kansas or Virginia. In fact, in the 1850s, Thayer actively sought non-Garrisonian abolitionist support for his projects and cooperated closely with Brown. In regard to Kansas, Thayer successfully solicited large donations of Smith's time and money, received material aid from Lewis Tappan, and established ties to such second-generation immediatists as Samuel Gridley Howe and George L. Stearns. Thayer also took a leading role in acquiring arms for Brown to use in Kansas.[24] It was, therefore, hardly surprising that in April 1857 he called on Smith and Brown to help with his Virginia scheme in language quite different from his public reassurances to the South.

Most significant, Thayer disclosed that the term *neighbors*, which he used to placate white Virginians, had for him a deeper, more ominous meaning. He told Smith and Brown that he derived his use of the word from the parable of the Good Samaritan in which Christ asks "'Which thinkest thou was *neighbor* to him who fell among thieves?'" In light of the abolitionist assumption that it was the slave who had fallen among thieves, Thayer was saying that he expected northern colonists to help the slaves. His comment to Brown, who had killed proslavery men in Kansas, that "you must have a home in Western Virginia" indicates that Thayer expected the help to be forthright and aggressive.[25]

Abolitionists responded in a variety of ways to Thayer and Underwood's requests for support. They were either silent, provided limited support, or were enthusiastic about the Emigrant Aid and Homestead Company. Radical political abolitionists and Garrisonians were similar in their hesitancy to embrace Thayer and Underwood's contention that northern colonies could redeem the South from slavery. For years Gerrit Smith had believed that so long as slavery were strong it would subvert northern colonies in the South. The colonies' "bold tone of freedom," Smith predicted in 1841, would become fainter and fainter as time passed. A few years later the *Liberator* published a letter opposing emigration from New England to eastern Virginia. In language similar to Smith's, the correspondent declared that not even ten thousand emigrants could "extirpate slavery from the Ancient Dominion." Instead they would be "speedily absorbed into part and parcel of the slave system."[26]

Such views persisted among immediatists in the late 1850s. In "remarks" appended in 1857 to an account of northern colonization efforts in Virginia, the *Standard* declared that "any attempt to regenerate or reform Virginia whilst it is under the absolute control of the slaveocracry will end in utter defeat and mortification." Lydia Maria Child communicated similar sentiments to Underwood in 1860. There was also sentiment that Thayer placed too much emphasis on profits and not enough on morality.[27] Such sensitivities limited radical political abolitionist and Garrisonian enthusiasm for Thayer and Underwood's plan. Smith did not respond to Thayer's request for assistance, Smith's associate William Goodell failed to include a single item about the project in the *Radical Abolitionist*, no Garrisonian became involved in the scheme, and neither of these groups passed resolutions supporting it.

There was, nevertheless, a positive side to their reactions. Smith remained friendly with Thayer and Underwood, Goodell initially responded "warmly" to Underwood's request for help, and both of the New Yorkers were supportive of more openly abolitionist calls for northern emigration to Kentucky. Moreover, Thayer in his later life greatly exaggerated Garrisonian antipathy toward him and his antislavery endeavors. According to him, the hostility had arisen during the struggle over Kansas Territory in 1854. In the 1880s he contended that when Garrisonians had denounced racism among free-state settlers in Kansas Territory, they were actually attacking him and his New England Emigrant Aid Company. But, in page after page of invective characterizing the Garrisonians as ineffective fanatics, Thayer failed to produce a single direct Garrisonian criticism of him or his company.[28]

Actually, the *Standard* had praised Thayer's Kansas effort as compatible with "moral agitation" against slavery, and when Thayer and Underwood began their Virginia venture Oliver Johnson—unlike Goodell—carried out his promise to give it extensive coverage, copying material from the *Evening Post, New York Times, New York Herald*, and *New York Tribune*. Garrison provided less coverage of the Virginia scheme in the *Liberator* but did not oppose it. Instead he published the hyperbolic threats of Virginian journalists against Thayer in the *Liberator*'s "Refuge of Oppression" column. Garrison's comment that "it is evident [from such threats] that the North Ameri-

James G. Birney, prototype of the northern abolitionist image of a southern white emancipator. Dwight L. Dumond, ed., *Letters of James G. Birney, 1831-1857.* 2 vols. New York: D. Appleton-Century, 1938, frontispiece, vol. 1.

John G. Fee, southern abolitionist missionary and advocate of northern migration to Kentucky. [Fee], *Autobiography of John G. Fee, Berea, Kentucky,* Chicago: National Christian Association, 1891, frontispiece.

Cassius M. Clay, the most influential of the southern political abolitionists. Original photograph owned by the author.

Thomas Garrett, northern abolitionist, who as a resident of Wilmington, Delaware, helped fugitive slaves on their way to the North. Courtesy of the Historical Society of Delaware.

James and Lucretia Mott, northern abolitionists whose speaking tour in Maryland convinced southerners to take up the cause. Anna Davis Hallowell, ed., *James and Lucretia Mott: Life and Letters,* Boston: Houghton Mifflin, 1885, frontispiece

Gamaliel Bailey, editor of the *National Era* in Washington, D.C., and advocate of abolitionist organization in the southern states. *Cosmopolitan* 8 (1890): 438.

Left, Adam Crooks, Northern abolitionist missionary active in North Carolina and Virginia. *Right,* Daniel Worth, southern-born, northern-trained abolitionist missionary active in North Carolina. Roy S. Nicholson, *Wesleyan Methodism in the South,* Syracuse, N.Y.: Wesleyan Methodist, 1933, 30, 78.

Alanson Work, James E. Burr, and George Thompson, the first slave
rescuers to gain renown among abolitionists, confined with slaves at the
jail in Palmyra, Missouri. George Thompson, *Prison Life and Reflections,*
Hartford, Conn.: A. Work, 1855, frontispiece.

Charles T. Torry, slave rescuer
whose death in a Maryland
prison made him a martyr
among abolitionists. J.C.
Lovejoy, *Memoir of Rev.
Charles T. Torrey,* 1847;
reprint, New York: Negro
Univs. Press, 1969,
frontispiece.

Calvin Fairbank, persistent slave rescuer and long-term prisoner of the Commonwealth of Kentucky. [Fairbank], *Rev. Calvin Fairbank during Slavery Times,* 1890; reprint, New York: Negro Univs. Press, 1969, frontispiece.

Daniel Drayton, slave rescuer whose pecuniary motives did not prevent northern abolitionists from celebrating his courage. Drayton, *Personal Memoir of Daniel Drayton,* 1855; reprint, New York: Negro Univs. Press, 1969, frontispiece.

William Lloyd Garrison, perhaps
the most influential of the northern
immediatists and the principal
leader of the AASS in the 1840s
and 1850s, shown in a repro-
duction of "a daguerreotype
taken in Dublin Oct. 1846."
Wendell Phillips Garrison
and Francis Jackson Garrison,
William Lloyd Garrison,1805-1879.
4 vols. New York: Houghton Mifflin,
1894, vol. 3, frontispiece.

Lewis Tappan, the principal leader
of the AFASS and the AMA.
Cosmopolitan 8 (1890): 440.

Henry Highland Garnet,
advocate of slave resistance.
William J. Simmons, ed., *Men
of Mark: Eminent, Progressive,
and Rising,* 1887; reprint,
Chicago: Johnson, 1970, 452.

Maria Weston Chapman, a
leading Garrisonian and a
critic of Cassius M. Clay.
Garrison and Garrison,
*William Lloyd Garrison,
1805-1879,* vol. 2, facing 34.

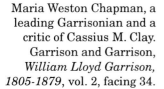

Frederick Douglass, prominent black abolitionist. Douglass, *My Bondage and My Freedom,* 1855; reprint, New York: Arno, 1968, frontispiece.

Gerrit Smith, wealthy philanthropist, leader of the radical political abolitionists, and advocate of rescuing slaves. Octavious Brooks Frothingham, *Gerrit Smith: A Biography.* New York: Putnam, 1878, frontispiece.

Henry Bibb, advocate of the Bibles for slaves campaign. Bibb, *Narrative of the Life and Adventures of Henry Bibb, an American Slave,* 1850; reprint, Miami: Mnemosyne, 1969, frontispiece.

can Homestead Company must seek another field for their operations" has been interpreted by historians as opposition to the company. Garrison was in.fact sarcastically ridiculing the Virginians' claims
that they could stop Thayer and Underwood's activities.[29] Despite their
misgivings, immediatists relished opportunities to confront slavery
on its own ground.

While the Smith and Garrisonian circles were far less hostile to
plans to create northern colonies in the South than has been sup
posed, other abolitionists greeted the plans with enthusiasm. This
was certainly the case for Gamaliel Bailey and Daniel R. Goodloe, the
editor and editor pro tempore of the *National Era* in Washington,
D.C. Northern-born Bailey had, like Underwood, married a Virginian, acquired slaveholding in-laws, and moved into the South. Goodloe
was a North Carolinian who had become an abolitionist and moved
to Washington in the 1840s.

The two journalists shared Underwood's sympathy for the oppressed as well as his contradictory belief that the upper South would
be freed from slavery through the sale of slaves into the deep South.
As long-time advocates of the peaceful destruction of slavery in the
border region through economic processes and increasing freedom
of discussion, Bailey and Goodloe welcomed Thayer and Underwood's
effort as hastening the inevitable. "The demand for slave labor in the
more Southern States will be supplied from Virginia, Maryland, Kentucky, and Missouri; and the latter will substitute the labor of free-
men for that of slaves," Goodloe predicted in 1854. "This is the natural
course of events," he continued. The process would not cease "until
the last withering track of the slave has been effaced" from Virginia
and the rest of the upper South. Goodloe even anticipated Underwood
in calling for organized emigration to carry "the church, the school,
and freedom of speech," along with free labor, into the South.[30]

Bailey and Goodloe, who had close relationships to the Free Soil
and Republican parties and feared open confrontation with
slaveholders, had distanced themselves philosophically as well as
geographically from the centers of abolitionism in the North. But a
new group of militant northern abolitionists also supported Thayer
and Underwood's plans. Concentrated like first-generation
immediatists in New England and New York, these second-generation immediatists were either younger or came to the movement later

in life than their predecessors. They were more likely to advocate violence and to participate in physical resistance to the Fugitive Slave Law of 1850. They were also prone to juxtaposing expressions of doubt concerning black abilities with support for egalitarian racial policies and were more likely than first-generation immediatists to cooperate with Republicans.[31]

Among the second-generation immediatists, Thomas Wentworth Higginson, Samuel Gridley Howe, and George L. Stearns were involved in Thayer's emigration effort for Kansas, and James Redpath played a minor role in support of Thayer and Underwood's plan for Virginia.[32] More notable was Theodore Parker's use of a Garrisonian gathering to promote the Virginia colonization scheme. Parker, a Bostonian minister, a transcendentalist literary figure, and an active defender of fugitive slaves, regarded Thayer and Underwood's advance into the South as a demonstration of what he assumed to be the superior energy of northern Anglo-Saxons in comparison to southern African Americans. Speaking at the Massachusetts state house in January 1858, he praised Thayer's effort "to Northernize the South" and gloried in Thayer's emphasis of the profit motive in replacing "'negro power'" with steam engines. Parker declared, "This is an antislavery argument which traders can understand. Mr. Thayer is not so much a talker as an organizer: he puts his thought into works. You know how much Kansas owes him for the organization he has set on foot. One day will he not revolutionize Virginia?"[33]

It was in regard to Kentucky, however, that abolitionists most strongly demonstrated an interest in establishing northern outposts in the slave states. In 1847 John C. Vaughan had called on northerners to come to Louisville, and in the 1850s there were two attempts to establish northern colonies in the state. The first was a small affair that is significant for the involvement of such church-oriented abolitionists as Lewis Tappan, New York philanthropist Lee Claflin, and AMA president Lawrence Brainerd. This effort began in 1852 when former slave-rescuer Delia A. Webster purchased a six-hundred-acre farm in northwestern Kentucky, which she—like Underwood in the 1840s—planned to work with free labor. In 1854 Webster was repeatedly imprisoned on charges that she used the farm to help slaves escape, and before the year ended she had retreated to Indiana. Four years later, Tappan and the others organized the Webster Farm Association to attract northern settlers to Webster's property. Like Underwood and Thayer, they emphasized economic development and profits rather than explicit abolitionism, but, from its start, the Webster Farm project was overshadowed in Kentucky by a more emphatically abolitionist colonization plan.[34]

Begun by John G. Fee and supported by other AMA agents in the state, this campaign brought to the fore the abolitionist aims that were implicit in other plans to establish northern colonies in the South. It is important as an especially strong illustration of the relationship between southern antislavery action and the values of northern abolitionism. Influenced by what he believed to be Thayer's successful colonization of Kansas and by Webster's ideas for Kentucky, Fee began in November 1855 to call for northern settlers to come to Kentucky to make it a free state. Fee's appeal, seconded by James Scott Davis, Peter H. West, Otis B. Waters, William E. Lincoln, John A.R. Rogers, George Candee, and others, had similarities to Underwood and Thayer's. Like Underwood, Fee and his missionary associates placed considerable emphasis on establishing northern culture. They reassured prospective emigrants that the missionaries had already made progress in creating the rudiments of northern civilization amidst the frontier conditions of Kentucky. They boasted of their free churches and schools "taught by antislavery teachers" as well as the protection for freedom of speech and other personal freedoms that existed on a limited basis in portions of the state. They contended that they needed northern settlers to expand this base, demonstrate the value of free institutions, and, as Candee put it, "build a righteous society."[35]

Fee and his coadjutors—like Underwood and Thayer—saw no inconsistency in combining appeals to selfish, pecuniary interests with more idealistic appeals to potential settlers. Fee's priority was to establish a community at Berea that would sustain a college committed to antislavery, egalitarian, temperance, and nonsectarian principles. To achieve this he did not hesitate to promise large profits to those who would invest and/or relocate. He assured Gerrit Smith that Smith could make a fine return on an investment in 250 acres of land at Berea as the development of a college and village were bound to raise the price for lots. Fee and Davis also attempted to attract settlers with glowing descriptions of farming opportunities, mineral wealth, and

local free-labor resources. They presented visionary plans for turn-
pike and railroad connections, and appealed to "enterprising men" to
come to Kentucky. In December 1857, colporteur Peter H. West declared, "Oh that the friends of Freedom North & East would turn an
eye to Kentucky for a time. . . . What we want is men to come and
form a collony [*sic*] and show Kentucky what Free labor can do."[36]

There were, however, important differences in emphasis between
the missionaries' call for northern emigrants and that of the Emigrant Aid and Homestead Company, and it is significant that those
differences forced Thayer and Underwood to clarify their rhetoric.
Like Underwood prior to his identification with the Republican party,
Fee and his coadjutors appealed to committed abolitionists to move
to the South. The missionaries never disguised their abolitionist motives and emphasized that it was the duty of northern Christians to
make sacrifices by going south to confront slavery and help those in
bonds. "Will not the same principle of action which prompts free state
men to go to Kansas to *exclude* slavery, lead others to come to Kentucky to help *abolish* slavery?" Fee asked in January 1857. This was
no scheme for free white workers gradually to *replace* blacks. Fee
and his colleagues were immediatists daring northerners to join them
in the front lines. "Come on, then, let us be Abolitionists together," he
said in March 1857. That same month, Waters anticipated Underwood
in declaring, "If northern men, and especially northern Christians,
are in earnest in their opposition to slavery, why should they not avail
themselves of the opportunity to settle in its midst, meet it face to
face, and bring 'the weapons of their warfare' to bear upon it?"[37]

Invocations of free-labor values and profits were decidedly sec-
ondary in this effort. Rather, as Waters put it, the emphasis was on
creating "a Christian anti-slavery colony in this State." He, Fee, and
the others wanted "earnest, experienced Christians, who will come
and lend a helping hand" in establishing northern settlements—centered on racially integrated, antislavery churches—that would impact
public opinion and serve as bases for antislavery politics. Fee and the
others assured prospective emigrants that they could be safe, pros-
perous, and enjoy some of the amenities of northern culture, but they
did not hide the prevalence of mob violence in Kentucky nor the need
to replace antislavery Kentuckians who had fled the state. The Kentucky missionaries said bluntly that emigrants would have to emu-

late Christ's sacrifices. "We want earnest, prayerful, devoted Christians, who do not come to increase their wealth, or to live at ease, but to do good—who are not afraid of reproach, of opposition, of toil and privation," Waters wrote in May 1857.[38]

The AMA, which by the mid-1850s represented a large portion of church-oriented abolitionists, fully supported the efforts of its Kentucky agents to attract settlers from the North. It endorsed Christian colonization in each of its annual reports from 1855 to 1858. From December 1855 through January 1860 the association's monthly *American Missionary* circulated among approximately twenty thousand northern abolitionist families the Kentuckians' calls for high-minded emigrants.[39]

A variety of other abolitionists also looked favorably on the undertaking. As soon as Fee began calling for emigrants, the *Standard* expressed "a very deep interest in the effort of Rev. John G. Fee and his heroic coadjutors to disseminate anti-slavery Christianity in Kentucky." The Reverend Charles B. Boynton of Cincinnati, a church-oriented abolitionist associated with the AMA who had earlier promoted "Christian colonization" in Kansas, assured Fee that he would do the same for Kentucky. "He [Boynton] thinks the emigration ought now be turned speedily as possible to this region," Fee told Cassius M. Clay in October 1857. A year later a correspondent of the evangelical *Independent* reported from Berea, "It is an omen of much importance commercially, but far more morally that the people of New England are beginning to turn their eyes to this region in a slave state. We trust that this very reason, because it is a slave state, will send many of the sons of the Puritans to a land where by their habits and example they may do much."[40]

Fee and Davis received a stream of inquiries from the type of abolitionist northerners they desired, and there were visits. The only cautionary words came from Lewis Tappan, who in May 1857 mildly upbraided Fee for his promotional efforts. Tappan commented that he had "but little confidence in Mr. Eli Thayer's style of doing things." But far fewer northerners went to Berea between 1857 and 1860 than to Ceredo. In part his was because Fee and his associates limited their prospects for success by failing to establish a land company to commercialize their plan and by restricting their appeal to abolitionists.[41]

Just as important, the missionaries' settlement scheme was undermined by anti-abolitionist violence in Kentucky during 1857 and 1858. Well-publicized assaults on Fee and the burning of one of his churches contradicted the missionaries' claims that there had been progress in protecting freedom of speech and property rights in the commonwealth. "I have heard some of our Northern friends say there are men that would come but they are afraid they would be burnt up," Peter H. West told Jocelyn in December 1857. At first, Fee attempted to use the mobbings to the advantage of his cause. The founders of the antislavery movement had suffered such mob outrages in the North in the 1830s, he recalled. "Should not their sons and daughters continue the work, 'carry the war (of words, of arguments) into Africa?'" But calls for emigrants in the *American Missionary* declined, and by February 1858 Fee confessed to Jocelyn, "I feel depressed because friends north are so slow to come here and help." Just as several abolitionists had predicted, it would not be until slavery had been abolished that significant numbers of the type of morally, economically, and politically committed men and women he sought would go south.[42]

In their disappointment, the missionaries bitterly and hyperbolically compared their colony to Ceredo. "Eli Thayer calls people to Virginia," Lincoln observed. "Thousands obey. Christ calls his church to send soldier volunteers to Kentucky, and lo, *not one*. The logical, strict deduction . . . is, the world obeys its god, the all-mighty Dollar, more than the church obeys its God, Jesus Christ."[43]

Yet Fee and Lincoln underestimated the impact of their colony. The number of immediatists at Berea probably never exceeded thirty-six men, women, and children, and only about twelve of these arrived in response to the call for northern abolitionist settlers. But the total free-labor, antislavery population of Berea was close to two hundred. In addition, the twelve northern settlers all arrived in the fall of 1859, which, as Richard D. Sears suggests, created in the minds of local slaveholders an image of an ominously increasing abolitionist presence just as news of John Brown's raid shocked the South. When vigilantes forced the Berean immediatists out of Kentucky in late 1859 and early 1860, they cited, among other reasons for their action, the "constantly increased accessions of northern men."[44]

In addition, the Berea colony's Christian abolitionist emphasis had a direct influence on Thayer and Underwood, demonstrating thereby the force of religious morality within the antislavery movement. By 1858, the advocates of northern settlement in Virginia had joined the missionaries in overt appeals to abolitionism. The change in Thayer was the more striking as he began to stress an element of evangelical morality he had previously subordinated to economic self-interest.

Thayer had, in fact, never ignored the concept of Christian colonization. In September 1854, he advised Jocelyn that the New England Emigrant Aid Company's effort in Kansas was "hardly more a civil one than a religious" and pledged to work with the AMA "in disseminating the true principles of Christianity." In 1857 he invited AMA leader Charles B. Boynton to visit Ceredo to report on its progress. But it was in conjunction with Fee that Thayer actually merged his colonization plans with those of the abolitionists. On September 30, 1858, the AMA held its annual meeting in Thayer's hometown of Worcester, Massachusetts, with Thayer as an invited speaker. In his remarks, Thayer called for "Christian Colonization" of the South, which he maintained could combine profit-making with the spread of freedom and true religion. In a subsequent speech at the meeting, Fee "warmly" endorsed these precepts, and Thayer, who had been condemned in 1857 by some antislavery advocates for his materialism, by 1859 had gained abolitionist praise for doing "the Lord's work" in Virginia.[45] It was, therefore, not surprising that Thayer's colleague Underwood used missionary terminology to appeal to Garrisonians for aid in abolitionizing Virginia in his 1859 letter to Oliver Johnson noted at the beginning of this chapter.

Plans to send free-state settlers into the South were hardly comparable to slave rescue attempts, images of southern white emancipators and southern black liberators, or more traditional abolitionist missionary efforts in the South as indications of abolitionist interest in southern antislavery action. Neither economic nor moral appeals convinced large numbers of northerners to risk their financial and physical security by emigrating into slave states. But, in linking the efforts in Virginia and Kentucky, it is clear that these attempts to encourage organized northern settlements in the South were a part of an aggressive abolitionist reform culture. Underwood's motives for his work in Virginia were deeply rooted in his abolitionist experience in New York. Fee and his brethren were active immediatists with close connections to the Gerrit Smith circle as well as to Lewis

Tappan and the others who ran the AMA. Even Thayer, who is usually portrayed as an opportunist or a realist disenchanted with abolitionist extremists, appealed to a variety of abolitionist groups for support and altered his rhetoric for the sake of the AMA. While some first-generation immediatists had misgivings about the utility of sending northern settlers into the South prior to general emancipation, church-oriented abolitionists, second-generation immediatists, and especially border-slave-state abolitionists persistently regarded organized emigration into the upper South as a potentially effective means of directly confronting slavery.

Chapter Seven

THE INTERSECTIONAL POLITICS OF SOUTHERN ABOLITIONISM

"I greatly rejoice at your visit to our state. The effect has been, and will continue to be most salutary," John G. Fee told George W. Julian of Indiana in November 1852. Julian was the Free Soil vice presidential nominee that year, and by coming to Kentucky he became the first member of an antislavery national ticket to campaign in a slave state. Historians of the sectional conflict have regarded such forays of northern antislavery politicians into the upper South as quixotic. They have portrayed the hopes of Liberty abolitionists, Free Soilers, and Republicans for political antislavery progress in the South as visionary, and it is certainly true that Fee greatly exaggerated in saying "slavery recd a shock[,] an attack, such as she never felt before" when he and a few other Kentuckians voted for Julian and Free Soil presidential candidate John P. Hale that year. Yet, like Fee, many northern abolitionists believed that an aggressive political "war" against slavery in the border region was essential to the success of their cause. Along with other types of southern antislavery action, this conviction had a major role in abolitionist reform culture.[1]

Although Fee was best known as an AMA agent, he and several others who emerged in the 1840s and 1850s as political abolitionist leaders in the upper South distinguished themselves from more conventional southern antislavery politicians by maintaining close ties to northern abolitionism. By advocating legislation to abolish slavery within their states, by refraining from overtly racist rhetoric, and by rejecting the expatriation of blacks as a prerequisite for emancipation, they qualified as political abolitionists and as heroes among the immediatists. They represented a type of southern political action that was complementary to the activities of black liberators, slave rescuers, abolitionist missionaries, and advocates of northern settlements in the upper South.

The existence of indigenous antislavery politics in the upper South in the 1840s and 1850s inspired northern political abolitionists to venture into that region to establish newspapers, to help organize branches of northern antislavery parties, and to put proslavery politicians on the defensive. Although such native and northern-based political antislavery efforts in the border region did not usually attract strong local support, they provided tangible—if exaggerated—evidence of progress against slavery in the South. That evidence in turn helped shape the development of political abolitionism and of mass political antislavery action in the North. This chapter aims to explore the relationship between southern political abolitionism and northern immediatism, indicate how northern abolitionists used that relationship to promote their organizations, and describe how northern political abolitionists intervened in the South.

Among the prominent southern political abolitionists were several individuals who gained renown among northern abolitionists as southern emancipators. Besides Fee, there were Cassius M. Clay, Joseph Evans Snodgrass, and William S. Bailey. Of these, Clay was by far the most influential in both the South and the North. Forging ties to northern abolitionists in the early 1840s, he led an effort to create an antislavery party in Kentucky and encouraged political abolitionism in other slave states. Despite his service in the Mexican War, which southern abolitionists criticized almost as sharply as their northern counterparts, Clay set an example that other southern antislavery politicians followed.[2]

Fee was also extremely active in politics. In addition to his service in the Free Soil campaign of 1852, he attempted to organize a Free Soil ticket in Kentucky in 1848, joined with Clay and much more conservative opponents of slavery in an attempt to add an emancipationist clause to the Kentucky constitution in 1849, and provided important support for Clay's emancipationist gubernatorial campaign in 1851. By 1855, Fee had become the leading southern spokesperson for the radical political abolitionists. Snodgrass, following the termination of his editorial career in 1847, became increasingly active in antislavery politics. He served as a Free Soil spokesperson in Maryland and Virginia until, in 1854, he moved to New York City, where he worked to promote northern migration to Kansas. Finally, William S. Bailey gained renown among radical political abolitionists and Republicans as the 1850s progressed.[3]

Two northern abolitionists also were prominent for their political activities in the upper South. The more influential of them was Gamaliel Bailey, who moved from Cincinnati to Washington, D.C., in late 1846 to establish the *National Era* as a Liberty newspaper. The other was John C. Underwood, who helped organize a Republican party in Virginia at the same time that he urged northerners to settle there.[4]

Of course, many political abolitionists in the upper South had only local reputations and received scant recognition in the North for their political efforts. Most of Fee's fellow AMA agents joined in his political campaigns. David Gamble, who served the AMA in Maryland, also promoted Free Soil and Republican organization in that state. Samuel M. Janney quietly helped organize a Free Soil presidential ticket in Virginia in 1848, and in the 1850s George Rye suffered persecution in Virginia for his antislavery politics without a fraction of the recognition Underwood received in the northern antislavery press for similar affliction.[5]

Other more prominent southern political abolitionists had little direct contact with their northern counterparts. North Carolina-born Daniel R. Goodloe, who served as an antislavery journalist and political organizer in Washington, D.C., during the 1840s and 1850s, had ties to John Quincy Adams, Gamaliel Bailey, the Free Soil party, and the Republican party rather than to northern abolitionists. Washington native Lewis Clephane, who served as the chief clerk for the *National Era* and who—along with Goodloe—was the leader of the extremely influential Republican Association of Washington, was in a similar position. He learned his abolitionism from his employer, Gamaliel Bailey, and from Bailey's more prominent associate, Salmon P. Chase. Although Goodloe and Clephane advocated abolition and on occasion expressed sympathy for the enslaved, neither of their careers generated the drama required to make them heroes to northern abolitionists.[6]

The two men also alienated northern abolitionists when their efforts to organize a Republican party in the border region led them into cooperation with Francis Preston Blair of Maryland and—less directly—with Francis P. Blair Jr. of Missouri. The Blairs represented a significant indigenous southern Jacksonian demand for the emancipation and expulsion of blacks for the sake of white safety and advancement that had negligible connections to northern immediatism.[7]

While the Blairs' appeal was acceptable to most Free Soilers and Republicans and could frighten proslavery southerners, northern abolitionists were reluctant to embrace anyone associated with it. It is true that northern abolitionists occasionally detected signs of progress in the Blairs' activities, and in the late 1850s such immediatists as Elihu Burritt, Gerrit Smith, and Theodore Parker reached out to them in search of intersectional and peaceful solutions to the problem of emancipation. But, generally, northern abolitionists ignored the Blairs and their associates as well as Archibald W. Campbell and other Whiggish Republicans in western Virginia, who made the expulsion of African Americans a political objective.[8]

In some respects similar to the Blairs and their Whiggish counterparts who cooperated with the Republican party in the 1850s were a class of southern political reformers who emerged in the 1830s and may be called pseudo-emancipationists. Like the Blairs, these individuals denied that slaveholding was innately sinful, ignored the rights of the slaves, advocated colonizing former slaves beyond the borders of the United States, and emphasized the interests of whites. But, unlike the Blairs, they worked within the existing major parties, usually sought to discourage rather than abolish slavery, and excoriated all northern abolitionists as violent fanatics. It was politicians of this type who responded to Nat Turner's rebellion of 1831 by attempting to persuade the Virginia assembly to gradually abolish slavery and expel blacks from that state. In Kentucky, individuals of similar persuasion passed the "Law of 1833" banning the importation of slaves into the state. The law aimed chiefly at reducing white fear of a growing black population and at helping local slaveholders by increasing the value of slaves who were already in Kentucky. But the law's proponents also presented it as a step toward the ultimate emancipation and expulsion of black Kentuckians. Among the Kentuckians identified with this and similar measures were Robert J. Breckinridge, James Madison Pendleton, and United States Senators Henry Clay and Joesph R. Underwood. Virginians who held compatible views included William B. Preston, John Letcher, and John Minor Botts.[9]

With the exception of Breckinridge, none of these pseudo-emancipationists engaged in a dialogue with northern abolitionists. In none of them, including Breckinridge, did northern abolitionists perceive a potential for progress toward immediatism. Despite his moral tone, his expressions of sympathy for black suffering, and his advocacy of emancipation in the 1830s and 1840s, Breckinridge alienated abolitionists by attacking them and by his firm allegiance to the ACS. By the 1850s his defense of slavery expansion and his bitter criticism of Republican party leaders William H. Seward and Charles Sumner identified him with the proslavery cause. Much more so than the Blairs and their allies, individuals such as Breckinridge and Letcher, who had retreated from earlier antislavery commitments, came to symbolize among northern abolitionists the difficulty slaveholders had in overcoming their proslavery culture.[10]

In contrast, in the 1840s Cassius M. Clay, Fee, Snodgrass, and some obscure Liberty party organizers of western Virginia engaged with northern abolitionists in a generally harmonious dialogue. Such intersectional ties moderated outlooks on both sides. But the major tendency was to draw the southerners involved into a northern abolitionism that contrasted with the indigenous reformism of the pseudo-emancipationists and the Blairs. Northern abolitionism influenced the political conduct of those southerners it attracted, whether they acted as radical political abolitionists or as Free Soilers and Republicans.[11]

The northern abolitionist influence was most clear in Fee and his associates who, beginning with the emancipationist campaign of 1849 to amend the Kentucky constitution, carried a moral demand for immediate emancipation into border-slave-state politics. By 1856, William S. Bailey's increasing dependence on northern abolitionist financial support led him to follow Fee into immediatism. If other politically oriented southerners who joined in dialogue with northern abolitionists did not become immediatists, they did repudiate racist schemes to deport former slaves and embraced emancipation on the soil. John Gilmore, John Emery, and Samuel M. Bell of the western Virginia Liberty party, for example, in 1844 implicitly rejected the expatriation of blacks when they called on slaveholders to "give fair wages to your laborers, and let their services be not compulsory but voluntary." John C. Vaughan of the *Louisville Examiner*, who had been a supporter of the ACS in 1839, by 1847 argued that the material and religious improvement of Kentucky's slaves had prepared them for freedom in America. Under Fee's constant prodding, Vaughan's successors as editors of the *Examiner* also distanced themselves from the colonizationists.[12]

Even more than was the case with their northern counterparts, however, appeals to white interests remained crucial to southern political abolitionists. Slavery, they maintained, was detrimental to the southern economy, to public education, to free white labor, to white civil liberties, and to white morality. They frequently asked their northern friends for statistical comparisons of the North and South to support such claims. When it embraced emancipation on the soil, the *Examiner* was careful to reassure its readers that blacks in freedom would continue to do the menial work. Even Fee was willing to endorse legislation designed to control black behavior after emancipation.[13]

It is Cassius M. Clay, nevertheless, who serves best to illustrate the tension southern political abolitionists felt between northern abolitionist morality and what they perceived to be southern reality. Well into the early 1840s, he had much in common with the pseudo-emancipationists. In 1845 he claimed to have become a life member in the ACS. But he simultaneously rejected African colonization as a means of general emancipation and endorsed freedom for blacks in the United States. Colonization, he suggested, might be useful as a means of Christianizing Africa, but otherwise it was a proslavery fraud. Its advocates, he charged, relied on Negrophobia to make whites unwilling to contemplate sharing the future with former slaves, then used the prohibitive costs of transporting blacks to Africa to guarantee perpetual slavery. He caricatured colonizationists as saying, "I am as much in favor of liberty as you, if you will send the blacks to the moon; but unless you send them to the moon, I'll see you damned before I assent to their liberation among us."[14]

In 1846 Clay said that immediate emancipation would be best for all but that because of the selfishness, irreligion, and unyielding habits of white Kentuckians, he accepted gradual abolition as a political goal. Caught between immediatist principles and his perception of white fear of black economic competition and race war, Clay in 1845 and 1851 produced muddled plans to end slavery in Kentucky that called for gradual emancipation on the soil while fruitlessly soliciting colonizationist support by suggesting that masters might sell their chattels out of state before slavery ended.[15]

Despite compromises and qualifications, Clay and the other political abolitionists of the upper South were able to move as far as they did toward immediatism because they shared religious precepts with their northern counterparts. Several historians have noted that northern Liberty party politicians attempted to apply Christian morality to American politics, and this was true of southern political abolitionists as well. The fact that the southerners' politics were religiously motivated explains their failure to form effective alliances with colonizationists and suggests that generalizations concerning their self-serving motives are inadequate.[16]

That religious faith accounted for the political activities of John G. Fee, John C. Vaughan, Samuel M. Janney, and Joseph Evans Snodgrass is clear. But Clay too mixed religion and politics. Although he was not a church member by the 1840s, Clay shared an evangelical background with other abolitionists and frequently employed religious arguments against slavery. In 1841, as a Kentucky legislator, he contended that slavery perverted the "moral inculcations" of Christianity. Four years later, he declared slavery to be "our great national sin" and called on "every follower of Christ to bear testimony against this crime against man and God: which fills our souls with cruelty and crime." Shortly thereafter, Clay revealed his similarity to northern immediatists in declaring that all slaveholders were sinners because they denied the brotherhood of God's children, destroyed "the moral government of God," and "subverted the principle of free agency."[17]

Much as was the case among Liberty abolitionists in New York and New England, southern political abolitionists blurred the distinction between religious and political antislavery organizations. In the 1840s and 1850s, Clay—primarily as a politician—and Fee—primarily as a missionary—cooperated closely. Fee regarded Clay's political campaign to add an emancipationist clause to the Kentucky constitution as part of a "moral reform" movement, and Fee's churches served as the core of Free Soil, Republican, and Radical Abolition party organizations in the commonwealth. Clay, in turn, actively promoted Fee's free churches. Even after the two men's political philosophies diverged in the mid-1850s, Fee scheduled Clay's political speeches in conjunction with his own sermons, advised Clay on choosing local Republican candidates, and promoted Clay's candidacy for the Republican vice presidential nomination in 1860.[18]

Of the two Kentucky leaders, Clay at least was aware of a distinction between religious and political spheres. He publicly identified himself as a politician, not as a moralist. But he was never able to put such a distinction into practice. His speeches often combined denials that slavery was a matter of conscience with him with strong indications that it was and that he was indeed a moralist shaped by a very Christian conscience. "Clay is not a Christian but he ought to be," Fee told George Whipple in 1859.[19]

While a close relationship between southern political and religious abolitionism is clearest in Kentucky, it existed in other states of the upper South as well. When the Liberty abolitionists of western Virginia met in 1844 to choose a slate of presidential electors, they recognized the government of God and grounded their action on the contention that "slaveholding is clearly condemned in the Bible." In North Carolina, the Wesleyan missionaries and their parishioners openly engaged in Free Soil politics from 1848 through 1853. Like abolitionists in his native Ohio, Jesse McBride argued that religious men had an obligation to vote against slavery and to elect antislavery candidates to state and national office. In Washington, D.C., in the late 1850s, antislavery church organizer Edward L. Stevens and AMA missionary George W. Bassett cooperated with Gamaliel Bailey in establishing close ties between themselves and Republican politicians. And, in Missouri, AMA missionary Stephen Blanchard in 1860 wrote about Biblical opposition to slavery for the *Saint Joseph Free Democrat*—a newspaper identified with Francis P. Blair Jr.'s emancipationist organization, which historians rarely associate with moral opposition to slavery.[20]

Because they mixed religion and politics, it is not surprising that southern political abolitionists carried advanced concepts of black rights into their political campaigns. Fee, who was as committed to equal rights for blacks as any white American of his time, in 1856 went so far as to object to a section of the Kentucky Republican Association's platform, which suggested that its members would help quell slave revolts. Snodgrass, who in the 1840s advocated the rights of Baltimore's free blacks, as a Free Soiler in 1852 called for the passage of a Maryland state law recognizing the common descent and brotherhood of the races. William S. Bailey denounced slavery as a system that required whites to oppress blacks.[21]

Nor were Daniel R. Goodloe and Cassius M. Clay unsympathetic to black aspirations for freedom and advancement in the United States. They resisted theories of black inferiority advanced by Louis Agassiz and the American School of Ethnology. Writing in the *National Era* in the 1850s, Goodloe endorsed the capacity of blacks to become useful citizens and warned against "Negrophobia." Clay said in 1854, "It is one of the boldest absurdities to suppose that the liberties of the white race are more sacred than those of the blacks." Goodloe and Clay were certainly ambivalent concerning issues of race, and they—along with other southern Republicans—joined northern Republicans in the late 1850s in a racist retreat from egalitarian rhetoric in response to Democratic charges that the Republicans favored blacks over whites. But Clay continued to oppose the expatriation of blacks and was never comfortable with denials of the doctrine that all men were created equal.[22]

The relationship between these southern political abolitionists and their northern counterparts had begun shortly after the formation of the Liberty party in 1840 as the first American antislavery party. When Clay emerged as an antislavery politician in a slave state, Liberty abolitionists attempted to lure him from the Whig party to their ranks and use his prestige as a southern emancipator to attract northern voters. Foremost in this effort were Gamaliel Bailey and Salmon P. Chase, who at the time resided in Cincinnati just across the Ohio River from slaveholding Kentucky. These leaders, in their physical proximity to slavery, in their legalism, in their disinclination to antagonize slaveholders, and in their willingness to compromise moral principle to appeal to white interests, had much in common with Clay and other southern abolitionists.[23]

Bailey and Chase especially hoped to use Clay to attract northern abolitionists to a political program of federal action against slavery in the national domain combined with political organization in the southern states to end slavery within them by state legislation. Chase initiated a correspondence with Clay in 1842 and, on the basis of Clay's response, told abolitionist powerhouse Lewis Tappan in early 1843 that "there are many, very many slaveholders who believe slavery to be a curse and a . . . violation of the code of equal rights who would willingly concur in putting an end to its existence by legislative enactment." If the Liberty party became strong enough to challenge slavery within the jurisdiction of Congress, Chase told Tappan, its efforts "would . . . soon [be] reinforced by the friends of Liberty in the Slave States who would act, not only against National but against State Slavery and the overthrow of both would be reached."[24]

Chase's vision of political antislavery progress in the South, based on his interpretation of Clay's actions and hopes, drew a reluctant Tappan into active support of the Liberty party. Tappan was so taken with Chase's letter that he repeated much of it verbatim to John Scoble of the British and Foreign Anti-Slavery Society in March 1843. Shortly thereafter Tappan began corresponding with Clay and by the mid-1840s had initiated an ambitious project aimed at promoting antislavery sentiment in the South.[25]

Other Liberty abolitionists were similarly impressed with the possibilities Clay's emergence suggested. In 1843 and 1844 his outspoken opposition to the annexation of slaveholding Texas, his open declaration that he was an abolitionist, his emancipation of his slaves, and his praise of the Liberty party as a growing force for emancipation inspired Liberty leaders across the North. In February 1844 Henry B. Stanton of Massachusetts attributed much of Clay's progress to Chase's influence and added to Chase, "I hope you will keep in close correspondence with Mr. Clay—for, if he keep on the High Road, he will yet do wonders for Humanity."[26]

So attractive was the promise Clay represented of political organization against slavery in the South that it was difficult for him to alienate Liberty advocates. They had some concern for his increasingly close ties to leading Garrisonians. Lewis Tappan and others were put off by his advocacy of violent self-defense and gradualism. But Joshua Leavitt of the *Emancipator* and James C. Jackson of the *Albany Patriot* admired his threat to use "cold steel" against those who threatened his antislavery effort, and Gamaliel Bailey argued that Clay had to be judged by different standards than northern abolitionists.[27] Much more distressing, however, were Clay's devotion to the Whig party during the presidential campaign of 1844 and his service in what abolitionists perceived to be a proslavery war against Mexico in 1846.

Throughout the first half of the 1840s, Clay made no secret of his belief that, despite his respect for the Liberty party, the Whigs represented the best hope for achieving general emancipation. He corresponded with Ohio's antislavery Whig congressman Joshua R. Giddings, and, like Giddings and other evangelical northern Whigs, Clay believed that what republican virtue and Christian morality existed in American politics resided in their party. The northern Whigs in turn were as aware as the Liberty abolitionists of Clay's appeal in the North as a southern emancipator. In 1844 they convinced him to undertake an extended speaking tour across Michigan, Ohio, New York, and Massachusetts in behalf of Whig presidential candidate Henry Clay, who was his distant cousin. Cassius M. Clay's ostensible purpose in this tour was to convince northern antislavery voters, who might otherwise prefer Liberty nominee James G. Birney, that it was justifiable to vote one last time for a slaveholding Whig like Henry Clay in order to prevent the election of Democrat James K. Polk, who was certain to push for the annexation of slaveholding Texas.[28]

During the course of Cassius M. Clay's speaking tour, Liberty and Garrisonian spokespeople rebuked his moral inconsistency as an abolitionist urging other abolitionists to vote for a candidate who owned at least sixty slaves. Yet the large and enthusiastic crowds Clay attracted underscored his standing among rank-and-file antislavery voters. Joshua Leavitt said people came to hear Clay "not because he was a Whig, but because he was an emancipator of slaves," and the appearance Clay created of antislavery progress in the South persuaded most Liberty leaders that his political usefulness for the third party outweighed his liabilities. "We of the *forlorn hope* may suspect him of wavering, at a most critical point in the march—may accuse him of faithlessness to his principles," commented the *Liberty Press* of Utica, New York, in July 1844, "but may we not justly pardon in him what we would not in ourselves, or in any Northern man?" Noting that Clay refused to criticize the Liberty party during his tour, Leavitt went so far as to claim that Clay's speeches helped the third party more than the Whigs.[29]

Northern abolitionists focused on Clay as the major proponent of political antislavery progress in the South through early 1846. His establishment of the *True American* as an abolitionist newspaper in the heart of a slave state in June 1845 and his willingness to risk his life to maintain his right to publish it that August thrilled all northern abolitionists. In January 1846 his reputation peaked as he addressed an audience of four thousand composed of Whigs, Liberty abolitionists, African Americans, and Quakers at New York City's Broadway Tabernacle. Speaking of every man's right to himself, his wife, his children, his Bible, and the fruits of his labor, Clay struck cords of morality that appealed to evangelicals. Lewis Tappan exclaimed, "C. M. Clay has done nobly here. . . . Think of the magnitude of the Tabernacle (the largest audience I ever saw there) applauding to the skies—the roof—ultra abolition doctrines!"[30]

A few months later Clay enlisted in the war against Mexico, and his standing among most abolitionists plummeted. But by then he had already established a role for southern abolitionists in northern antislavery politics. Upon his return from Mexico in 1848, Clay himself remained in demand as an antislavery campaign speaker, and he had substantial support as a possible Free Soil vice presidential nominee in 1852, as well as for the Republican nomination for that office in 1860.[31]

Clay's continued popularity in the North supported the assumption among abolitionists and antislavery politicians that an individual's heroism or martyrdom in the cause of emancipation in the South could attract voters to antislavery parties in the North. Unlike Clay, Joseph Evans Snodgrass was not an imposing physical presence, rather he was small in stature and sickly. The concern for black interests that he embodied has not usually been associated with Free Soilers. But Snodgrass spoke at the Free Soil convention at Buffalo in 1848, and— at the urging of that party's leaders—undertook an extensive speaking tour across Pennsylvania and Ohio in behalf of the party that fall. In 1852 he campaigned in New York and Illinois.[32]

In 1856 it was John C. Underwood's speech at the Republican national convention at Philadelphia, in which he attacked slavery for its brutal oppression of blacks as well as its negative impact on Virginia's economy, that led to his expulsion from that state. Expulsion in turn made him a popular campaign speaker in the North. As the "'hero of Virginia Republicanism,'" Underwood represented in New York and New England the proposition that the Republican party aimed not only at excluding slavery from the territories but at transforming the South as well.[33]

In fact, since the time of Salmon P. Chase's first contacts with Cassius M. Clay, northern political abolitionists and antislavery politicians encouraged indigenous emancipationist political organization in the states of the upper South. There, local party activists—whether Liberty, Free Soil, or Republican—could promote abolitionist legislation unhindered by constitutional restrictions that left slavery in the southern states legally beyond the control of either the northern state legislatures or Congress.

In the 1840s, the Cincinnati leadership of the Ohio Liberty party promoted the assumption that the success of their party in the North would lead directly to the formation of Liberty organizations in the South. But the Cincinnatians took more aggressive action as well. Chase became actively involved in the formation of a Liberty party in Virginia in 1844 and actually wrote that organization's address to the people of Virginia. "Your anti slavery feelings together with your knowledge of the history of both Virginia & Kentucky give you a superiority over all the friends that are labouring in the good cause," western Virginia Liberty organizer Samuel M. Bell told Chase. Meanwhile Gamaliel Bailey succeeded in expanding the circulation of his *Cincinnati Weekly Herald and Philanthropist* throughout the upper South.[34]

These efforts, combined with continuing hopes that Cassius M. Clay would join their party, encouraged Bailey, Chase, and other Cincinnati Liberty abolitionists to organize the ambitious Southern and Western Convention of the Friends of Constitutional Liberty of June 1845. Aimed at attracting antislavery Whigs and Democrats to the Liberty ranks, the convention—as its name suggests—had a southern orientation. In publicizing the call for the convention, Bailey emphasized that its objects were the same as Clay's: "VIZ: the extinction by *fair, and honorable and constitutional means,* of slavery in the State[s], and its reduction to its constitutional limits in the Union." Of the five hundred signatures on the call for the convention, sixty were from Virginia, and Bailey expected a large delegation from Kentucky. Fee attended the convention, and Clay, who did not waver in his loyalty to the Whig party, sent a letter commending the Ohioans' efforts. Chase in his address to the three thousand assembled in Cincinnati declared that it was the duty of the nonslaveholders of the South to act against slavery. Would southern whites, Chase asked, "be restrained from speaking . . . by the consideration that the enslaved will be benefited as well as themselves?" If so, he warned, they risked "a bitter retribution."[35]

Leading Liberty abolitionists of Massachusetts and New York advocated helping slaves to escape as a tactic better designed to weaken slavery in the upper South than encouraging political antislavery action in that region. Yet they too admired Clay's bravery if not his legal positivism and endorsed the necessity of political action in the South to end slavery. In terms similar to those William L. Chaplin would later apply to Charles T. Torrey, James C. Jackson of the *Al-*

bany Patriot responded to Clay's refusal to give in to mob demands by promising, "Liberty men. . . . will not forget that he stands in the breach in their stead—that his bosom is exposed to the dagger of the assassin instead of theirs." When Clay appeared to falter in 1846, Liberty abolitionists throughout the North rallied to subsidize John C. Vaughan as Clay's successor as editor of the *True American* and later as publisher of the *Louisville Examiner*.[36]

As significant as these initiatives by northern political abolitionists to help their counterparts in the South were, a joint venture by Liberty abolitionists of the Old Northwest and the AFASS to establish a southern-oriented national Liberty newspaper in slaveholding Washington, D.C., constituted the major northern abolitionist effort to foster antislavery politics in the South. Since the mid-1830s abolitionists had pressed the issue of ending slavery and the slave trade in Washington on Congress. Since 1841 they had struggled to maintain a lobbyist at the capitol, and they had long believed the movement required antislavery reporters at sessions of Congress.[37] But it took a serendipitous convergence of factors related to southern antislavery action to get the plan for an abolitionist newspaper in Washington started.

In 1845, Amos A. Phelps reflected a growing abolitionist consensus when he considered moving to Washington to confront slavery journalistically in that southern city. At the end of the year, when he and John Greenleaf Whittier traveled to Baltimore in an unsuccessful attempt to secure the release of slave-rescuer Torrey from prison, they visited nearby Washington. There they met Massachusetts-born Jacob Bigelow, a congressional reporter, an advocate of establishing an antislavery church at the capital, and an active abettor of fugitive slaves. Bigelow convinced Phelps and Whittier that public opinion in Washington would permit the publication of an abolitionist newspaper there. Phelps responded by contacting his friend Lewis Tappan, who then brought northwestern Liberty leaders into the undertaking.[38]

As what Tappan called the "great plan" acquired substance during 1846, its supporters increasingly emphasized the impact a Washington Liberty newspaper would have in the South. Tappan chose Gamaliel Bailey to edit the paper because of Bailey's diplomatic style and his demonstrated ability to attract southern subscribers. Charles

V. Dyer, who headed a committee of northwestern Liberty abolitionists, engaged subscription agents not only in the North and upper South but in such deep South states as South Carolina, Alabama, and Mississippi as well. By the fall of 1846 Tappan was raising a fund totaling sixty thousand dollars in order to make the new paper the center of a national propaganda agency. When he and Bailey named the paper the *National Era*, they intended it to symbolize a new epoch in which the Liberty party would expand into the South and become truly national in scope.[39]

Bailey inaugurated the newspaper in January 1847 with an appeal to the southern people. While he repudiated abolitionist invective against slaveholding, he insisted that intelligent southerners must realize "that the haughty claim that slavery shall be exempt from investigation, discussion, opposition, is a gross absurdity." A "leading object" of his newspaper, he announced, was to present to southerners "such facts and arguments as may serve to throw further light upon the question of slavery, and its disposition." The *National Era*, he said, would advocate the "doctrines and measures" of the Liberty party, which he maintained would not "attempt to force the Federal Constitution from its obvious meaning" by calling for federal interference with slavery in the southern states. Instead it would rely on the establishment of Liberty parties in the South to achieve abolition.[40]

The *National Era's* theme was that the antislavery movement was not a sectional but a class struggle. Like antislavery newspapers edited in the South by native southerners, it called on the southern white masses to overthrow "the ruling caste, the Slave Power." Bailey emphasized that abolition would free whites from oppression, raise their wages, and encourage economic and cultural progress. But, like Chase before him, he also relied on the image of a southern black liberator to warn that so long as slavery existed southerners risked a "war of extermination and anarchy." Would it not be wise, he asked, to put an end to this threat through a policy of peaceful emancipation that would place southern blacks on the side of "law and order, instead of against it?"[41]

The *National Era* became the leading journal of southern political abolitionism. From its start in 1847 until it suspended publication in early 1860—nine months after Bailey's death—it recorded every sort of evidence of political antislavery action in the South. As the

Liberty party passed from the scene and Bailey advocated in succession the policies of the Free Soil and Republican parties, he argued that these parties too would gain footholds in the southern states as *abolition* parties. Because of this emphasis and because of the newspaper's phenomenal success in its early years, it contributed substantially to assumptions among northern antislavery politicians concerning unionist, if not explicitly antislavery, sentiment in the upper South. Starting with less than eight thousand subscribers, the paper gained five hundred in Maryland and Virginia when it absorbed Snodgrass's *Baltimore Saturday Visiter* in April 1847. By September its circulation was eleven thousand. By November it exchanged with over sixty southern newspapers, and, although its circulation was mainly in the North, Tappan correctly claimed that the *National Era* was "probably read by a much larger number of persons North and South, than any anti-slavery paper that has ever been established in this country." In 1853 its circulation peaked at twenty-eight thousand, making it the most widely read purely antislavery newspaper of all time.[42]

Proslavery southern whites reacted to the *National Era* with considerable alarm. In the wake of the *Pearl* slave rescue attempt, southern congressmen encouraged a Washington mob that attacked the newspaper's office and threatened Bailey at his home. There were unfulfilled threats of mob action against the newspaper in 1850 and 1859. In the former year a consortium of proslavery politicians established the *Southern Press* in Washington to counteract the paper's influence. Proslavery statistician Ellwood Fisher, who edited the *Press*, declared the *National Era* to be "clearly incendiary." In 1853 a former slave trader sued Bailey for libel and that same year the *Times* of Montgomery, Alabama, warned its readers that Bailey's ability to attract a southern audience "is furnishing the axe which is to cleave your heads and dismember the very cord of national existence."[43]

Abolitionists were, nevertheless, divided concerning the *National Era*. Those Garrisonians and northeastern Liberty advocates who believed invective was more effective than diplomacy in fighting the sin of slaveholding, who believed slave rescue attempts were more useful in destabilizing slavery than southern political organization, and who distrusted the Cincinnatians' legalism, were never friendly to the Washington paper's mission. While Garrisonians and radical political abolitionists perceived Cassius M. Clay, John C. Vaughan, and Joseph Evans Snodgrass as truth-seeking southerners, they regarded Bailey as a retrogressed northern immediatist who compromised moral truth for the sake of self-preservation at a southern latitude. The Garrisonian *Anti-Slavery Bugle* sarcastically commented that the conduct of the *National Era* was "exceedingly judicious" and that the paper would not be "indicted for incendiarism, fanaticism, and we had almost said abolitionism."[44]

Even when mobs threatened to destroy the *National Era* following the *Pearl* escape attempt, radical political abolitionists condemned the paper and its editor. Elizur Wright Jr., George Bradburn, and Frederick Douglass deplored Bailey's suggestion that Daniel Drayton and Edward Sayres were wrong to violate proslavery law. Meanwhile Garrisonian spokesperson Wendell Phillips called the *National Era* a "nuisance." Two years later when the paper objected to William L. Chaplin's similarly illegal attempt to help slaves escape, Hiram P. Crozier of New York called for sacrificing it to aid Chaplin.[45]

In contrast, most northern abolitionists recognized that the *National Era* had an important mission even as it moved into support of the Free Soil and—later—the Republican parties. In calmer moments Garrisonian and radical political abolitionists also conceded that the Washington paper served a useful purpose. More importantly, southern abolitionists overwhelmingly characterized it as eminently suitable to their needs. Samuel M. Janney of Virginia, for example, had no sympathy for Garrisonian disunionism. When Garrisonians questioned Gamaliel Bailey's abolitionist credentials, Janney told Sydney Howard Gay of the *National Antislavery Standard*, "I take the N. Era which is much approved by the anti slavery friends here & the wholesome truths it contains will, I hope, do much good. . . . Why not let Doct Bailey alone to labour in the field he has chosen? It is a locality in which *your society cannot labour* with your present views."[46]

Although Cassius M. Clay and John G. Fee each had personal reasons for distrusting Bailey, they joined other abolitionists of the border region in recognizing his antislavery leadership and in extending the circulation of the *National Era*. In particular, Bailey served as role model and mentor for other southern antislavery journalists ranging from John C. Vaughan and his successors as editors of the *Louisville Examiner*, to Thomas C. Connolly of the Leesburg, Virginia

Chronicle, to Daniel R. Goodloe, who replaced Bailey as editor of the *National Era.*[47]

As they moved successively into the Free Soil and Republican parties, Bailey and his former Cincinnati Liberty colleague Salmon P. Chase continued to lead northern efforts to encourage a wide spectrum of political abolitionism in the South. By the late 1850s William H. Seward and other conservative Republicans engaged in similar efforts as Republican organizations in the upper South became factors in the maneuvering for the 1860 Republican presidential nomination. Such efforts may be portrayed as aggressive antislavery action in the South. But, as Garrisonian and radical political abolitionists pointed out, they also involved considerable compromise of the principles of immediatism. Gamaliel Bailey, for example, had by 1851 gone well beyond Cassius M. Clay in embracing colonization of free blacks as a basis for antislavery progress in the border region, and Clay himself grew more cautious under Republican influences in the late 1850s.[48]

It was because they were aware of the practical necessity of such compromises that radical political abolitionists and Garrisonians never played so active a role in encouraging broad-based political abolitionism in the South as the Cincinnatians. By the mid-1850s Lewis Tappan also had become disillusioned by such compromises. Henceforth he and the church-oriented abolitionists he represented directed their support for southern initiatives into the AMA and the Radical Abolition party, both of which Tappan helped lead.[49] But prior to Tappan's change of heart, northern church-oriented abolitionists had been enthusiastic concerning broad-based political antislavery action in the South, and so too had Garrisonians.

In the 1840s, church-oriented abolitionist institutions such as the AFASS and the Wesleyan Connection applauded Liberty and Free Soil organization in the upper South as evidence of antislavery progress. In 1846, Free Mission Baptist minister William Henry Brisbane of Philadelphia—and formerly of South Carolina—went so far as to declare that, before antislavery missionaries could be sent into the South, abolitionists had to "prepare the way through the ballot-box, by which the barbarian lynch-law spirit of the South shall be first subdued." Church-oriented abolitionists followed the efforts of Cassius M. Clay and the political emancipationist movement in Kentucky with special interest. They joined in the general abolitionist disappointment with Clay's enlistment in the Mexican War but quickly regained confidence in him. As late as 1854, the AMA declared his efforts to be "signs of progress."[50]

The Garrisonian relationship to southern political abolitionism followed a similar pattern. Struck by Clay's dramatic antislavery speeches in the Kentucky legislature and by his publication of an antislavery newspaper in the 1840s, Garrisonians hoped through personal contact and gentle instruction to lead him to immediatism and disunionism. Like Liberty and church-oriented abolitionists, the Garrisonians were bitterly disappointed by Clay's active support of the war against Mexico. But as time passed, they increasingly regarded Clay and far less enlightened southern antislavery politicians in much the same way they regarded the Free Soil and Republican parties—as representatives of a selfish but potentially successful movement to destroy slavery. Most striking, in the late 1840s Garrisonians praised Henry Ruffner's campaign to gradually emancipate and expatriate the slave population of the western portion of Virginia. While admitting that Ruffner's plan was "vicious in the extreme, in the point of principle," the Garrisonian-dominated MASS suggested that his plan and similar ones in Maryland, Kentucky, Tennessee, Missouri, and North Carolina "may ere long be seen entering largely into the solution of the great problem of practical emancipation."[51]

In comparison to Ruffner's scheme, Cassius M. Clay's 1851 gubernatorial campaign, calling for gradual emancipation on the soil, struck Garrisonians as enlightened. There was no sarcasm when in 1853 William Lloyd Garrison joined African-American leaders Charles L. Remond, William C. Nell, and Lewis Hayden in expressing gratitude to Clay for "fearlessly" espousing the cause of "all in bonds." Although Garrisonians never lost their admiration for Clay or their hope that he could advance the cause of emancipation, they became more critical of him, as in the late 1850s he became committed to a nonextensionist interpretation of the mission of the Republican party.[52]

In contrast to other northern abolitionist groups, it was not until the 1850s that the Gerrit Smith circle of radical political abolitionists became active among southern political abolitionists. Previously Smith, William Goodell, William L. Chaplin, Frederick Douglass, and others associated with the New York Liberty party had been far less involved in encouraging political antislavery action in the South than had been the Cincinnati Liberty abolitionists, Lewis Tappan, or even the Garrisonians. They had been critical of Cassius M. Clay and Gamaliel Bailey's efforts to build an antislavery consensus in the border region and had relied instead on slave rescue attempts, appeals to the slaves, and advocacy of federal intervention against slavery in the southern states.[53]

It was primarily as a means of pressing first Free Soilers and later Republicans to take a more aggressive stance toward slavery in the South that Smith and Goodell developed a more positive interest in southern political abolitionism. Smith and Clay had been personal friends since the mid-1840s. But their different political orientations discouraged cooperation until the 1850s when Smith offered to support Clay's political ambitions, extended him a personal loan, and even visited Clay's home near Lexington, Kentucky, in an extended effort to lure Clay into the radical political abolitionist faction. That Smith hoped to both convert Clay and use the Kentuckian's popularity among antislavery activists became clear in 1851 when Smith offered his support of Clay as the 1852 Free Soil vice presidential nominee in return for Clay's endorsement of the radical doctrine that slavery could never be legalized.[54]

Clay was too politically ambitious to identify with Smith's tiny Radical Abolitionist party. He was also acutely aware that to suggest, as Smith and William Goodell did, that slavery could not enjoy the protection of the law was to invite its defenders to assert that neither did the law protect Clay. "I think we differ about slavery rather because we look at it from different points," he told Smith in 1855. "I think you view it rather speculatively—I practically. I must be cautious about nice metaphysical abstractions in law—whose life depends upon an appeal to the sacredness of law."[55] But Smith and his friends were more successful in making John G. Fee and William S. Bailey serve as vehicles for their campaign to confront slavery in the South and—what they regarded as—Republican recalcitrance.

Fee's evangelicalism drew him to Smith and Goodell's advocacy of "Bible politics" and "righteous government." Also, by the 1850s the northern leaders of the AMA, which funded his free church movement, were radical political abolitionists. Francis Hawley, who served with Fee as an antislavery missionary in the mid-1850s, was a member of that group as well. Most significant, Fee, beginning in the late 1840s, developed a deep admiration for Goodell, whom Fee attempted to lure to Kentucky as either a preacher or as an editor of an abolitionist newspaper. These associations and Fee's growing conviction that slaveholders would not respond to moral suasion led to his identification with the radical political abolitionists in the mid-1850s. Even so, he never fully understood Smith and Goodell's legal theory and was never comfortable with their claim that Congress could abolish slavery in the southern states.[56]

In early 1856, Fee formally joined Smith, Goodell, and Tappan's American Abolition Society. In July of that year, he precipitated a breach between his and Clay's Kentucky antislavery forces by publicly declaring that proslavery laws must not be obeyed. When Fee proceeded to organize a tiny Radical Abolitionist party in Kentucky, Clay withdrew his physical protection of Fee and his associates. This, as well as Fee's provocative rhetoric and the growth of the Berea colony, encouraged the proslavery mob attacks that culminated in the forced expulsion of Fee and others from Kentucky beginning in late 1859.[57] In all Fee well served Smith and Goodell's revolutionary goals by openly challenging the legitimacy of slavery in Kentucky, by attempting to push Clay and the Kentucky Republicans into a similarly confrontational stance, and in the end by creating more antislavery martyrs, whose sufferings could be used to excite antislavery and antisouthern sentiment in the North against oppression in the South.[58]

That the radical political abolitionists hoped to use the prestige of southern political abolitionists to increase their own influence in the North and to coerce the Republican party into a more aggressive policy toward the South is also clear in their relationship with William S. Bailey. Bailey, whom first Fee and then Clay came to distrust, sought financial support for his newspaper and large family from Garrisonians and Republicans as well as the Smith circle. But by 1856, Bailey had a special relationship with the radical political abolitionists. Toward the end of that year, Goodell began to write for Bailey's *Kentucky News*, and that paper began to criticize the Republican party for not seeking the abolition of slavery in the southern states.[59]

From early 1858 onward, as Republican leaders such as Senators William H. Seward and William Pitt Fessenden explicitly denied that their party would use federal power against slavery in the states, Goodell used the *News*'s protests of this position to emphasize the shortcomings of the Republicans as an abolitionist party. Goodell's *Radical Abolitionist* and *Principia* quoted Bailey's newspaper as it declared: "If we disclaim the right of [federal government] interference with slavery in the States where it exists, we virtually acknowledge that it exists there of right, and if we admit this, then the Republican party ceases to meet the views of those who have labored through long years to arouse the people of the slave States to a true appreciation of their degraded condition." Thus, a southern antislavery newspaper aided the radical political abolitionists in their efforts to counteract conservative tendencies in the Republican party and commit that party to "the entire overthrow of slavery."[60]

It was, therefore, from the emergence of Cassius M. Clay as a significant figure to the eve of secession and civil war that southern political antislavery action intertwined with the course of political abolitionism in the North. Southern political abolitionists reflected developments within northern abolitionism and in turn influenced the development of northern antislavery parties. They served as symbols of aggressive action against slavery on its own ground, prodded northern Whigs and later Republicans toward direct confrontation with slavery, and encouraged northern political abolitionists to extend their own activities into the South. Finally, like other abolitionist ventures in the upper South, that of the political abolitionists underlined the perceptions of proslavery leaders that their cherished institution was under direct attack on its borders and in need of a determined defense.

Chapter Eight

LEGACIES

In 1877, sixty-one-year-old Calvin Fairbank served as the superintendent of the Moore Street Missionary Society of Richmond, Virginia, which provided an industrial education to African Americans. Fairbank, who was remembered for the imprisonment he had suffered as a result of his efforts to rescue slaves, retained the respect of black leaders. He joined with them in the belief that the risks he took three decades earlier had helped prepare the way for general emancipation after the Civil War. He regarded that war as the culmination of his antislavery actions and revered Abraham Lincoln as the instrument of God's design. Fairbank also recognized that the "'good fight'" for black rights had not ended in 1865. When he published his autobiography in 1890, he dedicated it to the old Liberty party faithful of the 1850s and to "their Successors, who recognize 'the Fatherhood of God, and Brotherhood of Man.'"[1]

Fairbank's activities in his old age and his retrospective on abolitionism introduce two themes that are the focus of this final chapter. First, there is the causal relationship between southern antislavery action and the Civil War. Second, there is the continuity between those individuals who represented northern abolitionism in the antebellum South and those who continued to work in that section for black rights during Reconstruction. The former theme suggests that northern abolitionists, through their focus on the South, had a direct role in causing the Civil War. The latter supports a notion that northern efforts to transform the South following the Civil War had their deepest roots in abolitionist missionary activities stretching back to the 1830s.

These themes contrast with most current interpretations of the role of abolitionism in the sectional struggle. From James Ford Rhodes and other nationalist historians of the late nineteenth century, who portrayed the abolitionists as successfully arousing the North against the South, to Avery Craven and other Revisionists of the 1930s, who judged the abolitionists to be irresponsible fanatics needlessly fomenting sectional animosities, to the neoabolitionist historians of the 1960s, who equated abolitionism with the Civil Rights movement, there was a shared belief that—for good or ill—the abolitionists had played a major role in causing the Civil War and shaping the issues of Reconstruction. But as Lawrence J. Friedman, James Brewer Stewart, and James L. Huston have from varying perspectives pointed out, historians have for quite some time disengaged the abolitionists from the defining political events of mid-nineteenth century America.[2]

Since the late 1960s, students of the antebellum decades have increasingly emphasized that the abolitionists were not radicals—that they were predominantly conservative, white, middle-class evangelicals, whose opposition to slavery had more to do with their personal religious, class, racial, and sexual anxieties than with the sectional struggle. When in 1982 Friedman defined abolitionism as an inward search for personal piety in which southern slavery had mainly symbolic meaning, he reflected the best scholarship of the previous decade.[3]

What, besides increasingly sophisticated scholarship, caused this turnabout? In 1983 Stewart whimsically surmised that the tendency to regard abolitionists as not especially radical or influential was a product of aging historians mired in the conservative, egocentric culture of the late 1970s and early 1980s. Stewart suggested that as neoabolitionist historians aged and more sophisticated investigations of abolitionist motivation clouded their once clear moral vision—as the 1960s promise of a more egalitarian society disintegrated—they began to find in the abolitionists the same ambivalence and ineffectiveness they discovered in themselves.[4] But there was more to it than that.

In an extremely perceptive 1990 article, Huston argued that the turning point in historical perceptions of the abolitionists came much earlier. Although he was directly concerned with current understandings of the movement's origins, Huston's ideas have relevance for its relationship to the Civil War as well. He maintained that Ulrich B. Phillips's portrayal of slavery as a benign institution, which in itself could not have engendered strong opposition, led Gilbert H. Barnes and others in the 1930s to seek out exclusively *northern* causes for the rise of immediatism. Thus, Huston contended, began a process in which historians progressively disengaged the abolitionists from slavery, the South, and the sectional conflict.[5] Abolitionism became a phenomenon to be understood exclusively as an artifact of northern culture without meaning or influence outside of it.

Even earlier than Barnes, Albert Bushnell Hart contended that, after the failure of the great postal campaign of 1835, abolitionists deliberately concentrated exclusively on converting the North to immediatism, effectively ending their direct confrontation with slavery in the South. Strengthened by Bertram Wyatt-Brown in 1965, this interpretation has become a pervasive assumption among historians of the sectional conflict, although as much evidence for continued immediatist efforts in the South after 1835 can be found as for their desire to concentrate on the North. Even the neoabolitionist historians of the 1960s, by using psychological approaches to deny that abolitionists were unbalanced fanatics driven by feelings of personal guilt, began a process which, by emphasizing the abolitionists' conformity to the values of the northern middle class, culminated in studies which undermined their credibility as a radical force promoting sectional conflict.[6]

Finally, an increasingly precise terminology has limited perceptions of abolitionist influence. Historians since the 1960s have made a sharp distinction between members of immediate abolitionist organizations and politicians associated with the Republican, Free Soil, and even Liberty parties. Few historians still refer to William H. Seward or Charles Sumner as abolitionists, although to do so was once common practice. Even such antislavery politicians as Joshua R. Giddings and Salmon P. Chase, who belonged to immediatist societies at points in their careers, are denied the name. Consequently, the appearance of abolitionist influence on northern politics has been diminished by definition, and the most compelling recent accounts of the rise of the powerful and sectional Republican party dismiss an abolitionist or even a basic antislavery role in its formation.[7] Overall, from the vantage point of the 1980s, the abolitionists appeared to have had very little significance among the broad political, economic, and cultural forces that divided the Union in 1860 and 1861.

In the late 1970s and early 1980s both Friedman and Stewart called for new approaches in abolitionist studies that would save the field

from sterility as the abolitionists appeared to be less and less conse-
quential. Huston's essay, John R. McKivigan's investigation of the
relationship between abolitionism and the northern churches, and
recent books by Herbert Aptheker and Merton L. Dillon may be interpreted as responses. In 1989 Aptheker boldly restated the traditional interpretation of abolitionism as the major force leading the
North to war against slavery in 1861. In his *Slavery Attacked* of 1990,
Dillon emphasized the relationship between northern abolitionists
and growing slave resistance to their masters.[8]

Especially relevant to this study is Dillon's portrayal of a perennial southern white fear that external enemies would ally with the
slaves in the destruction of southern society. Recognition of that fear
and southern responses to it is compatible with an old theory of a
limited abolitionist role in Civil War causation. It holds that, while
abolitionists failed in a primary effort to unite public opinion in the
North against slavery in the South, southern leaders erroneously
assumed that the abolitionists wielded considerable power in the
North. As a result, southern leaders misinterpreted northern intentions toward slavery, overreacted to perceived threats, and insisted
on obnoxious policies to protect slavery. These policies, including
nullification, the gag rule, the Fugitive Slave Act of 1850, and, ultimately, secession, created in the North an image of southern aggression that, according to the theory, alienated increasing numbers of
nonabolitionist northerners and led to the Civil War.

George M. Fredrickson in 1968 used the theory to explain the
historical significance of William Lloyd Garrison, and as early as the
1930s Ulrich B. Phillips argued that the abolitionists, though weak in
the North, continued "to berate slaveholders and prod them into
counter-attacks." Even in 1853 Wendell Phillips observed that the
abolitionists had "made the trembling South demand the Fugitive
Slave Law," which, he said, in turn inspired Harriet Beecher Stowe to
write a novel that aroused the North against slavery. Friedman, however, is the most conscious articulator of the theory. He calls it the
"abolitionist push–southern shove interpretation" of Civil War causation. Noting recent research indicating an extremely limited abolitionist influence in the North, Friedman contends that this may be all
that can be claimed for the abolitionists in regard to Civil War causation. As Friedman notes, this "push-shove" thesis is compatible with

recent accounts of secession in the deep South that stress an irrational southern white fear of abolitionist encouragement of slave revolt.[9]

There is at least some resemblance between the "push-shove"
theory and Stephen A. Douglas's 1848 contention that sectional animosity was a product of irrational extremists in the North and South.[10]
Therefore, if the broad forces working toward sectional confrontation are isolated from the theory's model, the theory suggests a
neorevisionist image of unrestrained emotionalism producing a needless war. It rests on the assumption that southern leaders reacted
irrationally to the faraway rhetoric of ineffective dilettantes.

But was the threat so far away? Was the reaction so irrational?
The answer depends on the validity of the long-standing presump-
tion that after 1835 the abolitionists gave up direct efforts to influence the South, while unsuccessfully attempting to influence the
North. As the preceding chapters of this book indicate, the abolitionists actually intensified their efforts in the South after 1835 and persistently assumed that slaves would arise to take their freedom. In
other words, the abolitionist push against the South was neither distant, inadvertent, nor insubstantial. There was a real abolitionist presence in the border slave states, threatening the security of slave
property in that region, that led proslavery leaders of the deep South
to exaggerated but not unfounded fears of abolitionist agents. It also
led them to a quite rational realization that they needed drastic action
to stop the destabilization of slavery on its northern border.[11]

Although the thrust of this book has been to show that northern
abolitionist reform culture continued to value antislavery progress in
the South throughout the 1840s and 1850s, it has also noted the strong
local and sectional southern reactions to abolitionist initiatives below
the Mason-Dixon line. Well before John Brown's raid in 1859, such
reactions reverberated into a pervasive southern white fear of abolitionist attacks on slavery's periphery and threats to its heartland.
Abolitionist efforts in the border region provided a core of truth to
proslavery assertions that the South was in danger of subversion from
within, which advocates of secession used from the late 1840s through
the crisis of 1860-61 to promote their cause.[12] Just as the election of
Abraham Lincoln in 1860 was not in itself sufficient to explain the
successful secession movement of 1860-61, John Brown's raid was
not in itself a sufficient cause for a widespread southern white per-

ception of abolitionist aggression. Instead, fear of antislavery action in the South had roots decades deep.

Historians have traditionally stressed the struggle over the status of slavery in western territories as the issue that galvanized sectional differences and prepared the way for secession. But, since the late nineteenth century, they have recognized that southern perceptions of slavery's vulnerability in the border region also had an important role, and since the late 1960s they have focused increasingly on the decline of slavery on the South's northern flank. In 1970, William W. Freehling established that fear of losing the border region, which would have dire implications for slavery farther south, dominated secession literature in the deep South in the decades prior to the Civil War. Freehling, Barbara Jeanne Fields, and others have also given substantial support to traditional assumptions that fundamental economic change associated with the southward advance of a market economy and free labor was responsible for the weakening of slavery in the border slave states.[13] The point here is that northern abolitionists and their southern allies not only recognized what was going on but acted in the border region to hasten the disintegration of slavery by frightening local slaveholders. This in turn provoked a reaction in the South.

By the mid-1840s, the actions of Fairbank, Charles T. Torrey, and the other slave rescuers had empirically validated proslavery perceptions that abolitionist agents from the North were responsible for a steady northward exodus of slaves. *"Slave property in Maryland is becoming utterly worthless. The abolitionists are doing their work effectively, and in a few years more, Maryland will be numbered among the free states,"* lamented the *Baltimore Ray* in July 1845. Because the imprisonment and death of Torrey did not dissuade abolitionist "emissaries" from continuing "their stealthy efforts," the *Ray* feared nothing could stop the process. In late 1847 the *New Era* of St. Louis complained that black and white "emissaries of Abolition" in Missouri and Kentucky, by encouraging slaves to escape, had created "a strong and growing feeling of insecurity as regards slave property," and the newspaper suggested that "separation of the free and slave states might be the only cure."[14]

More than any other single event, it was the *Pearl* escape attempt of April 1848 that pressed concern for slavery's security in the border region on the more powerful of the deep South's proslavery leaders and made that concern a major factor in the secession movement. Massive, dramatic, and clearly carried out by "emissaries of the abolitionists," the *Pearl* episode occurred just as debate in Congress over the issue of slavery in the territories gained from Mexico grew heated. The escape attempt deeply disturbed John C. Calhoun, Jefferson Davis, and other influential southern congressmen, intensified their fear of abolitionist aggression, and directly injected concern for slavery in the border region into the developing sectional crisis of 1849-50. Davis warned in the Senate that the need of the South to protect itself against northern intruders, "acting, in fact and in morals, as incendiaries," was not a debatable issue but one upon which the people of the Union "may shed blood." Calhoun warned that the South could not permit itself to "sink to inferiority" by not acting to prevent such attacks on slavery. Disunion would result, he predicted, if such interference continued. In his famous "Southern Address" of January 1849, Calhoun actually gave priority to abolitionist efforts to undermine slavery in the South over the issue of slavery in the territories as proof of northern aggression.[15]

As the crisis of 1849-50 deepened, other southern leaders made similar analyses of the impact of slave rescuers on the stability of slavery in the upper South and on the perpetuity of the Union. Virginia's governor, John B. Floyd, declared in December 1849 that abolitionist activities belied northern claims that the exclusion of slavery from the territories was an end in itself. "They have," Floyd contended, "either resolved to dissolve the Union, or, believing that the South has not the spirit to resist, have determined to invade the sanctuaries of our homes and liberate our slaves." The *Richmond Enquirer*, referring indirectly to Torrey's activities in Maryland and Virginia, warned that, unless something were done, "the border states of Maryland and Delaware will, in ten years be denuded of their slaves, Virginia, now a serious sufferer, will find her slave property hardly worth the vexation and expense of preserving. It will seek the remote South with her best [slave] population, or [that population will] be lost to her by the silent and insiduous [*sic*] operations of the enemies of her peace."[16]

Dramatic apprehensions of northern abolitionists in the act of helping slaves escape from the South declined markedly in the early

1850s. But such actions continued, and the belief that abolitionists directly or indirectly inspired slaves to escape to the North had become deeply rooted in the southern consciousness. In September 1851 a farmer near Fincastle, Virginia, unsuspectingly told abolitionist missionary Jesse McBride, "abolitionists are so thick through here, that we cannot keep our servants; a number of mine ran off, so that I was compelled to sell or lose them all." In 1855 John G. Fee reported a rumor that a mere speech by Cassius M. Clay in Jessamine County, Kentucky, was enough to inspire twelve slaves to escape. By late 1856 such reports of abolitionist contacts with and influences on slaves had spread to the deep South, and—as several historians have noted— rumors of abolitionist-slave conspiracies became a principal factor in the successful secession movements in the states of that region in 1860-61.

Historians such as David Brion Davis and Steven A. Channing have argued that such southern perceptions of abolitionist agents in their midst were irrational or that, as in the case of other political witch hunts, southern elites used phantoms to enforce "ideological discipline" during crises caused by real threats from more distant places.[17] But, however exaggerated were accounts of abolitionist-slave conspiracies in the deep South on the eve of secession, they rested on a reality that had existed in the border region since the 1840s, that had been vividly reinforced by John Brown's raid in 1859, and which was ultimately founded on the real deterioration of slavery on its periphery.

Abolitionist efforts to help slaves escape provided the most tangible evidence to southern leaders that northern intruders were assaulting the institution of slavery on its home ground. But so did abolitionist missionary enterprises in the upper South. In conjunction with the southward expansion of antislavery politics and the promotion of northern colonies, these abolitionist initiatives contributed to a southern siege mentality that helped produce a successful secession movement in 1860-61.

Missionary abolitionism certainly helped convince staunch advocates of slavery that they must adopt the most resolute defense of that institution. In the 1830s, the great abolitionist postal campaign, Amos Dresser's mission to Tennessee, and David Nelson's introduction of northern abolitionists into Missouri helped provoke the bitter, although not entirely successful, proslavery reaction of that decade. By the late 1840s the AFASS and AMA had launched more determined campaigns to reach white and black audiences in the South, which convinced southern leaders that abolitionists had by no means abandoned direct action against slavery.

From the late 1840s to 1860, John G. Fee and other AMA agents in Kentucky openly sought white converts to abolitionist churches, circulated antislavery literature, contacted slaves, and made attempts to extend their activities into Virginia.[18] According to their own accounts as well as those of their proslavery opponents, Fee and his associates inspired some slaves to escape and actively helped others. So did AMA agents in Washington, D.C. The AMA-assisted Wesleyan missionaries in North Carolina and Virginia and the AMA missionaries in Missouri left little evidence to contradict their public denials of proslavery charges that they aided slaves to escape. But the Wesleyans openly met with slaves and distributed antislavery literature.

In all states where they were active, the missionaries evoked strong proslavery reactions. Many of their white southern neighbors regarded them to be as dangerous as Fairbank, Torrey, or even Nat Turner and John Brown. That the missionaries were involved in southern Free-Soil politics only made them appear to be more threatening. As a correspondent of a North Carolina newspaper put it in 1851, "The South may complain that the Fugitive slave law is not executed by the North, but while she cherishes free soilers in her bosom to poison the mind of the slave against his master and teach him to fly to a Free State, what can she expect but that he will be received and protected from his owner when he arrives there."[19]

When newspapers in the deep South copied accounts published in Kentucky, Virginia, and North Carolina of abolitionist missionary activities, the obvious message was that the threat to slavery lay not alone in distant regions of the North and West but in the South itself. It was also clear at the highest levels of southern leadership that abolitionists never gave up their intention to propagandize the South. In 1849, Sydney Howard Gay boasted of his ability to find exchanges for the *National Anti-Slavery Standard* in that section. More important, so influential an opinion-shaper as Jefferson Davis publicized the vigorous efforts of the AFASS to spread antislavery documents to a southern audience in the late 1840s and early 1850s. In 1849 Davis noted that the society's annual report endorsed helping slaves to escape, called for the employment of agents in the South, and contemplated the establishment of more southern antislavery newspapers in addition to the *National Era*. Consequently, Davis warned against southern concessions concerning western territories because an increasingly antislavery North was already strong enough to pose a direct threat to slavery in the South itself. A year later when New Hampshire's Free-Soil United States Senator John P. Hale claimed he knew "of no associations for the purpose of printing incendiary publications to be circulated in the South," Davis exclaimed, "Why, sir, the New York Anti-Slavery Society [AFASS] sends out more publications, I believe, than the Senate of the United States."[20]

The Fugitive Slave Act of 1850 and the later struggle in Kansas Territory between free and slave state forces temporarily shifted abolitionist emphasis away from the South. In contrast to the sectional crisis of the late 1840s, during the national election campaign of 1856 southern advocates of secession focused mainly on the Republican party's threat to slavery in Kansas. But fears that abolitionist activity threatened slavery on the South's northern periphery continued.[21] Such fears were confirmed a year later with the establishment of a northern free-labor colony in Virginia.

The initiation of Eli Thayer and John C. Underwood's settlement at Ceredo aroused an intensely bitter response from slavery's defenders. Thayer and Underwood's ambitious plans for other northern enclaves in eastern Virginia, where slaves were more plentiful than in Ceredo's environs, compounded the impact. The national publicity provided for these efforts by the *New York Herald* guaranteed that they would attract more attention in the South than Fee's much smaller—though more forthrightly abolitionist—colony at Berea, Kentucky. So did Thayer's notoriety throughout the South as the founder of the "Northern Kansas Emigrant Aid movement." Reflecting the border region's experience with slave rescue attempts, several Virginia journalists charged that Thayer and Underwood's talk of demonstrating the superiority of free labor was a ruse. The real aim, the journalists suggested, was to create refuges for runaway slaves, and, as the *Richmond Enquirer* contended, introduce "a horde of underground railroad agents and abolition incendiaries" into Virginia.[22]

Other southern journalists, however, took Thayer and Underwood's threat of peaceful competition between free and slave labor in the border region very seriously. Especially among slavery's more dedicated advocates in the deep South, proposals for free-labor colonies appeared to reflect fundamental climatic, demographic, economic, and political forces that threatened to tear away the northern rank of slave states. In spite of the outraged response to the northern colonization scheme by Virginia's leading newspapers, the *New Orleans Delta* declared "that Virginia is not fully awake as she should be to the great question of Southern interests. . . . The enemy is looking over the Border . . . and organizing their forces for an early invasion."[23]

Robert Barnwell Rhett's *Charleston Mercury* differed in some respects from the *Delta* in its response to northern colonization efforts in Virginia. The *Mercury* expressed more confidence than the *Delta* that Virginia would "crush the philanthropic experimenters." The newspapers also differed concerning the appropriate southern response to the colonies. The *Delta* called for stronger bonds among all slave states, while the *Mercury* advocated united action only among the states of the deep South. But, like the *Delta*, Rhett's paper feared that the free-labor colonization scheme was a concrete manifestation of "inevitable causes . . . which, ere long may convert the frontier [slave] States from warm and able co-operators into neutrals or worse."[24] The point is that it was abolitionist-inspired northern action on southern soil that evoked calls for a resolute stand by the South to defend slavery on it northern perimeter.

Because Underwood was closely associated with Virginia's fledgling Republican party, his slaveholding opponents had good reason to assume his free-labor colonization scheme had political implications. They charged that he and Thayer intended to build up an antislavery party in the state by importing northern voters, and northern immigrants did indeed contribute to the growth of the Republican party in Virginia. The efforts of Underwood and others to organize such parties on the northern fringe of the South were, of course, continuations of a southern political strategy originated by Liberty abolitionists in the early 1840s. By the late 1850s, Republican organizations existed in Delaware, Maryland, Virginia, and Kentucky, in addition to Francis P. Blair Jr.'s quite similar Free Democratic party in Missouri.[25]

These organizations were tiny and, with the exception of Blair's party, ineffective in electing candidates. They were also—by northern standards—extremely conservative on racial issues. Leaders such as Underwood, Cassius M. Clay, and Gamaliel Bailey, who shared an abolitionist background, were rare among Republicans of the border region. The emphasis was on protecting the interests of nonslaveholding whites and expelling free blacks. The Republican party itself, nationally and in the northern states, was primarily committed to banning slavery from the western territories, not immediately abolishing it in the South. Even before John Brown's raid, leading Republicans had denounced abolitionist initiatives in the South. Meanwhile Bailey's *National Era* was the chief advocate of Republican organization in the South. As Bailey's health and, consequently, his influence declined in the late 1850s, the party's national leadership grew less interested in contesting for the border slave states in the elections of 1860—in part because to have any chance of success in those states, the party would have to dilute further its antislavery platform.[26]

Yet the existence of Republican parties in the border slave states and southern perceptions of Republican intentions regarding slavery in the South played a role in the secession of the deep South states in 1860-61. Advocates of secession in late 1860 built on earlier southern arguments dating back to 1849 and 1856 that the establishment of Free Soil and Republican parties in the upper South justified disunion.[27] The question is, were such fears a corollary of the push-shove theory with southern spokespersons overestimating the power of abolitionism in these parties? Or were secessionists reacting rationally to a real political abolitionist threat within the upper South?

It is true that advocates of secession such as Jefferson Davis deliberately confused Republicans with abolitionists for dramatic effect. Three considerations, nevertheless, indicate that Davis, Rhett, and others were engaged in more than irresponsible rhetoric. In the first place, even the more conservative southern Republicans endorsed gradual emancipation, and Republican parties in the southern states faced no constitutional obstacles in passing abolitionist legislation.[28]

Second, southern secessionists and numerous Republican leaders agreed that a Republican president would appoint emancipationists as postmasters, United States marshals, district attorneys, customs collectors, and other federal officials in the South in order to create effective Republican parties in all the southern states. The *Richmond Enquirer* spoke for many throughout the South when in July 1860 it charged, "Upon the election of Lincoln to power, we would apprehend no direct act of violence against negro property, but by the use of federal office, contracts, power and patronage, the building up in every Southern State of a Black Republican party . . . to become in a few short years the open advocates of abolition . . . and eventually the ruin of every Southern State by the destruction of negro labor."[29]

Third, slavery's militant defenders on occasion did clearly distinguish between Republicans and abolitionists, while arguing that the election of a Republican president in 1860 would encourage further abolitionist ventures in the South. They assumed that a Republican victory would validate a climate of opinion in the North that was becoming more tolerant of such ventures, even as Republican leaders disavowed them. Abolitionists, they predicted, could expect leniency from Republican officials when charged with crimes against slavery. "The *under*-ground railroad, will become an *over*-ground railroad," contended the *Charleston Mercury*. "The tenure of slave property will be felt to be weakened; and the slaves will be sent down to the Cotton States for sale, and the Frontier [slave] States *enter on the policy of making themselves Free States*." The *Mercury* went on to predict that "unless some great movement . . . is made, so will the supporters of slavery be forced further and further south until they make their last and Thermopylaen stand on the shores of the Gulf."[30] John Brown's raid alone had not caused these fears and this resolve. Rather it was a pattern of abolitionist initiative in the upper South since the 1830s that accounts for the southern commitment to drastic action. While an abolitionist presence in the upper South was a product of more fundamental forces driving the North and South apart, that presence— in conjunction with the rise of the Republican party to national power— was beyond question a precipitative cause of secession and the Civil War.

As for the second theme of this chapter, there is clear continuity between antebellum southern antislavery action and the northern effort to transform the South during the Civil War and Reconstruction. The parallels between the eras, however, are not perfect, because the war dramatically changed the cultural environment within which efforts to reform the South took place. The destruction of slavery by northern armed might, for example, nullified the assumptions of religious, economic, and political antislavery advocates that they could peacefully transform the South. There was also a major change in personnel, as many northern reformers, politicians, and educators, who would not have ventured into the South before northern armies prepared the way, took up the work an older generation had begun. Yet a significant number of individuals, who had represented the aims of northern abolitionism in the South before the war, labored on. They firmly bound the two eras, as—for the most part—they used their knowledge of southern culture and their empathy for the newly freed southern black people to become influential advocates of racial justice.

In its broadest sense the war quickly became an endorsement of the more aggressive abolitionist tactics in the South. By the summer of 1861 the Union military campaign in Virginia and Missouri included a massive effort to help slaves escape as large numbers of "contrabands" crossed northern lines and were not returned to their masters. Although this logically required no antebellum precedent, the spirit of John Brown and to a lesser degree that of Charles T. Torrey lived on in the minds of the soldiers who marched to "John Brown's Body." Politicians representing the loyal border states of Maryland, Delaware, and Kentucky denounced the Union officers who executed the policy. President Abraham Lincoln, still hoping to conciliate the slaveholders of the upper South, forced General John C. Frémont to withdraw his proclamation encouraging Missouri slaves to desert their masters. But black and white abolitionists welcomed the mounting numbers of "contrabands" as the knell of slavery.[31]

By September 1862, Lincoln had formally joined with abolitionists and the Radicals in his own party, who from the war's beginning had insisted that it must be fought to abolish slavery as well as to preserve the Union. This change of policy—forced on Lincoln by the necessities of war, changes in northern public opinion, and the logic of events within the Union armies—led directly to the enlistment of black men as northern combat troops. As these African-American soldiers began to demonstrate their ability and bravery, the image of black liberators, fighting for the Union as well as the freedom of their people, briefly transcended the abolitionist movement and became part of northern popular culture. However, the army's reliance on white officers to lead black troops deeply flawed perceptions of black fighting men as representatives of black initiative. Although slaves throughout the South took the opportunity the war afforded to assert their rights, the antebellum abolitionist contention, exemplified by John Brown, that white men must direct black men in a violent conflict with slavery had prevailed over the other abolitionist view that southern black leaders would arise to violently seize freedom.[32]

The Civil War also settled several other disagreements among abolitionists concerning southern antislavery action. It vindicated the radical political abolitionists who, since the late 1830s, had contended that the federal government must act to abolish slavery in the southern states. It confirmed Garrisonian contentions that the destruction of slavery had to precede political and economic change in the South and contradicted those who had argued that the establishment of northern colonies or emancipationist parties could promote the peaceful abolition of the institution.[33] The election of a powerful Republican president in 1860 did lead to the formation of Republican organizations in the southern states as advocates of southern antislavery political action and secessionists predicted. But those organizations formed in the wake of Union armies. Even the Garrisonians were overly optimistic concerning the economic impact of abolition on the South. Emancipation left the great mass of southern blacks and many whites as subservient agricultural contractors rather than independent operators in a market economy.

Yet an emphasis on northern involvement in the South to effect fundamental change bridged antebellum abolitionism and northern policy during and after the war. This is especially clear regarding abolitionist missions in the South. Despite violent setbacks in Kentucky, North Carolina, and Missouri between 1859 and 1861, the AMA used the Civil War and Reconstruction to greatly expand tactics its agents had pioneered in the 1840s and 1850s. In the process, the AMA's northern abolitionist leadership shifted more of the association's limited resources to southern missions. During the war, it continued to employ missionaries to preach an antislavery gospel and distribute abolitionist literature to southern whites. It also continued to establish integrated churches and schools in the South, although during the later nineteenth century the congregations, schools, and colleges it supported increasingly served an exclusively black clientele. As the number of "contrabands" and black Union soldiers grew, it was the AMA that took the lead in providing them with religious, educational, and vocational instruction. The antebellum Bibles for slaves campaign became during the war an effort to provide Bibles and New Testaments to the freedpeople.

Although the AMA never escaped the paternalistic attitudes typical of white abolitionists, it served well into the twentieth century as an effective advocate of the human, civil, and economic rights of southern blacks. Young men and women, both black and white, during the Civil War and Reconstruction went south to serve as teachers and chaplains very much in the tradition of antebellum abolitionist missionaries who went before them.[34]

These younger missionaries represented a significant change in personnel in some of the southern states in which AMA missionaries had been active before the war. In Maryland, David Gamble, who had served as an AMA agent since the late 1840s, ended his ties to the association after December 1862. In North Carolina, new agents supported by the Union army completely replaced those associated with Daniel Worth and Daniel Wilson. But in Missouri and Kentucky, there was individual as well as institutional continuity. In Missouri Stephen Blanchard, who had been forced to leave the state under threat of indictment in January 1861, returned in April 1862 to help promote the campaign for statewide emancipation, which succeeded in January 1865.[35]

In Kentucky there was actually no break in the AMA missionary effort, despite the expulsion of the missionaries in late 1859 and early 1860. Throughout the early war years, John G. Fee, John A.R. Rogers, George Candee, and others periodically returned to the state to advocate immediate abolition and to minister to the needs of the freedpeople. Fee battled his own emotional depression and mobs during these years and returned permanently to Berea in the spring of 1864. During Reconstruction he and his colleagues continued to establish racially integrated schools, hospitals, and churches. They steadfastly confronted the Ku Klux Klan in the early 1870s, and they maintained Berea College as an integrated institution of higher learning until Kentucky forbade the practice in 1904—three years after Fee died.[36]

Fee also maintained his political radicalism into the war years and beyond. He forthrightly opposed President Abraham Lincoln's refusal to embrace equal rights for "the colored man" and the president's "abortive policies of expatriation." Fee believed that Lincoln's failure to press for immediate emancipation in the border slave states and his mild reconstruction policy would perpetuate oppression, aristocracy, immorality, and economic stagnation in Kentucky. Consequently, Fee joined Wendell Phillips and a minority of northern abolitionists in opposing Lincoln's renomination by the Republican party in 1864. Into his extreme old age Fee maintained his political commitment to reform. "We are all 'Radicals'—Prohibition— 'Suffragists'—government issue of currency—overthrow of tariffs & oppressive monopolies—Praise God for life," he told George W. Julian in 1897.[37]

Although Fee was not exceptional among southern abolitionists in his longevity, others who represented the aims of northern abolitionism in the South died before the Civil War or before Reconstruction. Early abolitionist missionary David Nelson died peacefully in 1844, and slave rescuer Charles T. Torrey, of course, died in a Maryland penitentiary in 1846. Jesse McBride and Jarvis C. Bacon succumbed as young men in the 1850s to diseases their friends claimed had resulted from their sufferings as missionaries in North Carolina and Virginia. Daniel Drayton of the *Pearl* killed himself in 1857. Southern emancipator James G. Birney passed away in New Jersey that same year after many years of poor health, Gamaliel Bailey died in 1859, and Daniel Worth in 1862 while serving as president of the Indiana Conference of the Wesleyan Methodist Church.

Each of these last three left personal legacies in the work of transforming the South. Birney's son William became a commander of United States Colored Troops fighting in Virginia, Bailey's son Marcellus served as one of the younger Birney's officers, and Bailey's wife, Margaret Shands Bailey, became an AMA teacher of black soldiers at "Camp Birney" near Baltimore. In a relationship more of the spirit than of blood ties, Worth's sufferings in North Carolina in 1859 directly inspired Radical Republican Albion W. Tourgée of New York to take up the struggle for the rights of blacks and poor whites in the same Guilford County where Worth, McBride, and Jacob Crooks had labored before him.[38]

Others who engaged in southern antislavery action in the 1840s and 1850s withdrew from active abolitionism into varying degrees of obscurity. Among the slave rescuers, James E. Burr and Alanson Work played only minor roles in the antislavery movement following their release from the Missouri penitentiary in the 1840s, although Work maintained a formal relationship with the AMA until 1878. After she gave up her effort to establish a free-labor farm in Kentucky in 1858, Delia Webster lived uneventfully in Madison, Indiana. Because he had been a major figure in abolitionism prior to his arrest for helping slaves escape from Washington, D.C., in 1850, William L. Chaplin's abrupt withdrawal from the cause was more dramatic. From the early 1850s onward Chaplin joined his friend James C. Jackson at Jackson's Glen Haven, New York, water cure institute and lectured in behalf of temperance. Nevertheless, at the time of Chaplin's death in 1871, Frederick Douglass among others continued to honor his active contribution to the struggle against slavery. Such was not the case for Eli Thayer. Defeated by his own Republican party for reelection to Congress in 1860 and financially ruined by the partial destruction of Ceredo during the Civil War, Thayer became increasingly bitter towards the abolitionists with whom he had cooperated in the 1850s.[39]

For the most part, however, those who had engaged in antebellum southern antislavery action and survived beyond 1861 remained, like Fee, committed to the cause of abolition and black rights. With the exceptions of former slave rescuer George Thompson, who during the Civil War confined himself to speaking engagements in the North, and southern emancipator John C. Vaughan, who by 1859 had become a member of James H. Lane's radical free-state party in Kansas, they also maintained a personal commitment to action in the South.[40] This was certainly true for former slave rescuers Jonathan Walker and Calvin Fairbank. Walker, who had settled in Wisconsin in the early 1850s, was in his mid-sixties and in poor health when in April 1864 he traveled to eastern Virginia to devote himself for several months "to the aid of the newly emancipated slaves of that part of the country in their industrial pursuits." Fairbank, who was released from the Kentucky penitentiary that same April, immediately began lecturing to black and white audiences across the North, as well as to an integrated group assembled at Wilmington, Delaware, by Thomas Garrett. Fairbank also renewed his association with Lewis Hayden and other prominent black leaders, including

Frederick Douglass and Henry Highland Garnet, before becoming an advocate for the freedpeople in Virginia in late 1868.[41]

There was similar continuity during the Civil War and Reconstruction among southern abolitionists who had emphasized political and economic action against slavery prior to the war. Joseph Evans Snodgrass, who spent the war years in New York City, had by 1865 coalesced with the AASS. In 1869 he promoted the formation of a company to purchase land in Virginia for sale "in small quantities to the freedmen, so that they may become landholders and thus, truly independent men." By 1871 he had returned permanently to the Baltimore-Washington area. Meanwhile, between 1864 and 1866 William S. Bailey—as ever an expert at raising northern financial support—had enlisted the aid of John A. Andrew, Samuel E. Sewell, George L. Stearns, Gerrit Smith, and others in a successful effort to revive his newspaper in Covington, Kentucky.[42]

It was, nevertheless, John C. Underwood who most forcefully illustrated the continuity of reform in the South in the 1860s with abolitionist-inspired antebellum political and economic action in that section. During the divisive presidential campaign of 1860, Underwood joined Lydia Maria Child of the AASS in a last futile effort to use moral suasion to convince Virginia slaveholders to peacefully free their slaves. Like Child and other formerly pacifistic abolitionists to his north, Underwood—an active Republican—enthusiastically supported Lincoln's war policy, and in May 1863 he accepted an appointment as the federal judge for the eastern district of Virginia. The appointment made him one of the more powerful figures in the state until his death in 1873.

Underwood used his judicial authority to protect blacks and loyal whites from excessive punishments for minor offenses. He became notorious in the South for gaining a treason indictment against former Confederate president Jefferson Davis in May 1866 and for his open denunciation of slaveholders for their sexual exploitation of black women. From December 1867 to April 1868 Underwood served as president of the Radical Republican-dominated Virginia constitutional convention, which produced the "Underwood Constitution," notable for its establishment of a system of public education, tax equalization, and protection for black rights, as well as for its drastic disfranchisement of white men.[43]

A common thread among these individuals—and Fee as well—

was their continuing commitment to black rights and to government enforcement of those rights. When Thompson, who had settled in Michigan following his return to the United States from missionary work in Sierra Leone, undertook an extensive speaking tour in the North in late 1865 he told Gerrit Smith, "Whenever I can do so, I take for my subject the great question of the Rights of the black man, and endeavor to show the folly, injustice & danger of neglecting his claims to full citizenship." Historians have often explained remarks like Thompson's in the mid-1860s as products of a hard-headed political calculation that black voters were needed to maintain Republican political power.[44] But Thompson was no politician. His remarks reflect a continuing abolitionist commitment to equal rights, which Underwood and the others carried into the upper South.

Underwood consciously drew on his New York Liberty party background as he assumed his duties as a federal judge. He determined to interpret the power of the national government as broadly as he could to defend the rights of the freedpeople. "I would be greatly obliged to you for some of your views so often given of the Anti Slavery character of the Constitution," he told Gerrit Smith. "I desire to interpret it in the light of its preamble, the Declaration of Independence, the Presidents proclamation of freedom & Popes Universal Prayer." Snodgrass expressed a similar outlook in May 1865 at the annual meeting of the AASS, where he joined Wendell Phillips in advocating what would become the Fourteenth Amendment. Snodgrass declared, "I hope to live to see the righteous and indispensable curtailment of what is popularly accepted as 'States Rights.' . . . Without it, I fear, the anti-slavery clause [Thirteenth Amendment] will have been confirmed in vain, so far as equality before the law is concerned in even certain 'free States,' to say nothing of 'slave States.'" Two months later Fairbank warned an abolitionist convention in Massachusetts that if Congress sustained Lincoln's plan of reconstruction, which left issues of black suffrage and black rights to the southern states, "the amount of suffering awaiting the recently freed people is incalculable."[45]

Their long-standing empathy with the oppressed and their first-hand observation of conditions in the postwar South, enabled those who operated within a tradition of southern antislavery activism to see that the federal government and northern friends of the freedpeople would have to be active for a long period if black rights were to be maintained. Underwood, Walker, and Fairbank, for example, were far more cognizant of this than such leading northern advocates of black rights as Wendell Phillips and Frederick Douglass. Arguing that the former slaveholders of Virginia were crueler than the biblical pharaoh, Underwood told Gerrit Smith in October 1868, "The grand scheme of these people is, how to get the most sweat & labor out of their late slaves with the least possible compensation . . . .I have several times heard the sentiment earnestly expressed that by proper legislation (meaning the most cruel legislation) they could get more out of the colored people than under the old system as they would not be required to provide food, clothing, houses, & medical attentions." Two months later Fairbank demonstrated his awareness that conditions in the South required more than the introduction of free labor and lip service to universal manhood suffrage. "The capitalist has the poor white and black in his fist. . . . And mixed blooded negroes throw their influence with their enemies to save their barbershops and popularity," he declared.[46]

Similar observations of conditions in Virginia informed Walker's endorsement in 1864 of pending Congressional legislation creating the Freedmen's Bureau. Before his deteriorating health forced him to give up his mission among the former slaves, he had visited several farms upon which blacks had been placed by the Union army. While he praised the various northern benevolent associations that helped the freedpeople, he found conditions on the farms deplorable. The soil was poor, tools were "badly worn," women, children, and the aged did much of the work, disease was rampant, pay was inadequate or nonexistent, and the northern "overseers" were abusive. In the short run Walker recommended "remunerative employment" and "trusty advisers" to protect the freedmen. But he clearly believed that the full realization of black potential would require decades of active northern intervention in the South, which as it turned out the North was unwilling to provide.[47]

The careers of Cassius M. Clay and Daniel R. Goodloe during Reconstruction do not entirely fit this pattern of continuity among those who represented northern abolitionism in the South before the Civil War. Goodloe prepared the Lincoln administration's plan for compensated emancipation in the District of Columbia during the war, and in 1866 President Andrew Johnson appointed him United States Marshal for North Carolina, where Goodloe soon became embroiled in local politics. Clay, who had actively campaigned for Lincoln in 1860, became United States Minister to Russia from 1861 to 1862 and from 1863 to 1869, when he returned to Kentucky. Shortly after each man took up residence in his native state, he began a qualified retreat from an advanced position on black rights. Both men came to question the wisdom of unrestricted black suffrage, and Goodloe vocally opposed the social and educational integration of blacks and whites as well. He and Clay supported the Liberal Republican effort to end Radical Reconstruction in 1872, and in 1884 an elderly Clay contended, "It was a mistake to invest an ignorant and lately enslaved race at once with the franchise of the ballot. Time proved that they were incompetent to govern themselves or whites."[48]

Clay and Goodloe were motivated by racism, by a sincere belief that black enfranchisement was fomenting an uncontrollably violent white reaction, and by fear that arbitrary Republican rule in the South threatened the racial and sectional harmony they had long argued would be the result of emancipation. Clay, who was certainly the more significant of the two figures and who had much closer ties than Goodloe to northern abolitionist reform culture, was also influenced by his fruitless quest for elective office in his old age. But, as historian Louis S. Gerteis has indicated, Clay and Goodloe were very much in accord with northern antislavery reformers such as Charles Sumner and George W. Julian—if not with major northern abolitionists—in their desire to reestablish national harmony by terminating aggressive federal protection of black rights.[49]

It is also very important to note the *degree* of Clay and Goodloe's retrogression from their prewar views on race. Both of them, after all, endorsed the Fourteenth and Fifteenth Amendments. Both denounced Ku Klux Klan terrorism, and until he returned to Kentucky Clay provided an example comparable to that of Fee, Fairbank, and Underwood of consistent commitment to the goals of abolitionism. In 1861 and 1862, Clay once again won the praise of northern abolitionists for his forthright defense of Frémont's proclamation of freedom in Missouri, for his early advocacy of the enlistment of black soldiers, and for his demand that Lincoln's war to save the Union also become a war to end slavery.[50]

In August 1862 Clay openly criticized the Lincoln administration for its efforts to preserve both the Union and slavery as well as for its commitment to the colonization of former slaves beyond the country's borders. "As for myself," he said in a Washington, D.C., speech, "never, so help me God, will I draw a sword to keep the chains on another fellow-being." He flatly stated, "As regards the negro, I am opposed to colonization, because it will be a means of delaying emancipation." A few months later in a raucous New York City debate with Massachusetts Democrat George Francis Train, who argued that God had designed Africans for slavery, Clay embraced traditional abolitionist precepts of racial equality. "If you want to make an infidel of me," he declared, "convince me that slavery is Divine . . . .When I believe that God can doom millions of his creatures to the unutterable woes of such a terrifying system—contrary to the decalogue and to the whole morality of the Christian faith—I will be ready to praise the Devil. . . . God . . . has fashioned man of every clime and color in his own image."[51]

In February 1867, two years before his return to the United States from St. Petersburg, Clay emphasized that "we have four millions of colored citizens; they are with us, and of us, for good as [or] evil. I think that it is the duty of all good citizens to try and elevate the African race in America . . . and prepare them for the ultimate influence which they must sooner or later have upon the political and economical interests of the United States."[52] This outlook, paternalistic and hopeful, was similar to that of others who had under the influence of northern abolitionism struggled against slavery in the old South. Clay in his old age might publicly repudiate this optimism, the North might fail to maintain an active commitment to this vision, but the legacy of southern antislavery action would endure to influence younger generations of blacks and whites.

NOTES

Note: For complete publication information, see Bibliography, 219-236.

ABBREVIATIONS

AASS	American Anti-Slavery Society
AFASR	*American and Foreign Anti-Slavery Reporter*
AFASS	American and Foreign Anti-Slavery Society
AM	*American Missionary*
AMA	American Missionary Association
AMAA	American Missionary Association Archives
AMM	*American Missionary Magazine*
AP	*Albany Patriot*
ASB	*Anti-Slavery Bugle*
ASR	*Anti-Slavery Reporter*
BCA	Berea College Archives
BPL	Boston Public Library
BSV	*Baltimore Saturday Visiter [sic]*
CG	*Congressional Globe*
CM	*Charleston Mercury*
CWHP	*Cincinnati Weekly Herald and Philanthropist*
DAB	*Dictionary of American Biography*
DNCB	*Dictionary of North Carolina Biography*
FDP	*Frederick Douglass Paper*
GUE	*Genius of Universal Emancipation*
HSPa	Historical Society of Pennsylvania
LC	Library of Congress
LE	*Louisville Examiner*
MASS	Massachusetts Anti-Slavery Society
MHS	Massachusetts Historical Society
NASS	*National Anti-Slavery Standard*
NCHR	*North Carolina Historical Review*
NE	*National Era*
NEASS	New England Anti-Slavery Society
NS	*North Star*
NYH	*New York Herald*
NYHS	New York Historical Society
NYTi	*New York Times*
NYTr	*New York Tribune*

OE	*Oberlin Evangelist*
PF	*Pennsylvania Freeman*
RA	*Radical Abolitionist*
RE	*Richmond Enquirer*
SC	Friends Historical Library, Swarthmore College
SU	Syracuse University
TA	*True American*
TW	*True Wesleyan*
UNC	University of North Carolina
WRHS	Western Reserve Historical Society

INTRODUCTON

1. D.B. Davis, *Problem of Slavery in Western Culture* and *Problem of Slavery in the Age of Revolution*; Zilversmit, *First Emancipation*.

2. Salmon P. Chase to Charles Dexter Cleveland, Oct. 22, 1841, Chase Papers, LC; *OE*, Sept. 14, 1859; McPherson, *Struggle for Equality*, 3; Kraditor, *Means and Ends*, 8; D.B. Davis, "Antislavery or Abolition?" 95-99; Blue, *Free Soilers*, 2; Walters, *Antislavery Appeal*, xiii; Friedman, *Gregarious Saints*, 1. Friedman notes recent dissent from this narrow definition of abolitionism. See also Stewart, *Holy Warriors*, 77-78; Foner, *Politics and Ideology*, 211n.

3. Foner, *Free Soil*; Friedman, *Gregarious Saints*, 225-52; Howard, *Religion and the Radical Republican Movement*.

4. Curry and Goodheart, "'Knives in their Heads,'" 401-14; Stewart, "Young Turks and Old Turkeys," 226-32.

5. W.W. Freehling, *Road to Disunion,* esp. 1:17-19, 31-35, 197-201, 538-41; Fields, *Slavery and Freedom on the Middle Ground,* esp. 4-7, 12-14, 55-56; Berlin, *Slaves without Masters*, 27-35, 231. For examples of abolitionist awareness of slavery's vulnerability in the border South, see AFASS, *Thirteenth Annual Report,* 29; *NE*, Dec. 10, 1857.

6. Walters, *Antislavery Appeal*, esp. 70-87. The definition of the term *reform culture* used in this book derives from the concept of political culture developed by anthropologists and adapted to the study of nineteenth-century American history by Daniel Walker Howe and others. See Howe, *Political Culture of the American Whigs,* esp. 2-3; Alan M. Kraut, "Partisanship and Principle: The Liberty Party in Antebellum Political Culture," in Kraut, *Crusaders and Compromisers*, 71-99.

7. Huston, "Experiential Basis," 609-20; Merton L. Dillon, review of Herbert Aptheker, "Abolitionism: A Revolutionary Movement," in *JAH* 76 (Mar. 1990): 1229-30; Formisano, "Political Character," 704-6; Walters, *Antislavery Appeal*, 70-100; H. Davis, *Leavitt*, 39-40, 99-100; McKivigan, "Antislavery 'Comeouter' Sects," 142-60.

8. On the disengagement of black and white abolitionists, see August Meier and Elliot Rudwick, "Role of Blacks in the Abolitionist Movement," in Bracey, *Blacks in the Abolitionist Movement,* 112-22; Pease and Pease, "Ends, Means and Attitudes," 117-28; Friedman, *Gregarious Saints,* 160-95. My findings are compatible with those presented in Aptheker, *Anti-Racism in U.S. History,* esp. 129-54; and Jacobs, *Courage and Conscience.*

9. Not all southerners who had close ties to northern abolitionism were themselves immediatists. A primary object of this book is to demonstrate that, while such southerners were not immediatists, northern abolitionist influence led them to *approach* immediatism.

10. Not all Liberty abolitionists belonged to immediatist societies, and many who did complicated their status when they joined the essentially nonextensionist Free Soil and Republican parties. I include immersion in abolitionist reform culture, the virtual identity of the New York Liberty party and that state's immediatist antislavery society, and the affiliation of the Cincinnati Liberty leaders with the AFASS in the late 1840s in defining such individuals as immediatists.

1. THE SOUTH IN ANTISLAVERY HISTORY

1. Fields, *Slavery and Freedom on the Middle Ground*; W.W. Freehling, *Road to Disunion,* 1:98-118, 455-74; Dillon, *Slavery Attacked,* esp. 208, and Dillion, "Abolitionists: A Decade of Historiography," 514 (hereafter cited as Dillon, "Abolitionist Historiography").

2. For examples representing major abolitionist factions years after the initial period of optimism for rapid advancement of antislavery sentiment in the South, see *Emancipator,* Apr. 3, 1844; *CWHP,* Apr. 23, 1845; *AP,* May 26, 1847; *NASS,* Apr. 12-May 10, 1849; MASS, Sixteenth Annual Report, 23-24; AFASS, *[8th] Annual Report,* 34-37.

3. For examples from the major abolitionist factions, see MASS, *Eighteenth Annual Report,* 24-26; *NE,* Oct. 2, 1851; Bell, *Minutes and Proceedings,* 13; Gerrit Smith to William Lloyd Garrison, July 18, 1854, Garrison Papers, BPL.

4. Holst, *Constitutional and Political History,* 3:429-30.

5. Hart, *Slavery and Abolition,* 206, 232, 234, 315, 322; Barnes, *Antislavery Impulse*; Walters, *Antislavery Appeal,* 37-145; Friedman, *Gregarious Saints,* esp. 5; Stewart, "Young Turks and Old Turkeys," 226-32; Huston, "Experiential Basis," 609-20.

6. Walters, *Antislavery Appeal,* 131; Stewart, *Holy Warriors,* 70, 209.

7. Goodell, *Slavery and Antislavery,* 385-87 (1st quotation); May, *Recollections,* 10-13; H. Wilson, *Slave Power,* 1:166-69 (2d quotation).

8. W.P. Garrison and F.J. Garrison, *Garrison,* 1:87-94; Willey, *Antislavery Cause,* 28-29 (1st and 2d quotations); Holst, *Constitutional and Political History,* 2:81-82 (3d quotation); McMaster, *History of the People of the United States,* 5:208-11.

9. Hart, *Slavery and Abolition,* 158-61, 166 (1st and 2d quotations), 173-74; A.D. Adams, *Neglected Period of Anti-Slavery,* 17, 29-38 (3d-5th quotations, 29), 206, 249-50.

10. Dumond, *Antislavery Origins of the Civil War,* 49 (1st quotation), and *Antislavery,* 95; Stewart, "Evangelicalism and the Radical Strain in Southern Antislavery Thought," 379-96 (2d quotation, 380); Dillon, *Lundy,* v-vi (3d quotation), 15-19, 99, 126-39; Aptheker, *Abolitionism,* 2-3 (4th quotation).

11. Goodell, *Slavery and Anti-Slavery,* 95-117, 385-89; May, *Recollections,* 2-5, 15; H. Wilson, *Slave Power,* 1:176-88; Stanton, *Recollections,* 46-47, Pillsbury, *Acts of the Anti-Slavery Apostles,* 2; Hart, *Slavery and Abolition,* 166, 170-72 (quotation).

12. Goodell, *Slavery and Anti-Slavery,* 1-3; May, *Recollections,* 1-5, 126; H. Wilson, *Slave Power,* 1:184; Hart, *Slavery and Abolition,* 174-75; Stewart, "Young Turks and Old Turkeys," 229-30; Aptheker, *Abolitionism,* xi-xiii.

13. Julian, "Genesis," 533-55; O. Johnson, "Osborn's Place in Anti-Slavery History," 191-206, and *Garrison,* 22 (quotation).

14. Goodell, *Slavery and Anti-Slavery,* 385; Greeley, *American Conflict,* 1:107-14 (quotation 112); May, *Recollections,* 12-15; Holst, *Constitutional and Political History,* 2:81-83; H. Wilson, *Slave Power,* 1:167, 177-81; W.P. Garrison and F.J. Garrison, *Garrison,* 1:87. Early historians of abolitionism also note the shock Garrison experienced observing slavery in Baltimore. In an article that influenced this chapter, James L. Huston argues that physical contact with slavery was at the heart of northern commitment to abolitionism. See Huston, "Experiential Basis," 609-40.

15. A.D. Adams, *Neglected Period of Anti-Slavery,* 17, 249-52. For contemporary examples of the myth, see *Philanthropist,* Oct. 27, 1841; CIVIS to Editors, n.d., in *LE,* Aug. 28, 1847. For antebellum and modern exposure of the myth, see *NE,* June 4, 1857; Rhodes, *History,* 1:58; Stampp, "Fate of the Southern Anti-Slavery Movement," 12-16.

16. U.B. Phillips, "Plantation as a Civilizing Factor," 262, "Conservatism and Progress," 3-8, and *Course of the South to Secession,* 85-89, 95, 110, 158.

17. Scarborough, *Opposition to Slavery in Georgia,* 179-97; Whitfield, *Slavery Agitation in Virginia,* 47-61; Merkel, *Antislavery Controversy in Missouri,* 2. On the unlikelihood that amelioration would have led to abolition, see Genovese, *Roll, Jordan, Roll,* 49-58.

18. Pressly, *Americans Interpret Their Civil War,* 291-328; Higham, *History,* 200-201, 212-16; Huston, "Experiential Basis," 609-11; Randall, *Civil War and Reconstruction,* 100-107; Craven, *Coming of the Civil War,* 134-50.

19. Dumond, *Antislavery,* 88-95; Birney, *Birney,* 163-70, 431-35; Tyler, *Freedom's Ferment,* 482; Thomas, *Weld,* 3-42; Donald, *Lincoln Reconsidered,* 19-36; Filler, *Crusade against Slavery,* 17-19 (quotation), 25-27. Hart was probably more correct than Dumond when he wrote of northward-bound southern abolitionists: "Nearly all of these men joined themselves to an abolition movement

which they found in full action in the north." See Hart, *Slavery and Abolition*, 179-80.

20. Stewart, "Evangelicalism and the Radical Strain in Southern Antislavery Thought," 379-80; Dillon, *Lundy*, 49, 64-67, 96-97, 149-50, "Abolitionist Historiography," 514-15, "Three Southern Antislavery Editors," 47-56, and *Abolitionists*, 35; Stewart, *Holy Warriors*, 41 (quotation).

21. Aptheker, *Abolitionism*, xiii, 59; Dillon, *Slavery Attacked*, esp. 114; Quarles, *Black Abolitionists*, 3-41.

22. Wyatt-Brown, *Tappan*, 1-73; Dillon, *Abolitionists*, 27-30; Stewart, *Holy Warriors*, 33-49.

23. As Finnie points out, Lundy's estimate has been frequently cited. See "Antislavery Movement in the Upper South," 319; H. Wilson, *Slave Power*, 1:697-70; Birney, *Birney*, 74-82; A.D. Adams, *Neglected Period of Anti-Slavery*, 17-24, 37-56, 127-39; 249-52; Dillon, *Lundy*, 14 (quotation), 21, 78, 85, 92-101, and "Three Southern Antislavery Editors," 47n; Weeks, "Anti-Slavery Sentiment in the South," 89; Simms, "Critical Analysis of Abolitionist Literature," 380-81; Hickin, "Antislavery in Virginia," 28.

24. Rhodes, *History*, 1:58; U.B. Phillips, *Course of the South to Secession*, 104-10, 158; Dillon, *Lundy*, 10-12, 49-54, 105-10, 140-41, 150-51; May, *Reminiscences*, 5-7; W.P. Garrison and F.J. Garrison, *Garrison*, 1:89n; McMaster, *History of the People of the United States*, 5:212; A.D. Adams, *Neglected Period of Anti-Slavery*, 17, 249-52 (quotation).

25. Finnie, "Antislavery Movement in the Upper South," 319-42 (quotation, 341). For indications of Finnie's impact on Dillon and Stewart, see Dillon, "Abolitionist Historiography," 514-15; Stewart, *Holy Warriors*, 208.

26. Finnie, "Antislavery Movement in the Upper South," 341-42 (quotation); Hesseltine, "New Aspects of the Proslavery Argument," 1-14; Dillon, *Slavery Attacked*, 87-161; Wyatt-Brown, *Southern Honor*, 402-34; Nye, *Fettered Freedom*; Eaton, *Freedom-of-Thought Struggle*, 3-26.

27. Stampp, "Fate of the Southern Anti-Slavery Movement," 10-22; Hickin, "Antislavery in Virginia."

28. The following ignore or only briefly allude to prominent late antebellum southern abolitionists: Goodell, *Slavery and Antislavery*; Greeley, *American Conflict*; H. Wilson, *Slave Power*; O. Johnson, *Garrison*; Rhodes, *History*; Barnes, *Antislavery Impulse*; Dumond, *Antislavery Origins of the Civil War*; Foner, *Free Soil*; Sewell, *Ballots for Freedom*; Stewart, *Holy Warriors*; Dillon, *Abolitionists* and *Slavery Attacked*; Aptheker, *Abolitionism*.

29. U.B. Phillips, *Course of the South to Secession,* 108-10; Stewart, *Holy Warriors*, 59 (1st quotation); Degler, *Other South*, 47-96 (2d quotation, 79; 3d quotation, 75; 4th quotation, 18). Earlier Hart said that after 1830 only "feeble efforts at a gradual emancipation were permitted" in the upper South. See Hart, *Slavery and Abolition*, 175.

30. H. Wilson, *Slave Power*, 2:628-35, 668-70; W.P. Garrison and F.J. Garrison, *Garrison*, 3:379 (quotation); Hart, *Slavery and Abolition*, 234; Tyler, *Freedom's Ferment*, 481, 521-22; Eaton, *Freedom-of-Thought Struggle*, 185; Dumond, *Antislavery Origins of the Civil War*, 28.

31. Degler, *Other South*, 18, 21, 75-79; Dillon, *Abolitionists*, 40; Lerner, *Grimké Sisters*; Fladeland, *Birney*; d'Entremont, *Southern Emancipator*; Bailey, *Helper*; Fredrickson, *Arrogance of Race*, 28-53. Fee has been the subject of at least one dissertation and is a prominent figure in several studies of antislavery in Kentucky. But no one establishes his significance within the broad context of antislavery in America. Even less attention has been given to Janney. See Loesch, "Kentucky Abolitionist"; English, "Fee"; Tallant, "Slavery Controversy in Kentucky"; Sears, *Day of Small Things*; Hickin, "Gentle Agitator," 159-90. Sears's book has been republished in slightly different form as *Kentucky Abolitionists in the Midst of Slavery, 1854-1864: Exiles for Freedom* (Lewiston, N.Y.: Mellen, 1993).

32. Holst, *Constitutional and Political History*, 3:118-27; Harrison, "Clay and the *True American*," 30-49; Smiley, "Clay and Southern Industrialism," 315-27; Howard, "Clay and the Origins of the Republican Party," 49-71; Harrison, "Anti-Slavery Career of Cassius M. Clay," 259-317; Smiley, *Lion of White Hall*; Pease and Pease, *Bound with Them in Chains*, 60-89.

33. Smiley, *Lion of White Hall*, esp. 22-23, 50-58; Pease and Pease, *Bound with Them in Chains*, 60-89; Degler, *Other South*, 55-60.

34. Holst, *Constitutional and Political History*, 3:118-27 (1st quotation, 121), 430-35; W.W. Freehling, *Road to Disunion*, 1:117 (2d quotation), 455-74; Berlin, *Slaves without Masters*, 184-86 (3d quotation); Smiley, *Lion of White Hall*, 139-41; Martin, *Antislavery Movement in Kentucky*, 130-32; Tapp, "Breckinridge," 146-50; Tallant, "Slavery Controversy in Kentucky," 282-308. Freehling notes that proslavery forces were able to bring strong counter pressure to contain Clay's efforts.

35. Berlin, *Slaves without Masters*, 186; W.W. Freehling, *Road to Disunion*, 1:114, 462, 465-66 (quotation), 472-74.

36. Degler, *Other South*, 91; Stewart, *Holy Warriors*, 59; May, *Recollections*, 131-32; O. Johnson, *Garrison*, 190; Merkel, *Antislavery Controversy in Missouri*, 9; Barnes and Dumond, *Letters of Theodore Weld, Angelina Grimké and Sarah Grimké*, 1:202n (hereafter cited as *Weld-Grimké Letters*); W.P. Garrison and F.J. Garrison, *Garrison*, 3:379; Harrold, "Clay on Slavery," 42-56; Snodgrass to Gamaliel Bailey, Feb. 28, 1846, in *CWHP*, Mar. 11, 1846; Hickin, "Gentle Agitator," 164; Harrold, "Violence and Nonviolence in Kentucky Abolitionism," 18, 33-35; C.H. Johnson, "Abolitionist Missionary Activities," 305-9; Mabee, *Black Freedom*, 59; P. Thompson, "Harriet Tubman, Thomas Garrett, and the Underground Railroad," 1-21 (hereafter cited as "Tubman and Garrett").

37. Takaki, *Iron Cages*; Litwack, *North of Slavery*; Pease and Pease, *They Who Would Be Free*, 68-94; Fee to George Whipple, Aug. 26, 1853, Fee to Simeon

S. Jocelyn, Dec. 4, 1858, AMAA, Amistad Research Center, Tulane University; *BSV*, Mar. 4, 1843, Aug. 17, 1844, July 5, 1845; Harrold, "Clay on Slavery," 42-56; Fredrickson, *Arrogance of Race*, 28-53; D.G. Matthews, "Abolitionists on Slavery," 180.

38. May, *Recollections*, 203; O. Johnson, *Garrison*, 190; Holst, *Constitutional and Political History,* 3:431-32; Foner, *Free Soil*, 120-21; Sewell, *Ballots*, 319-20; Smiley, *Lion of White Hall*, 22-23, 50-58; Pease and Pease, *Bound with Them in Chains*, 60-89; Degler, *Other South*, 13-96. Filler, *Crusade against Slavery*, 74; Dumond, *Antislavery Origins of the Civil War*, 28; and Stewart, *Holy Warriors*, 60, all quote Birney.

39. Dillon, *Abolitionists*, 231 (quotation); W.W. Freehling, *Road to Disunion*, 1:455, 462-73.

2. AN IMAGE OF A SOUTHERN WHITE EMANCIPATOR

1. Foote to W.S. Bailey, Oct. 6, 1857, in *Liberator*, Oct. 30, 1857.

2. Finnie, "Antislavery Movement in the Upper South," 319-42; Degler, *Other South*, 13-96; Stewart, *Holy Warriors*, 58-61; Pease and Pease, *Bound with Them in Chains*, 60-68.

3. For comments on the impact of the southern reaction on the abolitionists, see Wyatt-Brown, "Abolitionists' Postal Campaign," 227-38; Kraditor, *Means and Ends*, 255-60; Stewart, *Holy Warriors*, 60-61, 70-71; Dillon, *Abolitionists*, 64-66. For examples of northern abolitionists linking the progress of their movement with events in the South, see *Emancipator*, June 14, 1838; *NASS*, Mar. 3, 1842, Sept. 13, 1849; AFASS, *[10th] Annual Report*, 85-90; *FDP*, Aug. 6, 1852; *Liberator*, Feb. 13, 1857.

4. William Lloyd Garrison to Samuel J. May, July 28, 1834, Garrison to Henry E. Benson, Aug. 21, 1834, in Merrill and Ruchames, *Letters of William Lloyd Garrison*, 1:392, 2:165-66 (hereafter cited as *Garrison Letters)*; *GUE*, Aug. 26, 1834; *NE*, Feb. 22, 1849; *ASB*, Aug. 11, 1855; Lerner, *Grimké Sisters*; D'Entremont, *Conway*; Bailey, *Helper*; Hickin, "Gentle Agitator," 159-90; Thomas Garrett to Aaron M. Powell, Apr. 5, 1870, in *NASS*, Apr. 16, 1870; Dillon, *Lundy*; Harrold, *Bailey*. Abolitionists also rejected the antislavery pretensions of border-slave-state politicians such as Henry Clay and Thomas Hart Benton. For example, see *NASS*, 19 July 1849; MASS, *Eighteenth Annual Report*, 27-33.

5. Abzug, "Fear of Slave Violence," 15-28; Aptheker, "Militant Abolitionism," 456-59; MASS, *Fifth Annual Report*, xxi-ii, xxxv-vi; *Philanthropist*, Feb. 5, 1839; *CG*, 30 Cong., 1 sess., 672; *NE*, Nov. 16, 1848, Feb. 10, 1849.

6. Fladeland, *Birney*; Smiley, *Lion of White Hall*; Harrold, "Clay on Slavery and Race," 42-56, and "Intersectional Relationship between Cassius M. Clay and the Garrisonian Abolitionists," 102-3 (hereafter cited as "Clay and the Garrisonians"); Sears, *Day of Small Things*; Fee, *Autobiography*; Fee's letters in the AMAA, Amistad Research Center, Tulane University, and the Fee-Clay Correspondence, Berea College Archives. I reached a rough quantitative estimate of

the impact of the individual southern antislavery leaders—while they were in the South—on the minds of northern abolitionists by checking the number of letters posted in the southern states from each of the southerners listed in the index of John W. Blassingame and Mae G. Henderson, eds., *Antislavery Newspapers and Periodicals* (5 vols.; Boston: G.K. Hall, 1980-1984). In descending order of frequency the numbers of the entries are as follows: C.M. Clay: 144; Snodgrass: 53; Fee: 38; W.S. Bailey: 16; R.J. Breckinridge: 8; Birney: 7; Janney: 4; Daniel Worth: 3; Francis P. Blair Jr.: 2; Daniel R. Goodloe: 2; James M. Pendleton: 2; J.R. Underwood: 2, B.S. Hedrick: 2; A.W. Campbell: 1; William H. Brisbane: 0; Moncure Conway: 0; Frederick Douglass: 0; Grimkes: 0; Hinton R. Helper: 0; Henry Ruffner: 0; Vaughan: 0. Birney's letters cover only a period of a year and a half, two of Janney's letters are from the late 1860s, and the lack of letters from Vaughan is offset by high interest expressed in him by northern abolitionists in the late 1840s.

7. Snodgrass to Dr. Bailey, Feb. 28, 1846, in *CWHP*, Mar. 11, 1846; *BSV*, Sept. 21, 1844; *NASS*, Aug. 10, 1843, Jan. 29, 1846, Apr. 22, 1847; *NYTr*, Jan. 31, 1846; *Emancipator*, July 8, 1846; *NE*, Feb. 25, July 1, 1847, Oct. 21, 1852; *TA*, Feb. 18, July 15, Aug. 26, Sept. 2, 16, 1846; *LE*, June 19, July 3, 10, 31, Aug. 7, 28, 1847; Gamaliel Bailey to Birney, Oct. 28, 1838, in Dumond, *Letters of James G. Birney*, 1:475-76 (hereafter cited as *Birney Letters*); *Philanthropist*, Apr. 9, 1839; Salmon P. Chase to Gerrit Smith, 1 Sept. 1846, Gerrit Smith Papers, SU; *Daily True Democrat* (Cleveland), Jan. 12, 1847; Lewis Tappan to Gamaliel Bailey, Nov. 6, 1848, Tappan Papers, LC; T.C. Smith, *Liberty and Free Soil Parties*, passim.

8. Fee to George Whipple, Feb. 15, 1853 (1st quotation), W.S. Bailey to Simeon S. Jocelyn, Feb. 11, 1856 (printed circular), AMAA; "Sketch of the Life of Wm. S. Bailey. By Himself for the Evening Post," *NASS*, Aug. 16, 1856 (2d quotation); *Free South*, quoted in *ASB*, Oct. 29, 1859; *ASB*, Nov. 5, 1859; *RA* 2 (Feb. 1857): 63; *Liberator*, Sept. 28, 1860. See also Steely, "Bailey," 274-81.

9. William Lloyd Garrison to Helen E. Garrison, 11 May 1835, Merrill and Ruchames, *Garrison Letters*, 1:475; *Emancipator*, quoted in *Liberator*, Oct. 18. 1834; Fladeland, *Birney*, 88-89; Theodore Weld to Birney, June 19, Sept. 4, Dec. 11, 1834, in Dumond, *Birney Letters*, 1:119-20, 132-33, 155; NEASS, *Second Annual Report,* 25-26; AASS, *Second Annual Report,* 37-38, 46; Kraditor, *Means and Ends,* 255, 269n; *Liberator,* Oct. 18, 1834, June 6, 1835; Stewart, "Peaceful Hopes and Violent Experiences," 298-99.

10. Theodore Weld to Birney, May 28, 1834, Aug. 25, 1834, in Dumond, *Birney Letters*, 1:112-13, 130-32; *Emancipator*, June 10, Aug. 12, Oct. 14, 21, 1834; *Liberator*, Nov. 29, Dec. 6, 1834; AASS, *Second Annual Report*, 37-38; Fladeland, *Birney*, 88-89; Dillon, *Abolitionists*, 60-61; MASS, *Fourth Annual Report*, 15-16; Nye, *Fettered Freedom*, 174-218; Stewart, *Holy Warriors*, 48-49, 69-73. In 1835, Birney himself minimized the violent threats he faced in Kentucky compared to anti-abolitionist mobs in the North. Nevertheless, Liberty party advocates in particular later held Cassius M. Clay up to what they contended was Birney's

higher standard. See *ASR* 1 (June 1835): 68-71; *Emancipator*, July 3, 30, 1845, June 24, 1846; *CWHP*, Jan. 28, 1846, Feb. 2, 25, 1846.

11. Gerteis, *Morality and Utility*, 25-26; Ward, *Jackson*, 246-47n; *NASS*, Sept. 4, 1845, Aug. 4, 1855; MASS, *Fourteenth Annual Report*, 22-23; *CWHP*, 4 Feb. 1846; Tappan to John Beaumont, 30 Jan. 1844, in Abel and Klingberg, *Side-Light*, 170-71 (1st quotation); Foote to Bailey, Oct. 6, 1857, in *Liberator*, 30 Oct. 1857 (2d quotation).

12. Weld to Birney, June 19, 1835, in Dumond, *Birney Letters*, 1:120 (quotations).

13. *NASS*, Aug. 28, 1845 (1st quotation), Aug. 1, 1857 (5th quotation); *ASB*, Sept. 19, 1845 (2d quotation); AFASS, *[8th] Annual Report*, 33 (3d quotation); AFASS, *[11th] Annual Report*, 67-68 (4th quotation).

14. *Liberator*, Dec. 26, 1835 (1st quotation); Andrews to Editor *Baltimore Visiter*, Sept. 3, 1844, in *NASS*, Oct. 10, 1844 (2d and 3d quotations); Stern, *Patriarch*. For a discussion of abolitionist ambivalence on this issue, see Kraditor, *Means and Ends*, 255, 269-70n.

15. NEASS, *Third Annual Report*, 13 (1st quotation); *ASB*, Sept. 19, 1845 (2d quotation); MASS, *Fifteenth Annual Report*, 27-29 (3d quotation); MASS, *Eighteenth Annual Report*, 24-27; *NE*, Aug. 19, 1847, Aug. 30, Sept. 6, 1849.

16. Simpson, "Slavery and the Cultural Imperialism of New England," 1-29; *ASB*, Sept. 19, 1845, Dec. 1, 1855; *NE*, June 28, 1849 (quotation), Oct. 16, 1853; AFASS, *[10th] Annual Report*, 103; *Liberator*, 3 Aug. 1855; "Cincinnati Correspondence," Mar. 18, 1857, in *NASS*, Mar. 28, 1857.

17. Weld to Birney, 16 Feb. 1835, in Dumond, *Birney Letters*, 1:180 (1st quotation); *NASS*, Feb. 27 (2d quotation), June 19, 1845; Tappan to Snodgrass, Oct. 18, 1844, lt. bk. copy, Tappan Papers; Bailey to *CWHP*, Nov. 5, 1844, in *CWHP*, Nov. 20, 1844; *ASB*, Sept. 5, 1845; MASS, *Sixteenth Annual Report*, 24 (3d quotation).

18. Birney to Lewis Tappan, Feb. 3, 1835, in *Liberator*, Apr. 4, 1835; Harrison, *Antislavery Movement in Kentucky*, 32; *St. Louis Daily Pennant*, quoted in *Liberator*, July 2, 1841; Salmon P. Chase to Gerrit Smith, May 14, 1842, Smith Papers; *Lexington Observer*, quoted in *NASS*, Mar. 6, 1845; CIVIS to Editors, n.d., in *LE*, Aug. 28, 1847; Nye, *Fettered Freedom*, 23-33, 38-39.

19. MASS, *Fourteenth Annual Report*, 26-27; *Liberator*, June 6, 1835, Aug. 29, 1848; *Emancipator*, June 10, 1834 (1st quotation), July 20, 1845; Robert H. Rose to Birney, Dec. 13, 1834, in Dumond, *Birney Letters*, 1:157 (2d and 3d quotations); *NYTr*, quoted in *TA*, Sept. 30, 1845 (4th-6th quotations).

20. *NASS*, July 1, 1847 (1st quotation); *Liberator*, Dec. 6, 1834; *ASB*, Sept. 19, 1845; MASS, *Fourteenth Annual Report*, 22-26, 52-54; Lewis Tappan to Leavitt, Feb. 28, 1847, in *Emancipator*, Mar. 10, 1847; Kraditor, *Means and Ends*, 257-59, 272n; Blassingame, *Douglass Papers*, 2:404-5; *Emancipator*, July 30, 1845 (2d-4th quotations).

21. MASS, *Fourth Annual Report*, 15-16 (1st quotation); *CWHP*, Nov. 20, 1844,

Feb. 4 (2d quotation), Mar. 11, 1846; *Liberator,* Jan. 30, 1846; *NASS,* Feb. 26, 1846. For examples of Birney's frequent appeals to white interests in the early 1830s, see Birney to Lewis Tappan, Feb. 3, 1835, in *Liberator,* Apr. 4, 1835; Birney to Gerrit Smith, Sept. 13, 1835, in Dumond, *Birney Letters,* 1:243.

22. MASS, *Sixteenth Annual Report,* 25-26 (1st quotation); *CWHP,* Feb. 4, Mar. 11-25, 1846; *GUE,* July 1834; *Emancipator,* Aug. 26, 1834; *NASS,* Aug. 4, 1855; Harrold, "Clay on Slavery and Race"; Clay to William C. Bloss, E. W. Chester, J. Miller, et al., Jan. 16, 1846, in *NASS,* Jan. 22, 1846; Clay to Salmon P. Chase, Mar. 20, 1846, Chase Papers, HSPa (2d and 3d quotations), *Liberator,* May 27, 1853 (4th quotation).

23. *Emancipator,* Aug. 12, 1834 (1st quotation); Johnson to Mrs. Henry G. [Maria Weston] Chapman, Jan. 27, 1846, Maria Weston Chapman Papers, BPL (2d quotation); Smith to Vaughan, July 28, 1851, Smith Papers; Charles Francis Adams, diary, Dec. 6, 1851, Adams Papers, MHS.

24. *Emancipator,* Oct. 14, 1834 (1st quotation); *NASS,* July 9, 1846 (2d quotation); *RA* 2 (Feb. 1857): 63 (3d quotation).

25. *GUE,* Feb. 19, 1830; *NASS,* Mar. 5, 1846 (lst quotation), Sept. 8, 1855 (2d quotation), Nov. 24, 1855; *Emancipator,* Aug. 12, 1834, Aug. 27, 1845; *Philanthropist,* Jan. 27, 1841; *Cincinnati Herald,* quoted in *Emancipator,* Apr. 24, 1844; *CWHP,* July 3, 1844; *Liberator,* May 27, 1853.

26. Nye, *Fettered Freedom,* 174-93; Dillon, *Abolitionists,* 64-66; Weld to Birney, Aug. 19 [1835], in Dumond, *Birney Letters,* 1:239; *Liberator,* Sept. 26, Dec. 26, 1835; *Emancipator,* Oct 1835; MASS, *Fourteenth Annual Report,* 21-22.

27. *NASS,* Aug. 28, 1845 (1st quotation), Jan. 29, 1846 (2d and 3d quotations), Aug. 1, 1857; *Liberator,* Feb. 28, 1845, Mar. 23, 1860 (4th quotation); AFASS, *Thirteenth Annual Report,* 129-30; Blassingame, *Douglass Papers,* 3:325 (5th quotation).

28. MASS, *Fourteenth Annual Report,* 26-27 (1st quotation); *Liberator,* Aug. 29, 1845 (2d quotation); *TA,* Sept. 30, 1845; *NASS,* Jan. 29, 1846, July 1, 1847; *NE,* Mar. 14, 1850, June 4, 1857, Aug. 23, 1858; *RA* 3 (Mch 1858): 57-58.

29. Stewart, "Peaceful Hopes and Violent Experiences," 299-300; *Emancipator,* Aug. 27, Oct. 1, 1845; *NASS,* Sept. 4, 1845, Feb. 26, 1846; *CWHP,* Mar. 11, 1846; MASS, *Fifteenth Annual Report,* 27, and *Sixteenth Annual Report,* 28 (1st quotation); *AM,* Nov. 1858, as quoted in Mabee, *Black Freedom,* 238 (2d quotation).

30. MASS, *Fourth Annual Report,* 15-16 (1st quotation), and *Twentieth Annual Report,* 64-65 (2d quotation); *ASB,* Aug. 15, 1857 (3d quotation); *Liberator,* Sept. 28, 1860 (4th and 5th quotations). On nineteenth-century concepts of masculinity and the abolitionists see: Yacavone, *May,* 95-103; Bertram Wyatt-Brown, "The Abolitionist Controversy: Men of Blood, Men of God," in Quint and Cantor, *Men, Women, and Issues,* 1:230-48; Wyatt-Brown, *Yankee Saints and Southern Sinners,* 123-26; Hoganson, "Garrisonian Abolitionists and the Rhetoric of Gender," 558-95; Pugh, *Sons of Liberty,* passim.

31. Chapman to Clay, July 25, 1846, in *Liberator,* Aug. 7, 1846.

32. *Liberator*, Feb. 2, Apr. 12 (quotation), 1844; *Emancipator*, Feb. 19, 1845. To a lesser extent abolitionists attempted to instruct Snodgrass. Also, Weld in the early 1830s privately presented arguments designed to convert Birney to immediatism. But I find no public appeals to Birney in the antislavery press, aside from those directed to the Kentucky gradual abolition society he founded. See Lewis Tappan to [Snodgrass], 30 Aug. 1845, Tappan Papers; Fladeland, *Birney*, 80-81; *GUE*, Mar. 1834.

33. *NASS*, Aug. 12, 1841, Sept. 4, 1845; *Emancipator*, Feb. 29, Sept. 25 (1st quotation), 1844, July 16, 1845 (3d quotation); *Liberator*, May 5, 1843, Feb. 2, 1844, Feb. 28, June 20, Aug. 29, Sept. 19, 1845 (2d quotation), June 19, 1846, Sept. 10, 1847; *Philanthropist*, quoted in *NASS*, June 8, 1843; *CWHP*, July 3, 1844; *ASB*, Sept. 19, Oct. 31, 1845, July 3, Aug. 21, 1846; Lewis Tappan to Robert F. Baird, 23 Oct. 1845, Tappan Papers; *Cincinnati Morning Herald*, quoted in *Emancipator*, 3 Sept. 1845; Harrold, "Violence and Nonviolence in Kentucky Abolitionism," 19-21. See also Harrold, "Clay and the Garrisonians," 101-19. Clay freed the slaves he personally owned, but could not legally emancipate those he held in trust for his children.

34. *Emancipator*, Feb. 19 (1st-2d quotations), Aug. 27 (5th and 6th quotations), 1845; *GUE*, Mar. 1834 (3d and 4th quotations, emphasis in original); Blanchard and Rice, *Debate on Slavery*, 270; *Cincinnati Morning Herald*, quoted in *Emancipator*, Sept. 3, 1845; *ASB*, Sept. 19, 1845 (7th and 8th quotations); *NASS*, Feb. 5, 1846 (9th-11th quotations). For Gay's revealing response to Clay's sale of a slave for whom Clay was the trustee, see *NASS*, 22 May 1845.

35. *LE*, June 19, July 3, 10, Aug. 7, 1847; *Liberator*, July 2, 1847; *NASS*, July 1, 1847 (quotations); Lewis Tappan to Fee, Nov. 2, 1847, lt. bk. copy, Tappan Papers; Fee to George Whipple, Mar. 8, 1849, AMAA; *NE*, June 28, 1849; MASS, *Nineteenth Annual Report*, 70. Lewis Tappan had lost his initial enthusiasm for the *Examiner* by the end of 1848, and northern abolitionist Gamaliel Bailey complained that, while he also edited a newspaper on slave soil, abolitionists held him to a higher standard than Vaughan. See Tappan to Bailey, 6 Nov. 1848, lt. bk. copy, Tappan Papers; *NE*, 18 May 1848.

36. "Address of the Liberty Party of Pennsylvania, of 1845," in *AP*, Aug. 6, 1845; Simpson, "Slavery and the Cultural Imperialism of New England," 1-29; Walters, *Antislavery Appeal*, 70-87, 111-28.

37. Weld to Birney, Dec. 11, 1834, in Dumond, *Birney Letters*, 1:155; *ASR*, 1 (Apr. 1835): 46-47; *TA*, Sept. 30, 1845; *Emancipator*, Apr. 24, 1844, July 8, 1846 (1st quotation); NEASS, *Second Annual Report*, 25-26 (2d quotation); AASS, *Second Annual Report*, 46 (3d quotation), 59-68; Garrison to unknown, July 25, 1845, in Merrill and Ruchames, *Garrison Letters*, 3:311; MASS, *Fourteenth Annual Report*, 28, and *Sixteenth Annual Report*, 25; *NASS*, Jan. 29, 1846, July 1, 1847; AFASS, *[8th] Annual Report*, 33; *RA* 2 (Feb. 1857): 63. See also Kraditor, *Means and Ends*, 253-60.

38. Elizur Wright Jr. to Amos A. Phelps, Oct. 6, 1834, Phelps Papers, BPL;

Fee to George Whipple, Oct. 10, 1848, AMAA; AFASS, *[9th] Annual Report* (New York: AFASS, 1849), 19, and *Thirteenth Annual Report*, 129-30.

39. Hickin, "Gentle Agitator," 174; *Liberator*, Feb. 28, 1845, July 2, 1847; Clay to Gerrit Smith, Feb. 18, 1845, in *Liberator*, Apr. 4, 1845; *NASS*, May 22, June 5, 1845; *Emancipator*, Aug. 27, Oct. 22, 1845; MASS, *Fourteen Annual Report*, 23-45; *ASB*, June 26, 1846; *TA*, July 15, 1846 (quotations); Salmon P. Chase to Charles Sumner, 26 Nov. 1846, in Bourne, "Diary and Correspondence of Salmon P. Chase," 2:111 (hereafter cited as "Chase Diary and Correspondence"); Lewis Tappan to George W. Alexander, Feb. 23, 1847, in Abel and Klingberg, *Side Light*, 219; Tappan to Leavitt, Feb. 28, 1847, in *Emancipator*, Mar. 10, 1847; Tappan to Gamaliel Bailey, Nov. 6, 1848, lt. bk. copy, Tappan Papers.

40. Fee to George Whipple, Oct. 28, 1852, Feb. 15, 1853, William S. Bailey to Simeon S. Jocelyn, Dec. 11, 1856, AMAA; Fee to Clay, Nov. 26, 1856, Fee-Clay Correspondence, BCA; Fee to Daniel Foster, Mar. 12, 1857, in *NASS*, Mar. 28, 1857; *NE*, July 1, 1847 (quotation), Apr. 9, 23, 1857, Oct. 14, 1858, Jan. 6, 1859; Rebecca Bailey to Charles F. Harvey, Jan. 10, 1859, Charles Francis Adams Papers; *Liberator*, Mar. 23, Sept. 28, Oct. 5, 1860; *RA* 2 (Feb. 1857): 63, and 4 (Dec. 1858): 37.

41. Sewell, *Ballots for Freedom*, 87, 314-20.

42. Hickin, "Antislavery in Virginia," 3-4; Martin, *Antislavery Movement in Kentucky*, 132-38; *ASB*, Aug. 16, 1851, Aug. 15, 1857, Nov. 5, 1859; MASS, *Twentieth Annual Report*, 64-65; *Liberator*, May 27, 1853, Aug. 3, 17, 1855; *NE*, Oct. 16, 1853, Nov. 15, 1855, Apr. 16, May 7, 14, 1857, Sept. 16, Dec. 23, 1858, Apr. 21, 1859; *Independent*, Aug. 2, 1855; *RA* 3 (Mar. 1858): 57-58.

43. After 1850 the MASS dropped the section on antislavery progress in the South that it had maintained in its annual reports since 1846. The *Liberator*, *NASS*, and *ASB* continued to copy reports of the activities of southern emancipationists from other papers in the 1850s, but their editorial comments declined after the late 1840s. In the late 1850s the following titles set the tone: "Penalty for Preaching the Gospel in Kentucky," "Lynch Law in Kentucky," and, following John Brown's Raid, "Reign of Terror in the South." See *NASS*, Aug. 1, 15, Sept. 5, 1857, Feb. 25, 1860; *ASB*, Aug. 15, 1857, Nov. 5, 1859; *Independent*, Sept. 10, 1857; *NE*, Feb. 25, 1858; *Liberator*, Sept. 9, 1859.

3. AN IMAGE OF A SOUTHERN BLACK LIBERATOR

1. Phelps, *Lectures on Slavery*, 208-11.

2. Slave resistance and revolt: Aptheker, *American Negro Slave Revolts*; Genovese, *Role, Jordan Role*; Genovese, *From Rebellion to Revolution*, which contains an extensive bibliography. Southern white fear of slave revolt: Eaton, *Freedom-of-Thought Struggle*, 89-117; Bruce, *Violence and Culture in the Antebellum South*, 125-31, 190. Bertram Wyatt-Brown regards southern white fear of slave revolt as a response to cyclical feelings of general insecurity rather than to a real threat of rebellion. See Wyatt-Brown, *Southern Honor*, 402-34.

3. Dillon, *Slavery Attacked*, 114-19. Abolitionists used the term *self-emancipation* frequently. See for example *Emancipator*, Feb. 17, 1842, Jan. 7, 1846, May 19, 1847.

4. See for example Walters, *Antislavery Appeal*; Friedman, *Gregarious Saints*; H. Davis, *Leavitt*. For a historiographical overview, see Huston, "Experiential Basis," 609-40.

5. Pease and Pease, "Antislavery Ambivalence,"682-95, and "Ends, Means, and Attitudes," 117-28; Friedman, *Gregarious Saints*, 160-222; Walters, *Antislavery Appeal*, 25-33, 56-60; Pease and Pease, *They Who Would Be Free*, 68-94, 233-50; Demos, "Antislavery Movement and the Problem of Violent 'Means,'" 501-26; Perry, *Radical Abolitionism*, 231-67; Dillon, *Abolitionists*, 219-43.

6. Abzug, "Fear of Slave Violence," 15-28; Rossbach, *Ambivalent Conspirators*; Pease and Pease, *They Who Would Be Free*, 233-50.

7. Dillon, *Slavery Attacked*, 130-242. Herbert Aptheker anticipates some of Dillon's and this chapter's themes in *Abolitionism*, esp. xii, 59. Also, Carleton Mabee, in a brief chapter on abolitionist views of slave revolt in his 1970 study of nonviolence among the abolitionists, contends that commitment to nonviolence always qualified black and white abolitionist contemplation of slave revolt as a means of ending slavery. See Mabee, *Black Freedom*, 51-66.

8. Takaki, "Black Child-Savage in Antebellum America," in Nash and Weiss, *The Great Fear,* 27-44, and *Iron Cages*, 108-44; Litwack, *North of Slavery*; Stanton, *Leopard's Spots*; Fredrickson, *Black Image in the White Mind*, 1-164 (quotation); Walters, *Antislavery Appeal*, 55-60; Friedman, *Gregarious Saints*, 165-74; Hoganson, "Garrisonain Abolitionists and the Rhetoric of Gender," 558-95; Richard Yarborough, "Race, Violence, and Manhood: The Masculine Ideal in Frederick Douglass's 'The Heroic Slave,'" in Sundquist, *Douglass,* 166-88.

9. Stowe, *Uncle Tom's Cabin*; Walker, *Walker's Appeal,* 62 (1st quotation); Garnet, "Address to the Slaves of the United States," Aug. 13, 1843, in Ripley, *Black Abolitionist Papers*, 3:410 (2d quotation).

10. Sanborn, *Life and Letters of John Brown*, 130 (1st quotation); Oates, *To Purge this Land with Blood,* 59-60; "Speech of Theodore Parker" Jan. 28, 1858, in *Liberator*, Feb. 19, 1858 (2d quotation).

11. Garrison to President of the Anti-Slavery Convention, Jan. 30, 1836, in Merrill and Ruchames, *Garrison Letters*, 2:32; Marsh, *Writings and Speeches of Alvan Stewart on Slavery*, 193; *Emancipator*, Sept. 29 (1st quotation), Oct. 21, 1846; Phillips, *Speeches, Lectures, and Letters* (Boston: Lee and Shepard, 1892), 108-9; Theodore Parker to Thomas Wentworth Higginson, Jan. 18, 1857, in *Liberator*, Jan. 23, 1857; "Great Anti-Slavery Meeting in Faneuil Hall," in *Liberator*, Feb. 4, 1842 (2d quotation).

12. Hunt, *Haiti's Influence on Antebellum America*, 147-63; Oates, *Fires of the Jubilee*; Aptheker, *American Negro Slave Revolts*, 325-39.

13. Jones, *Mutiny on the "Amistad,"* and Jones, "The Peculiar Institution and National Honor," 28-50; Dillon, *Slavery Attacked*, 202-3; *Emancipator*, Jan. 7, 13,

Mar. 10, 17, 1842; "Great Anti-Colonization Mass Meeting of the Colored Citizens of the City of New York," Apr. 22, 1849, in *NASS*, May 3, 1849; Wish, "Slave Insurrection Panic of 1856," 206-27; Dew, "Black Ironworkers and the Slave Insurrection Panic of 1856," 321-38. For examples of the impact of each of these events on abolitionist discussion of slavery, see *Emancipator*, Sept. 5-Oct. 31, 1839; *NASS*, Feb. 10-Apr. 14, 1842; *Liberator*, Jan. 23, Feb. 13, 1857.

14. Dillon, *Slavery Attacked*, 206-7; *FDP*, Sept. 25, Oct. 9, Dec. 25, 1851; Hiram Wilson to [Henry] Bibb, Jan. 1, 1853, in *FDP*, Feb. 4, 1853; Abzug, "Fear of Slave Violence," 17-21; Pease and Pease, *They Who Would Be Free*, 206-12, 236-39; *Liberator*, Sept. 3, 1831, Aug. 28, 1848.

15. Fredrickson, *Black Image*, 1-129; Walters, *Antislavery Appeal*, 56-69; Garnet, *Past and Present Condition and Destiny of the Colored Race,* 18-21.

16. *Liberator*, July 9 (1st quotation), Oct. 1 (2d quotation), 1831; *Emancipator*, June 1, 1833, Feb. 17, 1842 (3d quotation); Abzug, "Fear of Slave Violence," 17.

17. V., "'Walker's Appeal.' No. 2," *Liberator*, May 14, 1831 (quotations); Phelps, *Lectures on Slavery*, 210; *AP*, Jan. 26, Sept. 12, 1843; *AM* 10 (May 1856): 51; Dillon, *Slavery Attacked*, 184-85. Abolitionists also argued that the harsh environment of slavery drove blacks to revolt. For example see *Liberator*, Sept. 3, 1831.

18. Filler, *Wendell Phillips on Civil Rights and Freedom,* 74-75 (quotation); *Philanthropist*, Dec. 8, 1841; *CWHP*, Jan. 22, 1845.

19. "New York Anti-Slavery Society. . . . Speech by Rev. T.W. Higginson," May 12, 1858, in *Liberator*, May 28, 1858; Higginson, "Physical Courage," 732-33 (1st and 3d-6th quotations); Fredrickson, *Black Image in the White Mind*, 110-15 (2d quotation).

20. *AP*, Oct. 10, 1843; *Liberator*, Oct. 1, 1831, June 9, 1848; *CWHP*, Apr. 23, 1845; Underwood to William K. Strong, Jan. 1, 1857, in *NASS*, Jan. 10, 1857; Garnet, "Address to the Slaves," in Ripley, *Black Abolitionist Papers*, 3:410 (1st quotation); Garrison, "Address to the Slaves of the United States," May 31, 1843, in *Liberator*, June 2, 1843; Rogers, *Collections from the Miscellaneous Writings,* 20; Phillips, *Speeches, Lectures, and Letters* (3d ed.; Boston: J. Redpath, 1863), 86; Blassingame, *Douglass Papers*, 3:162 (2d quotation); Cheek and Cheek, *John Mercer Langston,* 354-55.

21. Strikes: Garnet, "Address to the Slaves," 408; *Emancipator*, July 30, 1845; Henry C. Wright to Garrison, Jan. 8, 1857, in *Liberator*, Jan. 23, 1857. Escapes: *Emancipator*, Feb. 19, 1845, Jan. 7, 1846; Charles T. Torrey to Gerrit Smith, Aug. 3, 1844, Smith Papers. Force: *Liberator*, Sept. 3, 1831 (1st quotation); Janney to Henry D. Sedgewick, 1831, in Tuckerman, *Jay,* 37 (2d quotation).

22. "Great Anti-Colonization Mass Meeting," in *NASS*, May 3, 1849 (quotations); Dillon, *Abolitionists*, 229, 235-36; Sanborn, *Brown*, 136-37; Phillips, *Speeches, Lectures, and Letters* (1863), 84-86; "New York Anti-Slavery Society. . . . Speech of Rev. T. W. Higginson," May 12, 1858, in *Liberator*, May 28, 1858.

23. *Philanthropist*, quoted in *Emancipator*, Sept. 12, 1839; Garnet, "Address

to the Slaves," 409; Sireno French, "The Peculiar Institution. An Original Tale,"
AP, Sept. 25, 1844; [Hammond], *Life and Opinions of Julius Melbourne,* 106-7, 139-
40; Sanborn, *Brown,* 136-37; "New York Anti-Slavery Society . . . . Speech of Rev.
T. W. Higginson," in *Liberator,* May 28, 1858; John G. Whittier to William C. Nell,
Jan. 29, 1858, in ibid., Mar. 12, 1858; Cornish, *Sable Arm.*

24. *RA* 2 (June 1857): 97 (1st quotation); Blassingame, *Douglass Papers,* 3:207-
8 (2d quotation); "Speech of Wendell Phillips at the Annual Meeting of the Massachusetts A. S. Society," Jan. 28, 1858, in *Liberator,* Mar. 5, 1858.

25. Abzug, "Fear of Slave Violence," 15-24; Walters, *Antislavery Appeal,* 27-
28; Dillon, *Slavery Attacked,* 172-74; Garrison to Henry E. Benson, Sept. 26, 1831,
in Merrill and Ruchames, *Garrison Letters,* 1:138; *Emancipator,* Aug. 8, 1834 (quotation); Arthur Tappan, et al., "To the Public," Sept. 3, 1835, in ibid., Oct. 1835.

26. Demos, "Problem of Violent 'Means,'" 503-4; *Liberator,* May 5, 1832 (1st
quotation); Stewart to Samuel Webb, June 25, 1840, Stewart Papers, NYHS (2d
quotation); "Wandering Gentile," in *Liberator,* Sept. 8, 1854 (3d quotation).

27. Abzug, "Fear of Slave Violence," 21; Aptheker, "Militant Abolitionism,"
456, 460-61; Whittier, *Conflict With Slavery.* 72-73; MASS, *Tenth Annual Report,*
10; *Liberator,* Feb. 4, 1842 (quotation); *Philanthropist,* Feb. 9, 1842; Pease and
Pease, *They Who Would Be Free,* 236-37; Walters, *Antislavery Appeal,* 26; "National Liberty Convention," Aug. 30, 1843, in *AP,* Sept. 5, 1843.

28. Perry, *Radical Abolitionism,* 232-33; Garrison to the editor of the Boston
Courier, [Mar. 11, 1837], in Merrill and Ruchames, *Garrison Letters,* 2:226-28 (1st-
3d quotations); Wright to Garrison, Jan. 8, 1857, in *Liberator,* Jan. 23, 1857; *AFASR*
(extra edition), Dec. 1840, quoted in Friedman, *Gregarious Saints,* 202 (4th-5th
quotations); Williamsburg, N.Y. Liberty Convention, Dec. 29, 1841, in *Emancipator,* Jan. 20, 1842.

29. Abzug, "Fear of Slave Violence," 19-21; Gerrit Smith to [?], n.d., in *Emancipator,* Sept. 19, 1839; Milo D. Codding to [editors], n.d., in *NASS,* Mar. 14, 1842;
John C. Underwood to T. S. Sizer, Aug. 14, 1856, in *NASS,* Sept. 6, 1856; Pease
and Pease, *They Who Would Be Free,* 236-44; William Jay to Rev. and Dear Sir,
Sept. 7, 1839, in *Emancipator,* Sept. 19, 1839; A Colored Philadelphian to the
editor, July 28, 1831, in *Liberator,* Aug. 20, 1831; ibid., Jan. 15, Sept. 3, 15, 1831;
Rogers, *Miscellaneous Writings,* 20; Jabez D. Hammond to Gerrit Smith, May 18,
1839, Smith Papers; "Great Anti-Colonization Mass Meeting," in *NASS,* May 3,
1849.

30. Abzug, "Fear of Slave Violence," 23 (1st quotation); *Emancipator,* June 7,
1838, Feb. 11, 1842; *Liberator,* Jan. 8, Oct. 1, 1831, Sept. 13, 1839 (2d quotation),
Feb. 13, 1857; "Resolutions of the New York Nominating Convention," in *Emancipator,* Feb. 11, 1842; George Perkins, "Can a Slave Rightfully Resist?" in Griffiths,
Autographs for Freedom, 33-38. In 1829 David Walker argued that blacks suffered
more in the nineteenth century than whites had prior to the American Revolution but never explicitly used this claim to justify slave revolt. See Walker, *Walker's
Appeal,* 74-76.

31. Hoganson, "Garrisonian Abolitionists and the Rhetoric of Gender," 574-

80; Bentley, "White Slaves," 501-22; *Liberator*, May 14, Sept. 17 (quotation), Oct. 1, 1831, Feb. 11, 1842; *ASR* 1 (Apr. 1835): 37-39, (Dec. 1835): 151-52; *Herald of Freedom*, quoted in *Liberator*, Sept. 13, 1839; G.X., "Dialogue between Toussaint L'Ouverture and Washington," in *Liberator.*, Mar. 10, 1832; "Tenth Annual Meeting of the Massachusetts Anti-Slavery Society," Jan. 26, 1842, in *Liberator*, Feb. 4, 1842; Garnet, "Address to the Slaves," in Ripley, *Black Abolitionist Papers*, 3: 409; Wendell Phillips, speech to Massachusetts Anti-Slavery Society, Jan. 29, 1857, in *Liberator*, Feb. 13, 1857; John C. Underwood to editor of the *NYTi*, n.d., in *NASS*, Feb. 21, 1857; Blassingame, *Douglass Papers*, 3:413-19; Garrison to Louis Kossuth, Feb. 1852, in Merrill and Ruchames, *Garrison Letters*, 4:174-76; Rogers, *Miscellaneous Writings*, 75-76. On Gabriel's Rebellion see Egerton, *Gabriel's Rebellion*. Nancy Bently in "White Slaves: The Mulatto Hero in Antebellum Fiction" suggests that only black abolitionists were able to portray "a forceful black protagonist of full African descent," but, at least in their nonfiction writings, white abolitionists were able to do so as well. On occasion they protrayed slave women as heroes. See *TW*, Oct. 30, 1847.

32. *Evangelist*, quoted in *Philanthropist*, Jan. 12, 1842 (1st quotation); *NASS*, May 3, 1849; *RA* 2 (June 1857): 97 (2d quotation); "New York Anti-Slavery Society . . . Speech of T. W. Higginson," May 12, 1858, in *Liberator*, May 28, 1858.

33. *Liberator*, Oct. 1, 1831 (1st-3d quotations); Remond, speech at Marboro Chapel, Boston, May 29, 1844, in Ripley, *Black Abolitionist Papers*, 3:442-43 (4th-6th quotations).

34. *Evangelist*, quoted in *Philanthropist*, Jan. 12, 1842 (quotations); [Higginson], "Nat Turner's Insurrection," 175-76.

35. Gerrit Smith, "Address to the Slave of the United States," in *NASS*, Feb. 24, 1842; *Emancipator*, Nov. 28, 1839; Lewis Tappan to Gerrit Smith, Feb. 7, 1842, Smith Papers.

36. Smith, "Address to the Slaves" (quotation). There seems to have been some coordination of Garrison's speech with Smith's. Dillon provides a thorough discussion of these speeches and their significance. See Smith to Oliver Johnson, Feb. 2, 1842, lt. bk. copy, Smith Papers; Dillon, *Slavery Attacked*, 201-16.

37. Theodore D. Weld to Angelina Grimke Weld, Jan. 30, 1842, in Barnes and Dumond, *Weld-Grimké Letters*, 2:907; *Philanthropist*, Feb. 9, Mar. 9, Apr. 6, 1842; *NASS*, Feb. 10, 1842; *Liberator*, Feb. 11, 1842; *Emancipator*, Nov. 28, 1839; Feb. 11, 1842; Lewis Tappan to Smith, Feb. 25, 1842, Smith Papers; W.G., "Addressing the Colored People," *Emancipator*, Aug. 19, 1835 (quotation). For an example of the abolitionist claim that they could not communicate with slaves, see Garrison to the editor of the *Boston Courier* [Mar. 18, 1837], in Merrill and Ruchames, *Garrison Letters*, 2:241. For the opposite claim, see *Emancipator*, Mar. 4, 1842; "New York Anti-Slavery Society . . . Speech of Rev. T.W. Higginson," May 12, 1858, in *Liberator*, May 12, 1858. On the missionary effort, see chapter five. See also James Redpath, *Roving Editor*.

38. Smith, "Address to the Slaves" (quotation); Garrison, "Address to the

Slaves of the United States," *Liberator*, June 2, 1843; Garnet, "Address to the Slaves," 407-9.

39. Garnet, "Address to the Slaves," 408-10 (quotations). I make a distinction between calls for slave action and less clear endorsements of the right of slaves to act. For example, *Walker's Appeal* caused considerable excitement in the South, but it is a long complaint rather than an explicit call to arms. Similarly, Garnet's address is often portrayed as more clearly a call for slave revolt than it is here described. There are two existing versions of the address, both published well after its 1843 delivery—one in 1848 and another in 1865. On the basis of internal and external evidence, I have relied on the more qualified 1848 version. Others have used the less qualified and more insurrectionary 1865 version. Mabee and Dillon point out that the address was closer to a call for a general strike than for a rebellion such as Nat Turner's. Finally, Douglass's May 31, 1849, speech at Faneuil Hall is sometimes regarded as a call for slave rebellion, although Douglass only says that he would "welcome the intelligence to-morrow, should it come, that slaves had risen in the South." See Walker, *Walker's Appeal*; Ripley, *Black Abolitionist Papers*, 3:403-12; Aptheker, *Documentary History of the Negro People*, 1:226-33; *Emancipator*, Mar. 4, 1842; "Minutes of the National Convention of Colored Citizens," Aug. 15-19, 1843, esp. 13, in Bell, *Minutes of the Proceedings of the National Negro Conventions*; Pease and Pease, *They Who Would Be Free*, 238-39; Schor, *Garnet*, 51-57; Quarles, *Black Abolitionists*, 226-28; Sterling Stuckey, "A Last Stern Struggle: Henry Highland Garnet and Liberation Theory," in Litwack and Meier, *Black Leaders of the Nineteenth Century*, 135-37; Mabee, *Black Freedom*, 60; Dillon, *Slavery Attacked*, 213-14; Blassingame, *Douglass Papers*, 2:216-17.

40. *Liberator*, Feb. 4, 1842 (1st quotation); *NASS*, Feb. 24, 1842; One Idea to *Liberty Press*, May 1843, in *Emancipator*, June 1, 1843 (2d quotation).

41. Oliver Johnson to [Lydia Maria Child], Feb. 17, 1842, in *NASS*, Mar. 3, 1842; *Liberator*, Feb. 4, 1842; Aptheker, "Militant Abolitionism," 466; Demos, "Problem of Violent 'Means,'" 524; Friedman, *Gregarious Saints*, 205-6; Stewart, *Holy Warriors*, 153-66; Dillon, *Abolitionists*, 223-36.

42. *FDP*, Sept. 5, 1850 (1st-3d quotations); *Minutes of the State Convention of the Colored Citizens of Ohio, Convened at Columbus, Jan 16, 17, and 18th, 1851*, 11; Phillips, *Speeches, Lectures, and Letters* (1863), 85. See for example, *FDP*, 1851-1855 for evidence of the lack of calls for slave revolt or resistance during this period.

43. Friedman, *Gregarious Saints*, 214-22; Wish, "Slave Insurrection Panic," 206-7; Dew, "Black Ironworkers and the Slave Insurrection Panic of 1856," 321-38; Blassingame, *Douglass Papers*, 3:147.

44. Wright to Garrison, Jan. 8, 1857, in *Liberator*, Jan. 23, 1857; *Liberator*, Feb. 13, 1857 (1st and 2d quotations); A.J. Grover to Garrison, Feb. 24, 1857, in *Liberator*, Mar. 13, 1857; "Disunion Convention," Oct. 28, 1857, in *Liberator*, Nov. 6, 1857 (3d and 4th quotations); *Liberator*, Aug. 13, 1858 (5th and 6th quotations). Remond usually put his faith in disunion rather than in calls for slave revolt. See

Liberator, June 16, July 10, 1857. For other examples of the impact of the slave revolt panic, see Blassingame, *Douglass Papers*, 3:147-48; "Speech of Wendell Phillips at the Annual Meeting of the Massachusetts A.S. Society," Jan. 28, 1858, in *Liberator*, Mar. 5, 1858.

45. Rossbach, *Ambivalent Conspirators*, 165; Perry, *Radical Abolitionism*, 239; Pease and Pease, "Confrontation and Abolition," 929-30 (quotation), and *They Who Would Be Free*, 250; Dillon, *Abolitionists*, 236-37; *Principia*, Apr. 28, 1860; Tappan to Lysander Spooner, Oct. 7, 1858, Spooner Papers, BPL; Blassingame, *Douglass Papers*, 3:162, 215; *Liberator*, Aug. 13, 1858, Dec. 9, 1859; Quarles, *Black Abolitionists*, 231-32.

46. *NASS*, Feb. 10, 24, 1842; *Liberator*, Sept. 22, 1843; Aug. 13, 1858; *Philanthropist*, Feb. 9, Mar. 9, Apr. 6, 1842; Brisbane to Bailey, n.d., in *Philanthropist*, Mar. 30, 1842; "Minutes of the National Convention of Colored Citizens, Held at Buffalo," Aug. 15-19, 1843, in Bell, *Minutes and Proceedings of the National Negro Conventions*, 12-24; Janney to J. Miller McKim, Dec. 1, 1843, Antislavery Collection, Cornell Univ.; Clay to John Adams, et al., July 16, 1855, in *Liberator*, Aug. 17, 1855; Fee to Simeon S. Jocelyn, June 23, July 18, 1855, July 15, 1857, AMAA.

47. Hammond to Gerrit Smith, May 18, 1839, Feb. 28, 1852, Smith Papers; Spooner, "To the Non-Slaveholders of the South: A Plan for the Abolition of Slavery," prtd. circular [1858], Spooner to Thomas Wentworth Higginson, Nov. 28, 1858, Spooner Papers; Rossbach, *Ambivalent Conspirators*, passim; Dillon, *Slavery Attacked*, 227-34.

48. Theodore Parker to Thomas Wentworth Higginson, Jan. 18, 1857, in *Liberator*, Jan. 23, 1857; "Annual Meeting of the Massachusetts Anti-Slavery Society," Jan. 27, 1859 in *Liberator,* Feb. 4, 1859; Phillips, *Speeches, Lectures, and Letters* (1863), 280-82; Oates, *To Purge This Land with Blood*; Boyer, *Brown*; Pease and Pease, *They Who Would Be Free*, 248-49; Dillon, *Slavery Attacked*, 234. "Talk! talk! talk!—that will never set the slaves free," Brown complained after leaving a Boston antislavery meeting in 1859. See Sanborn, *Brown*, 131.

4. JOHN BROWN'S FORERUNNERS
Note: This chapter is reprinted with changes with permission from MARHO: The Radical Historians' Organization. Originally published in Radical History Review 55 (winter 1993).

1. *Freeman*, quoted in *Liberator*, Dec. 20, 1844.

2. Wolf, *On Freedom's Altar*; Siebert, *Underground Railroad*, 150-89; Gara, *Liberty Line*, 69-90; Boyer, *Legend of John Brown*, 23, 87; Aptheker, *Abolitionism*, esp. 94-122.

3. Dillon, "Abolitionist Historiography," 500-22; Huston, "Experiential Basis," 609-20; Walters, *Antislavery Appeal*; Friedman, "'Historical Topics,'" 177-94; Friedman, *Gregarious Saints*; Stewart, "Young Turks and Old Turkeys," 226-32; Pease and Pease, *They Who Would Be Free*, 68-94. Huston provides, in far greater depth, a path-breaking analysis of most of the points made here.

4. Wyatt-Brown, "Abolitionists' Postal Campaign," 227-38; Stewart, *Holy*

Warriors, 60-61, 70, 173; Pease and Pease, "Confrontation and Abolition in the 1850s," 923-37.

5. See W.W. Freehling, *Road to Disunion*, 1:99-118, 162-210, 453-74.

6. Gara, *Liberty Line*, 90-91; Friedman, *Gregarious Saints*, 165-74. Neither Tubman nor other blacks—such as Josiah Henson and John Mason—who went from the North to the South to help slaves escape are indexed in the published volumes of Frederick Douglass's papers. Henson, for example, was known among his contemporaries as director of the British-American Institute at Dawn, Canada West, not as a slave rescuer. Summary executions truncated public knowledge of slave rescue attempts, and some slave rescuers simply failed to attract the attention of northern abolitionists. See Blassingame, *Douglass Papers*; Ripley, *Black Abolitionist Papers*, 2:106-7n; *AP*, Apr. 7, 1847; *New Orleans Picayune*, quoted in *Philanthropist*, Sept. 22, 1841; Pickard, *Kidnapped and Ransomed*, 280-306, 377-409; Lewis W. Paine to Wendell Phillips, June 22, 1852, Benjamin P. Hunt Collection, BPL.

7. MASS, *Seventeenth Annual Report*, 41; *Liberator*, Oct. 14, 1853; *ASB*, Dec. 1, 1855; Garrett to Gerrit Smith, Jan. 13, 29, Apr. 29, 1858; Garrett to William Lloyd Garrison, Jan. 24, 1860, in *Liberator*, Mar. 2, 1860; Garrett to Aaron M. Powell, Apr. 5, 1870, in *NASS*, Apr. 16, 1870; McGowan, *Garrett*; P. Thompson, "Tubman and Garrett," 1-21.

8. MASS, *Thirteenth Annual Report*, 39; *St. Louis Republican*, quoted in *Liberator*, Aug. 27, 1841; G. Thompson, *Prison Life*.

9. Lovejoy, *Memoir of Torrey*; *Philanthropist*, Jan. 4, 1843; Torrey to Gerrit Smith, Jan. 23, 1844, Smith Papers; *Chronotype*, quoted in *BSV*, May 23, 1846.

10. Walker, *Trial and Imprisonment of Jonathan Walker*; *Liberator*, Aug. 8 (1st quotation), 29, 1845; Walker to Horace Mann, Feb. 5, 1849, Mann Papers, MHS; Filler, *Crusade against Slavery*, 164 (2d quotation).

11. Fairbank, *Fairbank*, 1-57, 85-149; Coffin, *Reminiscences*, 719-21; Coleman, "Delia Webster and Calvin Fairbank," 130-32; Webster, *Kentucky Jurisprudence*; Francis Jackson and Ellis Grey Loring, "Fairbank," [1849] ms. in William Lloyd Garrison Papers, BPL; Fairbank to [Frederick Douglass], Nov. 13, 1851, in *FDP*, Nov. 20, 1851; Webster to Rev. Dr. Cheever, Oct. 19, 1855, in *FDP*, Dec. 7, 1855.

12. Drayton, *Memoir*, 24-35; Goodell, *Slavery and Antislavery*, 445-46; Chaplin to Gerrit Smith, Mar. 21, 1838, Mar. 25, May 17, 1848, W.R. Smith to Gerrit Smith, Feb. 19, 1851, Smith Papers; *Case of Chaplin*, 14-17; *Courtland Standard*, May 2, 1871, quoted in *New National Era*, May 11, 1871; Friedman, *Gregarious Saints*, 97-123; MASS, *Seventeenth Annual Report*, 40.

13. *NYH*, Apr. 19, 20, 1848; Drayton, *Memoir*, 38, 63-64; Harlow, *Smith*, 290-94 (quotation); *National Intelligencer*, quoted in *NE*, Aug. 15, 1850; *Liberator*, Aug. 16, 1850; *Case of Chaplin*, 22-33.

14. Of those not previously located, Burr was from western New York and Thompson from northern Ohio. See Drayton, *Memoir*, 24-25, 39; Joseph Evans

Snodgrass to Gerrit Smith, June 30, 1848, Smith Papers; *NE*, May 18, 1848; *Narrative of Facts Respecting Alanson Work, Jas. E. Burr, & Geo. Thompson*, 5; Stewart, *Holy Warriors*, 33-49, 67, 78.

15. Barnes, *Antislavery Impulse*; Stewart, *Holy Warriors*, 33-49; Lovejoy, *Torrey*, 1-2, 314; Cross, *Burned-over District*; Fairbank, *Fairbank*, 1-7; G. Thompson, *Prison Life*, 17, 22-23; *Case of Chaplin*, 14-16; Walker, *Walker*, 63-64; Joseph Mash to Dear Brother, Sept. 10, 1844, in *Liberator*, Sept. 17, 1844; *Vermonter*, quoted in *Liberator*, Oct. 4, 1844. For abolitionist criticism of Webster, see *Liberty Herald* (Warren, Ohio), Jan. 30, Apr. 3, 1845; *Liberator*, Aug. 1, 1845; *ASR*, quoted in *Liberator*, Dec. 26, 1845; *AP*, Feb. 11, 1846.

16. Dillon, *Slavery Attacked*, 206-7; G. Thompson, *Prison Life*, 17-25, 61-65, 317-18 (1st-3d quotations); Lovejoy, *Torrey*, 94-95, 102; *AP*, Dec. 26, 1846 (4th quotation); Fairbank to Citizens, Mar. 19, 1850, in *Liberator*, Apr. 5, 1850; Torrey to Smith, Nov. 16, 1844, Smith Papers; Walker, *Walker*, 11-12.

17. Lovejoy, *Torrey*, 89-95, 315; *Liberator*, July 2, 1841, Aug. 8, 1845; Chaplin to Gerrit Smith, Mar. 21, 1838 (1st quotation), Thompson to Smith, Oct. 31, 1846, Smith to David A. Hall, Mar. 27, 1852 (2d quotation), Smith Papers; MASS, *Tenth Annual Report*, 81-87; Walker, *Walker*, 63-64; Fairbank, *Fairbank*, 7, 63, 71, 150, 183; Fairbank to Garrison, Feb. 7, 1865, Garrison Papers; *AP*, Dec. 26, 1846; G. D. Jewett to [?], Nov. 4, 1844, in *Liberator*, Nov. 29, 1844. Aileen S. Kraditor and Lawrence J. Friedman indicate that empathy for blacks was characteristic of white abolitionists, and recent studies in social psychology support a thesis that those who aided slaves to escape were highly empathic. See Kraditor, *Means and Ends*, 20-22, 235-38; Friedman, *Gregarious Saints*, 16-21; Batson, "Is Empathic Emotion a Source of Altruistic Motivation?" 290-302.

18. G. Thompson, *Prison Life*, 17-27, 61, 347-48; Lovejoy, *Torrey*, 90, 105-25, 129-32, 166-68; Fairbank, *Fairbank*, 26-32; Chaplin to Gerrit Smith and Charles A. Wheaton, Feb. 15, 1848, in *AP*, Apr. 23, 1848; Chaplin to Smith, June 18, 1846, Mar. 25, May 17, Nov. 2, 11, 1848, Torrey to Smith, Jan. 23 (1st quotation), Aug. 3, 1844, Smith Papers; G. Thompson, *Prison Life*, 17-27, 61, 347-48; Lovejoy, *Torrey*, 129-30; Fairbank to Citizens of Boston, Mar. 19, 1850, in *Liberator*, Apr. 5, 1850; *Liberator*, Jan. 24, 1851 (2d quotation); Silvan Tompkins, "The Psychology of Commitment: The Constructive Role of Violence and Suffering for the Individual and His Society" in Duberman, *Antislavery Vanguard*, 270-98; Huston, "Experiential Basis," 619-40.

19. Walker, *Moral Choices*; Torrey to Gerrit Smith, Jan. 23, 1844 (1st quotation), Smith Papers; Lovejoy, *Torrey*, 87, 101-5, 165, 242; Torrey to James M. McKim, Nov. 29, 1844, Garrison Papers; *AP*, Dec. 16, 1846 (2d quotation), Jan. 20, 27, Feb. 17, 1847, June 7, 1848; Friedman, *Gregarious Saints*, 123. See also Weiss, Buchanan, and Lombardo, "Altruism is Rewarding," 1262-63.

20. Torrey to [Mary I. Torrey], Sept. 14, 1844, in *BSV*, Sept. 28, 1844; Torrey to [Amos A. Phelps], Nov. 4, 1844, Lewis Tappan to Phelps, Nov. 19, 1844, Jan. 24, 1845, Mary I. Torrey to Phelps, Sept. 15, 1846, Phelps Papers, BPL; James C.

Jackson to Gerrit Smith, [1850], Sept. 2, 1850 (1st quotation), Apr. 24, 1855, W.R. Smith to [Smith], June 9, 1851, William Harned to Smith, July 22, 1851, Smith to L H. Kousseau, Dec. 31, 1851 (4th quotation), Smith to David A. Hall, Mar. 27, 1852, Smith Papers; Harlow, *Smith*, 291-93; C.H. Johnson, "AMA," 150-53 (2d quotation); G. Thompson, *Prison Life*, 38 (3d quotation).

21. *Courtland Standard*, May 2, 1871, quoted in *New National Era*, May 11, 1871; A.B. Smith to Gerrit Smith, Sept. 26, 1841, Smith Papers; Kraditor, *Means and Ends*, 49-51; *Tocsin of Liberty*, Nov. 10, 1842; *AP*, Jan. 19, Apr. 27, 1843, Feb. 21, May 1, 15, 22, 29, Dec. 4, 1844; One Idea to *Liberty Press*, May 1843, in *Emancipator*, June 1, 1843; Truth to Joshua Leavitt, July 15, 1845, in *Emancipator*, July 30, 1845; Filler, *Crusade against Slavery*, 163-64; Stewart, *Holy Warriors*, 137. From February through March 1844 the *AP* published reports of Torrey's exploits under the title, "Notes of Southern Travel by a Negro Stealer."

22. Thompson to Smith, [1851], Sept. 6, 1852, Work to Smith, July 5, 1851 (quotation), Burr to Smith, July 9, 1850, Smith Papers; *New York Evening Post*, quoted in *Liberator*, Aug. 16, 1850; G. Thompson, *Prison Life*, vi, 17-39; Fairbank, *Fairbank*, 45, 66-71, 79-85; Blassingame, *Douglass Papers*, 2:220; Fairbank to Editor, July 24, 1850, in *Liberator*, Aug. 9, 1850; Joseph Mash to Dear Brother, Sept. 10, 1844, in *Liberator*, Sept. 27, 1844; MASS, *Fourteenth Annual Report*, 51-52; Walker to Sydney Howard Gay, Mar. 3, 1847, in *Liberator*, Apr. 9, 1847; George W. Clarke to William [L. Chaplin], Nov. 18, 1845, in *AP*, Dec. 3, 1845. It is worth noting that Thomas Garrett of Delaware was also very close to the Garrisonians. See Garrett to Garrison, Mar. 1, 1850, in *Liberator*, Mar. 8, 1850; P. Thompson, "Tubman and Garrett," 7-11; McKivigan, *War against Proslavery Religion*, 106.

23. Cover, *Justice Accused*, 149-58; Wiecek, *Sources of Antislavery Constitutionalism*, 172-287; *Liberator*, Aug. 31, Sept. 6, 20, 1844; Gerrit Smith to Salmon P. Chase, Nov. 1, 1847, in *AP*, Nov. 10, 1847.

24. Fairbank, *Fairbank*, 8-10 (1st quotation), 53; *AP*, May 26, 1847; *NASS*, Jan. 16, 1851; Lovejoy, *Torrey*, 134-46 (2d quotation), 164-65, 309-11; David Ruggles to [?], n.d., in *Liberator*, Jan. 3, 1845; *Philanthropist*, Oct. 13, 1841; Lewis Tappan to Gerrit Smith, Sept. 16, 1844, Torrey to Smith, Aug. 3, 1844, Smith to William H. Seward, Aug. 11, 1850, William R. Smith to Smith, Mar. 11, 1851, Smith Papers; Lewis Tappan to John Scoble, Nov. 9, 1844, in Abel and Klingberg, *Side-Light*, 193; MASS, *Seventeenth Annual Report*, 40-41; "National Convention of the Liberty League," in *AP*, June 14, 1848.

25. G. Thompson, *Prison Life*, 45; Lovejoy, *Torrey*, 125, 136-37 (1st quotation), 305-6; *Emancipator*, Feb. 19, 1845 (2d quotation); *AP*, quoted in *NE*, Aug. 15, 1850 (3d quotation); Gara, *Liberty Line*, 69 (4th quotation). See also Dillon, *Slavery Attacked*, 206-10, 232.

26. Wyatt-Brown, *Yankee Saints and Southern Sinners*, 183-213; Berlin, *Slaves without Masters*, 182-216; Fields, *Slavery and Freedom on the Middle Ground*, 63-89; W.W. Freehling, *Road to Disunion*, 1:453-535; Dillon, *Slavery Attacked*, 151-200; Benjamin O. Wright to Walker, Aug. 30, 1844, Garrison Papers; G. Thompson,

Prison Life, 19-21, 73-74 (1st quotation), 91, 384 (3d quotation); *St. Louis Republican*, quoted in *Liberator*, Aug. 27, 1841 (2d quotation).

27. Delia Webster to Harry F. Leavitt, Oct. 12, 1844, in *Liberator*, Jan. 10, 1845; *CG*, 30th Cong., 1st sess., 501-8, 652-62; *Lynchman*, quoted in *Liberator*, Aug. 16, 1850.

28. *NYH*, quoted in *Liberator*, Jan. 17, 1845, May 19, 1848; *Eagle*, quoted in *Liberator*, May 12, 1848; Gara, *Liberty Line*, 70-85; H. Davis, *Leavitt*, 215-17.

29. *Narrative of Facts Respecting Work, Burr, & Thompson*, 5-6; Norfolk to Editor, n.d., in *Emancipator*, July 17, 1844, Lewis Tappan to John W. Alden, July 8, 1844, lt. bk. copy, Tappan Papers; Gerrit Smith to Charles T. Torrey, July 8, 1844, Torrey Papers, Congregational Library, Boston; Torrey to Gerrit Smith, Aug. 3, 1844, Smith Papers; *Liberator*, Aug. 1, 1845 (quotation); MASS, *Nineteenth Annual Report*, 68; *NYTr*, quoted in *NS*, May 19, 1848; *NE*, May 18, 25, 1848; Lewis Tappan to John Scoble, Nov. 9, 1844, in Abel and Klingberg, *Side-Light*, 193-94..

30. Smith to William H. Seward, Aug. 11, 1850 (1st quotation), Smith Papers; *Liberty Herald* (Warren), Jan. 16, 1845; Lovejoy, *Torrey*, 299 (2d quotation), 304-5, 312; *Emancipator*, May 13, 20, 1846.

31. *Liberator*, Sept. 27, 1844; David Ruggles to [?], n.d., in *Liberator*, Jan. 3, 1845; *Liberty Party Paper*, quoted in *Liberator*, Jan. 24, 1851 (quotation); *NS*, May 5, 1848, Sept. 5, 1850.

32. Friedman, *Gregarious Saints*, 196-222; Smith to Joshua R. Giddings, Mar. 21, 1852, Smith Papers; *NS*, May 5, 1848; Lovejoy, *Torrey*, 310, 312, 355; *Liberator*, July 26, (1st quotation), Aug. 9 (2d quotation), 1844.

33. MASS, *Fourteenth Annual Report*, 51-54 (1st quotation); *Liberator*, Aug. 1, 8, 1845; John Thomas to Gerrit Smith, Sept. 6, 1850, Smith Papers; MASS, *Twenty-first Annual Report*, 42-43; Fairbank, *Fairbank*, 163-66; *NS*, Jan. 8, Feb. 4, 25, 1848; *Emancipator*, Dec. 25, 1844, July 30, 1845; *AFASR* 2 (Nov. 1845): 78; *Courier*, quoted in *NS*, May 28, 1848 (2d quotation).

34. Wolf, *On Freedom's Altar*, 4, 45-49; G. Thompson, *Prison Life*, 115-16; Torrey to Gerrit Smith, Nov. 16, 1844, Smith to William H. Seward, Aug. 11, 1850, James C. Jackson to Smith, Sept. 2, 1850, Smith Papers; *Liberator*, July 26, Aug. 16 (quotations), 1844, July 18, 1845, Aug. 16, 1850; MASS, *Thirteenth Annual Report*, 39-40; Blassingame, *Douglass Papers*, 1:224-26, 308-9.

35. Gara, *Liberty Line*, 81-88; Harrold, *Bailey*; Samuel Lewis to Editor *Cincinnati Chronicle*, n.d., in *Philanthropist*, Sept. 29, 1841; Clay to T.B. Stevenson, Jan. 8, 1845, in *Liberator*, Jan. 31, 1845; John G. Fee to E.C. Allen, June 25, 1844[5], Salmon P. Chase Papers, LC. Gara cites several nonabolitionists, including George W. Julian, Moses Corwin, and an anti-abolitionist Quaker, in support of his argument.

36. *Liberator*, Aug. 1 (1st quotation), Sept. 3, 1845 (2d quotation); Lewis Tappan to Smith, Sept. 16, 1844, William R. Smith to Smith, Nov. 26, [1850], Smith Papers; Tappan to Amos A. Phelps, Oct. 28, 1844, Phelps Papers; G. Thompson, *Prison Life*, 191, 312-17, 390; Lovejoy, *Torrey*, 235, 247-55, 283-85, 304, 335-36, 353;

NASS, Dec. 26, 1844; Mary I. Torrey to Governor of Maryland, n.d., in *Liberator*, Feb. 27, 1846; *Chronotype*, quoted in *BSV*, May 23, 1846; *Spirit of Liberty*, quoted in *Liberator*, Jan. 10, 1845.

37. *Philanthropist*, Oct. 13, 1841; *CWHP*, Apr. 23, 1845; *NE*, Jan. 7, 1847; Apr. 27, 1848; Aug. 15, Oct. 31, 1850; *CG*, 30th Cong., 1 sess., 654-57, 670-71, *Appendix*, 502-4; Trefousse, *Radical Republicans*, passim.

38. *Chronotype*, quoted in *NE*, May 18, 1848 (1st and 2d quotations); *NE*, May 18, 1848, Oct. 10, 31, 1850 (3d quotation); *Liberty Herald* (Philadelphia), quoted in *AP*, May 24, 1848; *Liberty Press*, quoted in *Emancipator*, June 18, 1848.

39. Lewis Tappan to Gerrit Smith, Sept. 16, 1844, William R. Smith to Smith, Nov. 8, 21, 1850, Francis Jackson to Smith, May 5, 1851, Smith Papers; *Liberator*, July 26, 1844; H.H. Brigham to Garrison, Nov. 7, 1844, in *Liberator*, Nov. 29, 1844; *Emancipator*, June 3, 1846; ibid., quoted in *Liberator*, Aug. 7, 1846; MASS, *Fifteenth Annual Report*, 62-63; Fairbank to Citizens, Mar. 19, 1850, in *Liberator*, Apr. 5, 1850; Drayton, *Memoir*, 61-62; Quarles, *Black Abolitionists*, 163-65; Bailey to William H. Seward, Dec. 6, 1850, Seward Papers, University of Rochester; *NE*, Mar. 31, Oct. 16, 1851, Jan. 29, 1852.

40. Lewis Tappan to John Scoble, July 31, 1844, in Abel and Klingberg, *SideLight*, 119; Stewart, *Giddings,* 152-53; Torrey to Gerrit Smith, Aug. 3, 1844; James C. Jackson to Smith, Sept. 3, 6, 8, 1850, Seward to Smith, Nov. 4, 1850, Walter Edgerton to Smith, June 4, 1851, Smith Papers; Seward to Charles T. Torrey, Sept. 2, 1844, Torrey Papers; Messerli, *Mann*, 460-531; *FDP*, Sept. 5, 1850. United States Senator Salmon P. Chase, who had close ties to organized abolitionism, was also active in behalf of accused slave rescuers. See Chase to Samuel E. Sewall, May 27, 1848, in Bourne, "Chase Diary and Correspondence," 133-34.

41. Oates, *To Purge This Land with Blood*, 30-63; Boyer, *Brown*, 78, 125-26, 154-55, 253-374, 426, 514.

42. Oates, *To Purge This Land with Blood*, 13-63, 310-18, 333-34; Boyer, *Brown*, 15, 23-24, 88, 100-98, 253-75, 359-460; Aptheker, *Abolitionism*, 123-27; Fairbank, *Fairbank*, 18-19, 148-49; Lovejoy, *Torrey*, 157-58; *Liberator*, Aug. 16, 1850; Friedman, *Gregarious Saints*, 210-11; Quarles, *Black Abolitionists*, 240-45; Trefousse, *Radical Republicans*, 129-30; Stewart, *Holy Warriors*, 172-75.

5. PREACHING AN ABOLITIONIST GOSPEL IN THE SOUTH

1. Lovejoy, *Torrey*, 68.

2. Clay, *Writings*, 358-61.

3. *Emancipator*, Nov. 18, 1846. See also John G. Fee to Salmon P. Chase, Dec. 25, 1845, Chase Papers, LC.

4. C.H. Johnson, "AMA," 512-64; Reynolds, "AMA's Antislavery Campaign in Kentucky"; Nicholson, *Wesleyan Methodism in the South*, 25-105; Green, "Northern Missionary Activities in the South," 147-72; McKivigan, *War against Proslavery Religion*, esp. 93-127; Howard, *Conscience and Slavery: The Evangelistic Domestic Missions, 1837-1861,* 63-72. Johnson does a fine job of placing the AMA itself in

the context of evangelical abolitionism in the North. Despite its title, Howard's book gives southern antislavery missions very little attention.

5. Mabee, *Black Freedom*, 235-41 (quotation); Wyatt-Brown, "Abolitionists' Postal Campaign," 227-38. Mabee exaggerates in claiming that the AMA did "wonders" in the South.

6. *ASR* 1 (Nov. 1835): 121-23 (quotation); O. Johnson, *Garrison*, 218; Stewart, *Holy Warriors*, 60-61; Mabee, *Black Freedom*, 31-37; *Emancipator*, Oct. 1835; Martineau, *Martyr Age of the United States*, 23-26. Although Quakers influenced Benjamin Lundy, he stressed the economic evils of slavery. See Dillon, *Lundy*, 75-78; May, *Recollections*, 12-13.

7. *DAB*, Allen Johnson, ed. (11 vols.; New York: Scribner's, 1957-1964), s.v. "Nelson, David"; Merkel, *Antislavery Controversy in Missouri*, 9-12; Nelson to Gerrit Smith, Aug. 1834, Smith Papers; *Emancipator*, Apr., June 16, 23, July 7, 14, 1836.

8. *OE*, June 10, 1857; Hickin, "Gentle Agitator," 159-90; Lucretia Mott to Maria Weston Chapman, Nov. 30, 1842, Chapman Papers, BPL; Hallowell, *James and Lucretia Mott*, esp. 210-19, 235-41; Janney to J. Miller McKim, Dec. 1, 1843, Antislavery Collection, Cornell University; George Truman to Janney, May 2-3, 1846, John Jackson to Janney, Sept. 20, 1849, [Janney] to Phineas Janney, Sept. 27, 1849, Janney Papers, SC; Janney to George Truman, Feb. 29, 1844, Truman Papers, SC; Janney to Sydney Howard Gay, July 4, 1846, Gay Papers, Columbia University.

9. McKivigan, *War against Proslavery Religion*, 93-101; "First Annual Report of the Board of Managers of the Missionary Society of the Wesleyan Methodist Connection in America," Nov. 9, 1846, in *TW*, Nov. 14, 1846; AFASS, *[9th] Annual Report*, 80-81; *AM* 2 (June 1848): 60 and 6 (June 1852): 57; AMA, *Third Annual Report*, 30-31; Fee to Jocelyn, May 1859, AMAA; Lewis Tappan to A.M. Chamerovzow, Oct. 29 [18]54, in Abel and Klingberg, *Side-Light*, 347-48; Fee to Gerrit Smith, May 18, 1855, Smith Papers.

10. Nicholson, *Wesleyan Methodism in the South*, 8-52; Matlack, *History of American Slavery and Methodism*, esp. 358-62; C.H. Johnson, "Abolitionist Missionary Activities," 295-99.

11. C.H. Johnson, "AMA," esp. 512-39; Sears, *Day of Small Things*, 113-212; E. Mathews, *Autobiography*, 327-407. For details on AMA efforts in Washington, D.C., Missouri, Tennessee, and Virginia, see the respective files for the district and states in the AMAA.

12. "First Annual Report of the Board of Managers of the Missionary Society of the Wesleyan Methodist Connection," in *TW*, Nov. 14, 1846 (quotation); *AM* 1 and 3 (Aug. 1847): 75, (Apr. 1849): 52; AMA, *Eleventh Annual Report*, 77-78, and *Thirteenth Annual Report*, 55-56.

13. Howard, *Conscience and Slavery*, 63-72; Sears, *Day of Small Things*, 80-83; Fee to Whipple, Oct. 10, 1848, AMAA; AMA, *Second Annual Report*, 4, 22, and *Third Annual Report*, 8; AFASS, *[10th] Annual Report*, 57-58 (quotation).

14. Examples of requests for assistance: [?] to Dear Sir, Oct. 25, 1845, in *TW*,

Nov. 14, 1846; Fee to Whipple, Oct. 10, 1848, AMAA. Impact on foreign missions: AMA, *Second Annual Report,* 24-27, and *Seventh Annual Report,* 19-20, 74-75. Nonslaveholders: Fee to Whipple, Mar. 8, 1849, AMAA; *OE,* Aug. 18, 1858. Impact on the North: *TW,* Nov. 9, 1850 (quotation), Goodell to Fee, Aug. 6, 1857, Fee Papers, BCA.

15. The growth of AMA commitment to southern missions may be traced in its annual reports from 1849 through 1860. On its decision to give southern missions priority, see AMA, *Tenth Annual Report,* 80 (quotations), *Eleventh Annual Report,* 20, and *Thirteenth Annual Report,* 55-56; *AMM* 2 and 3 (Nov. 1858): 269-70, (June 1859): 130-31.

16. Of fifteen permanent AMA, Wesleyan, and Free Baptist missionaries whose ages are known or can be approximated, eleven were thirty or younger when they began their work in the South. See *DAB* s.v. "Fee, John G."; Sears, *Day of Small Things,* 11, 141, 159, 169, 183, 191, 239; Tolbert, "Worth," 284; McLeister and Nicholson, *Conscience and Commitment,* 66; Nicholson, *Wesleyan Methodism in the South,* 39, 44-45, 65; E. Mathews, *Autobiography,* 26; William Kendrick to Jocelyn, Mar. 8, 1858, G.H. Pool to Jocelyn, Feb. 24, 1859, AMAA. On those born in the West: Sears, *Day of Small Things,* 169, 191; McLeister and Nicholson, *Conscience and Commitment,* 66, 557. On the importance of Oberlin: Mabee, *Black Freedom,* 153-54.

17. Sears, *Day of Small Things,* 145-240; *OE,* Apr. 1, Oct. 28, 1857, July 13, 1859; AMA, *Fourteenth Annual Report,* 74; Kendrick to Jocelyn, Mar. 8, 1858, Pool to Jocelyn, Feb. 24, Mar. 31, 1859, AMAA.

18. E. Mathews, *Autobiography,* 29, 32, 42-46; Loesch, "Kentucky Abolitionist," 18-19; Hawley to Smith, Aug. 13, 1847, Apr. 1, 1858, Smith Papers; William P. McConnell, E.L. Stevens, and B.P. Worcester to Executive Committee, Feb. 16, 1853, Smith to Whipple, June 9, 1854, AMAA; Smith to Fee, Feb. 23, 1855, Fee Papers; C.H. Johnson, "Abolitionist Missionary Activities," 305-7.

19. Barnes, *Antislavery Impulse*; Volpe, *Forlorn Hope of Freedom,* 74, 100; E. Mathews, *Autobiography,* 183, 187, 217-19; Fee to Dr. Bailey, Mar. 1, 1848, in *NE,* Mar. 9, 1848; Francis Hawley to Gerrit Smith, Aug 13, 1847, Smith Papers; *TW,* Nov. 4, 1848; ERASMUS to Bro. Lee, Nov. 10, 1848, in *TW,* Nov. 25, 1848; McBride to Lee, Aug. 2, 1851, in *TW,* Aug. 16, 1851; David Gamble to Lewis Tappan, Aug. 3, 1852, Daniel Wilson to Jocelyn, Nov. 30, 1853, Cassius M. Clay to Tappan, Oct. 24, 1852, E.L. Stevens to Jocelyn, July 28, 1855, Stephen Blanchard to Tappan, Apr. 2, 1860, AMAA.

20. Worth to Jocelyn, Apr. 19, 1858, AMAA (quotation); Harrold "Violence and Nonviolence in Kentucky Abolitionism," 33-37; *NS,* Sept. 5, 1850; Lincoln to Gerrit Smith, May 7, Dec. 5, 1859, Smith Papers; Brandt, *Town that Started the Civil War.* George Bassett, who briefly served as an AMA missionary in Washington, D.C., also had radical political abolitionist proclivities. See Bassett to Lewis Tappan, Jocelyn, and Whipple, Dec. 14, 1858, AMAA; Bassett, *Slavery Examined.*

21. I find only one incident in which Fee mentioned colonizationist leanings

of an AMA agent. See Fee to Whipple, Apr. 1853, AMAA. On dependence on northern financing: Fee to J.S. Batchelder, n.d., in *AM* 9 (Apr, 1856): 43; Fee to Whipple, Oct. 10, 1848, Apr. 10, 1850, Daniel Wilson to Whipple, July 22, 1852, Worth to Jocelyn, June 3, Aug. 5, Oct. 15, 1858, G.H. Pool to Jocelyn, May 4, 1859, AMAA.

22. Fee to Bailey, Dec. 8, 1847, in *NE*, Jan. 27, 1848; Fee to Lewis Tappan, Oct. 30, 1849, Fee to Whipple, Jan. 23, 1850, Sept. 24, 1852, Wilson to Whipple, July 22, Nov. 3, 1852, Aug. 22, 1855, Fee to [Jocelyn?], Aug. 20, 1858, Worth to Jocelyn, Sept. 6, Oct. 15, 1858, AMAA; AFASS, *[10th] Annual Report,* 49-50; *AM* 4 and 9 (June 1850): 69, (July 1855): 69; *AMM* 3 (Nov. 1859): 241; E. Mathews, *Autobiography,* 378; *Cincinnati Gazette,* quoted in *FDP,* Apr. 21, 1854; Lewis Tappan to Fee, July 10, 1855, lt. bk. copy, Tappan Papers; AMA, *Ninth Annual Report,* 76, *Tenth Annual Report,* 68-70, *Twelfth Annual Report,* 3-8, and *Fourteenth Annual Report,* 3.

23. McKivigan, "Gospel Will Burst the Bonds of the Slave," 62-64, 77 (1st quotation); Lovejoy, *Torrey,* 68, 83 (2d and 3d quotations); *Christian Freeman,* quoted in *Emancipator,* Mar. 18, 1846 (4th quotation); ibid., Oct. 1835. A number of books discuss the proslavery Bible argument. See H.S. Smith, *In His Image, But;* Tise, *Proslavery,* 124-79; Boles, *Masters and Slaves;* Wood, *Arrogance of Faith.*

24. *Emancipator,* Oct. 20, 1835 (1st quotation), Mar. 17, 1842 (2d quotation); Stewart to Dr. Bailey, Aug. 30, 1845, in Marsh, *Writings and Speeches of Alvan Stewart on Slavery,* 370-71.

25. TRAVELER [Crooks] to Lee, n.d., in *TW,* Nov. 13, 1847 (1st quotation); Wilson to Whipple, Aug. 10, 1852, AMAA (2d quotation); AMA, *Twelfth Annual Report,* 12-14 (3d quotation).

26. *AM* 8 (Apr. 1854): 43 (1st quotation); *OE,* July 4, 1855 (2d quotation); AMA, *Seventh Annual Report,* 59-62 (3d quotation); McBride to Lee, June 31 [*sic*], 1851, in *Liberator,* Aug. 15, 1851 (4th quotation); Fee to [?], July 19, 1853, in *AM* 7 (Sept. 1853): 90-91.

27. AMA, *Fourth Annual Report,* 35-36, *Seventh Annual Report,* 59-61, *Twelfth Annual Report,* 50-51, and *Thirteenth Annual Report,* 51-53; C.H. Johnson, "AMA," 532-35; Tallant, "Slavery Controversy in Kentucky," 317, 322-23; C.H. Johnson, "Abolitionist Missionary Activities," 298-99, 307; James Scott Davis to Jocelyn, Dec. 5, 1856, AMAA; E. J. Humlong to [?], Feb. 29 [*sic*], 1857, in *OE,* Apr. 1, 1857; *AMM* 2 (Sept. 1858): 232-33, (Nov. 1858): 281.

28. The Kentucky churches had a total of 184 members in 1859. McBride claimed nearly 600 church members for North Carolina in 1851, Daniel Wilson reported only 213 in 1856, and the numbers probably increased in that state thereafter. See C.H. Johnson, "AMA," 515, 518-20, 528. On itinerant preaching: Fee to Whipple, Sept. 24, 1852, James S. Davis to Jocelyn, June 20, Aug. 18, Sept. 1, Oct. 5, 1857; *AM* 7 and 8 (Sept. 1853): 90-91, (Apr. 1854): 43; AMA, *Tenth Annual Report,* 69-70. On informal talks with southerners: Fee to Lewis Tappan, Dec. 27, 1848, Fee to Whipple, Mar. 8, 1849, Worth to Jocelyn, Apr. 19, 1858,

AMAA; *AMM* 2 (May 1858): 113-14, (Dec. 1858): 305-6; AMA, *Eighth Annual Report*, 75-76. The missionaries highly valued the distribution of antislavery publications. See for example Fee to Tappan, Dec. 27, 1848, Wilson to Jocelyn, May 23, 1854, Worth to Jocelyn, July 5, 1859, AMAA.

   29. Janney to McKim, Dec. 1, 1843, Antislavery Collection, Cornell University; Fee to E.C. Allen, June 25, 1844[5], Chase Papers, LC; Fee to Tappan, June 10, 1847, AMAA; Crooks to Lee, Oct. 2, 1849, in *TW*, Oct. 20, 1849; McBride to *TW.*, n.d., in *NASS*, June 6, 1850; E. Mathews, *Autobiography*, 372 (quotation); David Gamble to Dear Sir, Oct. 28, 1847, Gamble to Lewis Tappan, Aug. 3, 1852, Merrell Humphrey to Tappan, Feb. 20, 1851, AMAA. Todd Armstrong Reynolds notes that Fee ordered 3,500 copies of a single antislavery pamphlet in 1853. See Reynolds, "AMA's Antislavery Campaign in Kentucky," 88. On southern state laws against circulating incendiary publications: Nye, *Fettered Freedom*, 153-59; Eaton, *Freedom-of-Thought Struggle*, 118-43.

   30. Fee to Lewis Tappan, Dec. 27, 1848, Aug. 4, 1851, Fee to Whipple, Sept. 24, 1852, Feb. 15, 1853, Jacob West to Whipple, July 25, 1853, AMAA; *AM* 3, 4, and 7 (Mar. 1849): 45, (July 1850): 77-78, (Sept. 1853): 91; AMA, *Eighth Annual Report*, 73-74 (1st quotation); Fee to American Tract Society, n.d., in *AMM* 3 (Sept. 1859): 200-1 (2d quotation).

   31. Fee to Lewis Tappan, June 10, 1847, Dec. 27, 1848, Aug. 4, 1851, Fee to Whipple, Mar. 8, 1849 (quotation), Aug. 20, 1850, Sept. 24, 1852; Crooks to Lee, Oct. 2, 1849, in *TW*, Oct. 20, 1849; McBride to *TW*, n.d., in *NASS*, June 6, 1850; Sears, *Day of Small Things*, 113; *AM* 3 and 4 (Mar. 1849): 45, (July 1850): 77-78; AMA, *Eighth Annual Report*, 73-74; AFASS, *Address to the Non-Slaveholders of the South*; AFASS, *[11th] Annual Report*, 68.

   32. Fee to Tappan, June 10, 1847, Stephen Blanchard to Jocelyn, May 18, 1850, AMAA; Sears, *Day of Small Things*, 113; C.H. Johnson, "AMA," 450; *NE*, Sept. 16, 1858; Helper, *Impending Crisis*. Helper's book masked its author's bitter racism and included a good deal of moral denunciation of slavery. Preferences aside, Fee did not hesitate to appeal to white economic and social interests against slavery. See Fee to Mr. Editor, Sept. 16, 1847, in *LE*, Oct. 2, 1847; AMA, *Eleventh Annual Report*, 67.

   33. TRAVELER [Crooks] to Lee, n.d., in *TW*, Nov. 13, 1847 (1st-3d quotations); Crooks to Lee, n.d., in *TW*, Aug. 12, 1848; E. Mathews, *Autobiography*, 374-76; Fee to Whipple, Oct. 15, 1851, Wilson to Whipple, Nov. 1, 1853 (4th quotation), AMAA; Fee to Cassius M. Clay, Apr. 18, 1856, Apr. 17, 1857, Fee-Clay Correspondence.

   34. Gerrit Smith, "Address to the Slaves," in *NASS*, Feb. 24, 1842; Owen Lovejoy to [?], n.d., in *AM* 2 (Jan. 1848): 19 (1st quotation); C.H. Johnson, "Abolitionist Missionary Activities," 299-300; McBride to Lee, May 13, 1851, in *TW*, June 7, 1851; Fee to Whipple, Mar. 1851, Worth and Vestal to Jocelyn, July 15, 1859, AMAA; AFASS, *[11th] Annual Report*, 77; Worth to [Whipple], Nov. 9, 1857, in *AMM* 2 (Jan. 1858): 21-22; Worth to *Wesleyan*, n.d., in *AMM*, 2 (Oct.

1858): 257; C.H. Johnson, "AMA," 527; McBride to Lee, June 31 [*sic*], 1851, in *Liberator*, Aug. 15, 1851 (2d quotation).

35. *AMM* 1-3 (Jan. 1857): 7-8, (Sept. 1858): 232-33, (Nov. 1858): 281, (May 1859): 112, 114, (July 1859): 162 (1st quotation); Fee to Lewis Tappan, July 28, 1851 (3d quotation), Fee to Whipple, Aug. 11, 1851 (2d quotation), James S. Davis to Jocelyn, Dec. 5, 1856, George Candee to Jocelyn, Dec. 2, 1858, Fee to Jocelyn, Dec. 4, 11, 1858, John A.R. Rogers to Jocelyn, Dec. 28, 1858, AMAA; AMA, *Eleventh Annual Report*, 64-65, *Twelfth Annual Report*, 68, and *Thirteenth Annual Report*, 58.

36. McKivigan, "Gospel Will Burst the Bonds of the Slave," 62-64, 77; *Emancipator*, Apr. 8-June 17, 1846, Feb. 10-Oct. 20, 1847; *Liberator*, Feb. 27, 1857; AFASS, *[7th] Annual Report*, 9; *AP*, Dec. 29, 1847; *AM* 2 and 3 (Apr. 1848): 46-47, 3 (Nov. 1848): 7, (June 1849): 70, (July 1849): 76-77; C.H. Johnson, "AMA," 447-49. On the development of the colporteur system in Kentucky: Fee to Whipple, Mar. 8, 1849, Fee to Lewis Tappan, Oct. 30, 1849, AMAA; AMA, *Third-Ninth Annual Reports*.

37. *Emancipator*, June 17, 1846 (1st and 2d quotations); AFASS, *[9th] Annual Report*, 6-10 (3d quotation). The *Emancipator* frequently described the scheme without reference to abolition.

38. Critics: *Emancipator*, June 17, 1846; AFASS, *[7th] Annual Report*, 27; *NS*, Jan. 14, 1848; Blassingame, *Douglass Papers*, 2:176-88. Douglass's experience as a slave in Maryland suggests that literacy was more obtainable for slaves in the border region than he later claimed as a Garrisonian ideologue in the late 1840s. See McFeely, *Douglass*, 30, 50; For examples of colporteurs' reports, see AMA, *Third Annual Report*, 30, and *Ninth Annual Report*, 73, 78-79.

39. James M. West to [?], Dec. 6, 1854 (1st quotation), Clarke to Jocelyn, Nov. 19, 1854 (3d quotation), AMAA; AMA, *Fourth Annual Report*, 11 (2d quotation). On slaves learning of sympathetic whites: Matilda H. Fee, "Thank Them for the Bible," *OE*, Mar. 4, 1857. On the charges against the colporteurs: Haines to Whipple, June 10, Dec. 5, 1850, Fee to Whipple, June 12, 1850, Aug. 17, 26, 1853; James M. West to Whipple, Sept. 1, 1853, R.G. Williams to Editor, Aug. 27, 1853, clipping, AMAA; Cassius M. Clay, "To the People of Kentucky," Sept. 2, 1853, in *Liberator*, Sept. 30, 1853; AMA, *Ninth Annual Report*, 73. Richard D. Sears chronicles the backgrounds and activities of the AMA colporteurs. See Sears, *Day of Small Things*, 113-39.

40. Fee to E.C. Allen, June 25, 1844[5], Chase Papers, LC; *Cincinnati Morning Herald*, quoted in *AP*, July 2, 1845; Fee to Whipple, June 12, 1850, Fee to Jocelyn, Jan. 22, 1855 (quotation), AMAA; Lewis Tappan to Jacob Bigelow, Dec. 3, 6, 1855, lt. bk. copy, Tappan Papers; Still, *Underground Railroad*, 150-52, 174-79; AMA, *Thirteenth Annual Report*, 54; TRAVELER [Crooks] to Lee, n.d., in *TW*, Nov. 13, 1847; McBride to Mr. Editor, Oct. 4, 1852, in *Liberator*, Oct. 29, 1852.

41. Crooks to Lee, Oct. 23, 1847, in *TW*, Nov. 13, 1847; Hawley to Jocelyn, Aug. 17 (1st quotation), Sept. 20, 1854; Stephen Blanchard to Jocelyn, Sept. 27,

1859, Jan. 1, 1861, Worth, "For the New York Tribune," ms. n.d., AMAA; AMA, *Fifth Annual Report,* 43 (2d quotation) and *Seventh Annual Report*, 59. On the South's reputation as the most violent region of the country, see Bruce, *Violence and Culture*, 3-18.

42. Clay to Fee, July 8, 1855, Fee-Clay Correspondence (1st and 2d quotations); *AMM* 2 (Oct. 1848): 257 (3d quotation); Pool to Jocelyn, May 5, 1859, AMAA; C.H. Johnson, "AMA," 537-38.

43. Nicholson, *Wesleyan Methodism in the South,* 32-75; McBride to Lee, Aug. 2, 1851, in *TW*, Aug. 16, 1851 (quotation) Crooks to Lee, Aug. 24, 1851, in *TW*, Sept. 31, 1851; E. Crooks, *Crooks*, 42-111; McBride to [Lee], Apr. 30, 1851, in *PF*, May 29, 1851; McBride to Mr. Editor, June 11, 1852, in *Liberator*, July 23, 1852; Daniel Wilson to Whipple, June 22, July 22, 1852, Mar. 30, 1853, May 19, 1855, Worth to Whipple, Jan. 1, 1858, AMAA.

44. *TA*, July 22, 1846; Fee to Lewis Tappan, Nov. 17, 1846, in *AM* 1 (Jan. 1847): 23-24; Fee to Tappan, Oct. 30, 1849, Fee to Whipple, Mar., June 13, July 3, 1850, McLain to Jocelyn, [May 1857] (2d and 3d quotations), AMAA; Fee to Cassius M. Clay, Jan. 19, 1858, Fee-Clay Correspondence (1st quotation). The best sense of the intensity and pervasiveness of anti-abolitionist violence in Kentucky is gained by reading the correspondence in the Kentucky file of the AMAA.

45. *ASR* 1 (Nov. 1835): 121-23; *Emancipator*, July 7, 1836; McBride to *TW*, May 6, [1851], in *NASS*, June 5, 1851; *Liberator*, Aug. 14, 1857; *Cincinnati Gazette*, quoted in *ASB*, Jan. 14, 1860; Crooks to Lee, Oct. 18, 1850, in *TW*, Nov. 9, 1850; C.H. Johnson, "AMA," 530, 555; Pool to Jocelyn, May 4, 1859, Wilson to Whipple, June 22, July 22, 1852, May 19, 1855, AMAA; *NYTr*, Apr. 12, May 8, 1860.

46. Peter H. West to Whipple, Dec. 25, 1853, AMAA (quotation); McBride to *TW*, May 6, [1851], in *NASS*, June 5, 1851; McBride to Lee, June 31, 1851, in *Liberator*, Aug. 15, 1851; Crooks to Lee, Aug. 24, 1851, in *TW*, Sept. 13, 1851; Nicholson, *Wesleyan Methodism in the South,* 49-71; Wyatt-Brown, *Southern Honor*, 435-61; Harrold, "Violence and Nonviolence in Kentucky Abolitionism," 17-18.

47. Harrold, "Violence and Nonviolence in Kentucky Abolitionism," 26-38; Fee, "Mt. Vernon Resolutions vs. Free Speech," broadside, July 18, 1855 (1st and 2d quotations), Fee to Jocelyn, July 15, 1857 (3d quotation), AMAA; C.H. Johnson, "AMA," 548-49; Tallant, "Slavery Controversy in Kentucky," 311-13.

48. Worth to Tappan, Apr. 3, 1860, AMAA (1st quotation); McBride to *TW*, May 6 [1851], in *NASS*, June 5, 1851; *OE*, Apr. 11, 1855; Wilson to Jocelyn, July 25, 1855 (2d and 3d quotations), Pool to Jocelyn, Apr. 20, 1859 (4th quotation), Fee to Jocelyn, [Feb. 5, 1858], AMAA; *AMM* 2 (June 1858): 138-39; Fee to Gerrit Smith, Mar. 29, 1862, Smith Papers (5th quotation); Fee to Cassius M. Clay, July 25, 1886, Fee-Clay Correspondence; Candee to Jocelyn, Mar. 14, 1861, AMA (6th quotation).

49. McBride to Lee, Mar. 26, 1851, in *TW*, Apr. 12, 1851 (1st quotation). On divine providence: Fee to Lewis Tappan, Nov. 17, 1846, in *AM* 1 (Jan. 1847): 23-

24; Alfred Vestal to Jocelyn, Oct. 19, 1859, AMAA. On the need to maintain northern support: AMA, *Fifth Annual Report*, 43, and *Twelfth Annual Report*, 51. On small victories: Fee to Whipple, Apr. 10, 1850, Worth to Jocelyn, Apr. 19, 1858, AMAA; McBride to Lee, Mar. 26, 1851, in *TW*, Apr. 12, 1851. On martyrdom: E. Mathews, *Autobiography*, 324; *OE*, July 4, 1855; Worth to Lewis Tappan, Nov. 26, 1859, AMAA (2d quotation).

50. AFASS, *[10th] Annual Report*, 57-59; *NE*, May 9, 1850, Sept. 16, 1858; *PF*, May 29, Aug. 12 (1st quotation), 1851; *NASS*, Aug. 1, 1857; *ASB*, Aug. 15, 1857 (2d quotation).

51. *Principia*, Jan. 7, 1860; *OE*, Aug. 18, 1858; Goodell to Fee, Aug. 6, 1857, Fee Papers; Goodell to Gerrit Smith, June 8, 1851, Smith Papers; AMA, *Ninth Annual Report*, 77; *AMM* 1 and 2 (June 1857): 21, (Nov. 1858): 280; AASS, *Second Annual Report*, 46 (quotation). The earliest version of this taunt that I find is in *Emancipator*, May 18, 1833; the latest is in *NYTr*, May 8, 1860.

52. *American Citizen*, quoted in *Emancipator*, Sept. 9, 1846; ibid., May 26, 1847; MASS, *Fifth Annual Report*, v; *NASS*, June 5, 1851; *Independent*, quoted in *OE*, Apr. 29, 1857; Wendell Phillips, "The Constitution—The Irrepressible Conflict," in *ASB*, Mar. 10, 1860; W.L. Garrison, *"New Reign of Terror,"* iii; O. Johnson, *Garrison*, 39-42, 217-19; W.P. Garrison and F.J. Garrison, *Garrison*, 3:379.

53. Wyatt-Brown, "Abolitionists' Postal Campaign," 237-38; W.W. Freehling, *Road to Disunion*, 1:383, 455-74; Dumond, *Antislavery Origins of the Civil War,* 53-54; Stewart, *Holy Warriors*, 70; Walters, *Antislavery Appeal*, 131-32; Friedman, *Gregarious Saints*, 4-5.

6. ANTISLAVERY COLONIES IN THE UPPER SOUTH
1. Underwood to Johnson, Apr. 14, 1859, in *NASS*, May 7, 1859.

2. G.W. Smith, "Ante-Bellum Attempts," 177-213. See also Gerteis, "Slavery and Hard Times," 317-19.

3. Foner, *Free Soil*, 40-70; Sewell, *Ballots for Freedom*, 314-20; Current, *Northernizing the South,* 32-41.

4. S.A. Johnson, *Battle Cry of Freedom,* esp. 8-9; O.K. Rice, "Thayer," 587-88, 595-96; G.W. Smith, "Ante-Bellum Attempts," 191-92, 206-7; Thayer to James Gordon Bennett, Mar. 12, Apr. 23, 1857, in *NYH*, Mar. 30, Apr. 25, 1857; Thayer, *Kansas Crusade*, 88-116, 146-62, 189-201; Filler, *Crusade against Slavery, 238-39*; Hickin, "Antislavery in Virginia," 636-37, 654-55, 671-72; Franklin P. Rice, "Thayer," chap. 20:1; chap. 21:5, 12-14, chap. 24:10-11. Franklin P. Rice wrote his unpublished biography of Thayer during the late nineteenth or early twentieth century. There is no modern biography of Thayer.

5. Walters, *Antislavery Appeal*, 70-81, 111-28, 137-40; D.G. Mathews, "Abolitionists on Slavery," 180; Floan, *South in Northern Eyes*, 7-35.

6. Benson, *Concept of Jacksonian Democracy,* 89-109, 212-13; Sorin, *New York Abolitionists*, 3-17; Stewart, *Holy Warriors*, 37-41; Friedman, *Gregarious Saints*, 11-44, 69-70, 88-99, 225-52; Alan M. Kraut, "The Forgotten Reformers: A Profile

of Third Party Abolitionists in Antebellum New York," in Perry and Fellman, *Antislavery Reconsidered*, 119-45; Hickin, "Underwood and the Antislavery Crusade," 3-21; Underwood to Gerrit Smith, Jan. 13, 1842, Smith Papers. See also Cross, *Burned-over District.*

7. Hickin, "Underwood and the Antislavery Crusade," 18, 22-24, 41-43; Underwood to Smith, Jan. 13, 1842, Mar. 4, 1848, June 10, 1850 (quotation), Oct. 22, 1850, Smith Papers.

8. Hickin, "Underwood and the Antislavery Crusade," 11-13, 25-26, 31-32, "Underwood and the Antislavery Movement in Virginia," 157-58, and "Antislavery in Virginia," 617-24; Underwood to Gerrit Smith, Jan. 13, 1842, Oct. 22, 1850 (quotation), Smith Papers.

9. Eaton, *Freedom-of-Thought Struggle*, 258-59; G.W. Smith, "Ante-Bellum Attempts," 187-88; Smith to Channing, Sept. 6, 1841, lt. bk. copy, Smith Papers; *AP*, Mar. 27, 1844, Nov. 19, Dec. 10, 1845. The 1841 effort in Virginia inspired at least one native southern abolitionist. See [Janney], *Yankees in Fairfax County.*

10. Underwood to Smith, Oct. 22, 1850 (quotation), June 3, 1851; Smith to Channing, Sept. 6, 1841, lt. bk. copy, Smith Papers; YANKEE to the editor of the *New England Farmer*, n.d., in *Liberator*, Dec. 6, 1844. On the tendencies of northern emigrants to adopt southern views and the impact of the South on northern abolitionists who moved there: Current, *Northernizing the South*, 35-37; Eaton, *Freedom-of-Thought Struggle*, 264-65; Underwood, "Republicans and the Slave States. Speech . . . at Belton, Virginia, Oct. 17, 1860," in *NYTr*, Oct. 23, 1860.

11. Underwood to Smith, June 10, 1850, Jan. 3, 1851 (quotation), Smith Papers; Hickin, "Underwood and the Antislavery Crusade," 35-36, 41; Underwood to William K. Strong, Jan. 1, 1857, in *NASS*, Jan. 10, 1857; Underwood to the editor of the *NYTi*, [Jan. 12, 1857], in *NASS.*, Feb. 21, 1857; Underwood to Cornelia Barbour, July 9, 1860, in *NASS.*, July 28, 1860; Underwood to [?], Apr. 5, 1852, unidentified newspaper clipping, scrapbook, p. 4, Underwood Papers, LC; Underwood to the editor of the *NASS*, Aug. 20, 1858, in *NASS*, Aug. 28, 1858.

12. Underwood to Smith, Oct. 22, 1850, June 3, 1851 (quotations), Smith Papers.

13. Hickin, "Antislavery in Virginia," 629-30; Underwood to Seward, Mar. 24, 1856, Seward Papers; unidentified newspaper clipping, n.d., scrapbook, p. 1, Underwood Papers (quotations).

14. The fullest account of these events is in Hickin, "Underwood and the Antislavery Crusade," 53-57, 63 (quotation). On Underwood's status as a hero among abolitionists: *ASB*, July 12, 19, 1856; *Liberator*, Aug. 15, 29, 1856, Dec. 19, 1856. On his separation from his family: Underwood to Thayer, Mar. 11, 1857 (2 lts.), Thayer Papers. On his campaign orientation and his desire for Republican support: *NYTr*, July 12, 17, 19, Aug. 30, Sept. 5, 1856; Underwood to T. S. Sizer, Aug. 14, 1856, in *NASS*, Sept. 6, 1856; Underwood to [?], Dec. 16, 1856, in *NASS*, Jan. 3, 1857; Underwood to Thayer, Feb. 7, 1857, Thayer Papers.

15. Underwood to the editors of the *NYTi* [Jan. 12, 1857], in *NASS*, Feb. 21,

1857; Berlin, *Slaves without Masters*, 351-52; G.W. Smith, "Ante-Bellum Attempts," 191-94, 210-11; F.P. Rice, "Thayer," chap. 20:1, 5, 11-12, chap. 21:12-14, chap. 36:2-3; Hickin, "Antislavery in Virginia," 635-51; Hickin, "Underwood and the Antislavery Crusade," 161-63; Underwood to Thayer, Feb. 7, Mar. 9, 11(2), 13, 21, 28, Apr. 1, 6, 11, 1847, Thayer Papers.

16. G.W. Smith, "Ante-Bellum Attempts," 194; F.P. Rice, "Thayer," chap. 20:14n, 21, chap. 21:4, 7-22, chap. 36:1-13; Hickin, "Antislavery in Virginia," 639-59; O.K. Rice, "Thayer," 591-95; *NYH*, Apr. 21, 1857; Underwood to editor, May 13, 1857, in *NASS*, May 23, 1857; Hickin, "Underwood and the Antislavery Movement in Virginia," 164-65; Thayer to Bennett, Apr. 23, 1857, in *NYH*, Apr. 25, 1857; Daniel R. Goodloe to Thayer, Aug. 4, 1858, Thayer Papers; Thayer to Bennett, Mch 12, 1857, in *NASS*, Apr. 4, 1857; McClintic, "Ceredo," 168-90, 198-200, 233-54. Numerous letters in the Thayer papers are from prospective colonists.

17. O.K. Rice, "Thayer," 586-91; G.W. Smith, "Ante-Bellum Attempts," 209-10; F.P. Rice, "Thayer," chap. 21:20-22; Underwood to Thayer, June 4, 1847, Thayer Papers; Underwood to William H. Seward, Jan. 26, Feb. 2, Nov. 12, 1858, Seward Papers.

18. *Ceredo Crescent*, Jan. 15, 1859; G.W. Smith, "Ante-Bellum Attempts," 177-86, 194, 200-202; Foner, *Free Soil*, 40-71; Underwood to [?], Dec. 16, 1856, in *NASS*, Jan. 3, 1857; Underwood to the editors of the *NYTi*, [Jan. 12, 1857], in *NASS*, Feb. 21, 1857; Thayer to Bennett, Mar. 12, 1857, in *NASS*, Apr. 4, 1857 (1st and 2d quotations); Thayer to Bennett, Apr. 23, 1857, in *NYH*, Apr. 25, 1857 (3d quotation); F.P. Rice, "Thayer," chap. 21:13 (4th and 5th quotations); *NYH*, Apr. 21 (6th quotation), 25, 1857; Hickin, "Antislavery in Virginia," 653-54. Letters of inquiry concerning Ceredo are typically from people considering investment or a new start in business. See for example: W. Boyd Wilson to Thayer, July 2, 1857, Benjamin White to Thayer, Mar. 22, 1859, Wilkinson Edes to Thayer, July 30, 1859, Thayer Papers.

19. *Point Pleasant Republican* quoted in F.P. Rice, "Thayer," chap. 21:15-16 (1st quotation); Hickin, "Antislavery in Virginia," 644-46; *Star* and *South* quoted in *Liberator*, Apr. 17, 1857 (2d and 3d quotations); *South Side Democrat* quoted in F.P. Rice, "Thayer," chap. 20:14-15 (4th quotation); *Whig* quoted in *NYH*, Mar. 10, 1857 (5th-7th quotations); W.W. Freehling, *Road to Disunion*, 1:455-74. See also Eaton, "Resistance of the South to Northern Radicalism," 228.

20. Hickin, "Antislavery in Virginia," 637-40, 648-59; G.W. Smith, "Ante-Bellum Attempts," 194; Underwood to the editors of the *NYTi*, [Jan. 12, 1857], in *NASS*, Feb. 21, 1857 (1st quotation); Underwood, "Republicans and the Slave States" in *NYTr*, Oct. 23, 1860 (2d quotation); Thayer to Bennett, Mar. 12, 1857, in *NASS*, Apr. 4, 1857 (3d quotation); F.P. Rice, "Thayer," chap. 20:16-19, chap. 21:13 (4th quotation), 18-20. See also Underwood to Samuel M. Janney, Aug. 9, 1856, Janney Papers; Thayer to Bennett, Apr. 23, 1847, in *NYH*, Apr. 25, 1857; Thayer, "Suicide of Slavery," speech delivered in Congress, Mar. 25, 1858, in F.P. Rice, "Thayer," chap. 24:10-12.

21. Underwood to Thayer, Feb. 7, 1857 (1st quotation), Mar. 9, 1857 (2d quotation), Thayer Papers; Thayer to Bennett, Mar. 12, 1857, in *NYH*, Mar. 30, 1857 (3d-6th quotations).

22. For examples of emphasis on action over rhetoric, see Sanborn, *Brown*, 131; Thayer to F.P. Rice, Apr. 20, 1888, enclosing a ms. copy of Theodore Parker's speech of Jan. 29, 1858, Thayer Papers.

23. Underwood to Thayer, Mar. 11, 1857, Thayer Papers; Garrison to Helen B. Garrison, May 13, 1857, in Merrill and Ruchames, *Garrison Letters,* 4:438 (quotation); Hickin, "Antislavery in Virginia," 667; Gerrit Smith to Sarah Pugh, Apr. 5, 1847, in *AP*, Apr. 14, 1847; Dillon, *Abolitionists*, 230-31; *Liberator*, Apr. 10, 1857.

24. Thayer to Gerrit Smith, Mar. 6, Aug. 13, 1856, Oct. 8, 1858, Smith Papers; Smith to Thayer, May 7, 1856, [Thayer] to the editors of the *Sun*, Jan. 4, 1888, Thayer Papers; Thayer, *Kansas Crusade*, 89-111, 115, 189-201; Harlow, *Smith*, 343-51; Tappan to Thayer, Jan. 15, 1856, lt. bk. copy, Tappan Papers; Sanborn, *Brown*, 380-85. Historians generally agree that while the Emigrant Aid Company had negligible direct impact on the Kansas struggle, it influenced popular opinion in the North and South. See, for example, Gienapp, *Origins of the Republican Party,* 168-69.

25. Thayer to Smith, Apr. 27, 1857, Smith Papers; Thayer to Brown, Mar. 30, Apr. 14, 1857, in Sanborn, *Brown*, 381-83 (quotations); Gerrit Smith, "Address to the Slaves," *NASS*, Feb. 24, 1842.

26. Smith to Channing, Sept. 6, 1841, Smith Papers (1st quotation); YANKEE to the editor of the *New England Farmer*, n.d., in *Liberator*, Dec. 6, 1844 (2d and 3d quotations). See also Negro Stealer, "Emigration to the South," *AP*, Mar. 24, 1844.

27. *NASS*, Mar. 14, 1857 (quotations), Apr. 4, 1857; Child to Underwood, Dec. 6, 1860, in Patricia G. Holland and Milton Meltzer, eds., "The Collected Correspondence of Lydia Maria Child . . . Microfilm Edition" (Millwood, N.Y.: Krang, 1980), (hereafter cited as "Child Collected Correspondence"); Resolutions of the 24th Anniversary Meeting of the AASS, in *NASS*, May 16, 1857; Wendell Phillips's speech at this meeting, in *NASS*, May 23, 1857; *Milwaukee Free Democrat*, quoted in *NASS*, May 2, 1857.

28. Smith to Thayer, Oct. 16, 1858, Underwood to Thayer, Mar. 11, 1857 (quotation), [Thayer] to the editor of the *Sun*, Jan. 4, 1888, Thayer Papers; Underwood to Smith, May 2, 1863, Smith Papers; Thayer, *Kansas Crusade*, 88-196.

29. *NASS*, June 10, 1854 (1st quotation), Feb. 21, Mar. 14, Apr. 4, May 2, 23, 1857, May 7, 1859; *Liberator*, Apr. 17, 24 (2d and 3d quotations, 1857). By taking material out of context, historians tend to miss nineteenth-century sarcasm. For claims that the quoted phrase from the *Liberator* constituted opposition to the Virginia colonization scheme, see G.W. Smith, "Ante-Bellum Attempts," 207; and Hickin, "Underwood and the Antislavery Movement in Virginia," 163.

30. Harrold, *Bailey*, 13, 84-88; *DNCB* (4 vols. to date; Chapel Hill: Univ. of North Carolina Press, 1979-91), s.v. "Goodloe, Daniel Reeves"; Degler, *Other*

South, 29, 419-53; *CWHP*, Apr. 16, 1845, Jan. 28, 1846; *NE*, Nov. 25, 1847, Mar. 16, Oct. 12, 1848, Aug. 24, 1854 (quotations), Jan. 1, Apr. 9-Nov. 19, 1857, Feb. 18, May 7, Sept. 16, Dec. 30, 1858, Jan. 27, 1859, Mar. 1, 1860.

31. Harrold, *Bailey*, 94-215. There is no study of second-generation immediatists as a group. See Edelstein, *Strange Enthusiasm*; Fellman, "Parker," 666-84; Higginson to Gerrit Smith, June 24, 1858, Smith Papers; Commager, *Parker*; Fredrickson, *Black Image in the White Mind,* 119-21; Friedman, *Gregarious Saints*, 207, 220-21; Foner, *Free Soil*, 302-3.

32. Sanborn, *Brown*, 163; Filler, *Crusade against Slavery*, 238; Underwood to Thayer, Feb. 16, 1857, Stearns to Thayer, Apr. 6, 1857, Thayer Papers. These same individuals were among the secret supporters of Brown's plan to invade the South. Howe and Stearns are often categorized as Republicans rather than immediatists, although it is a close call. See Rossbach, *Ambivalent Conspirators*, 3 and passim; Stewart, *Holy Warriors*, 154-59, 172, 184; Friedman, *Gregarious Saints*, 244; McPherson, *Struggle for Equality*, esp. 6.

33. *NASS*, May 27, 1854, May 16, 1857; Higginson, "Anti-Slavery Days," 47-57; Fellman, "Parker," 678-84; "Speech of Rev. Theodore Parker, Delivered in the Massachusetts Representatives Hall . . . Jan. 29, 1858," in *Liberator*, Feb. 26, 1858 (quotations); Parker to Thayer, Feb. 26, Apr. 5, 1858, in Thayer, *Kansas Crusade*, xvi-xviii.

34. *LE*, July 10, 1847; Coleman, *Slavery Times in Kentucky,* 239-41; *By-Laws of the Webster Kentucky Farm Association*; Webster to Tappan, Mar. 24, 1858, AMAA; Webster to Rev. Dr. Cheever, Oct. 19, 1855, in *FDP*, Dec. 7, 1857.

35. Fee to Dear Brother, Nov. 9, 1855, in *AM* 10 (Dec. 1855):13-14; Cassius M. Clay to Fee, Dec. 18, 1855, Fee-Clay Correspondence; Fee to Simeon S. Jocelyn, Dec. 1856, Fee Papers, quoted in Reynolds, "AMA's Antislavery Campaign in Kentucky," 101 (1st quotation); Fee, "Emigration to Kentucky," *AMM* 1 (Jan. 1857): 20-21; Fee, "A College in Kentucky—Needed," *AMM* 1 (May 1857): 104-5; Davis to [Jocelyn], June 20, 1857, in *AMM* 1 (Aug. 1857): 189; Fee to [Jocelyn], Nov. 24, 1857, in *AMM* 2 (Jan. 1858): 20-21; Fee to *NYTr*, Aug. 17, 1857, in *NASS*, Sept. 12, 1857; Candee to Jocelyn, Aug. 12, 1858, AMAA (2d quotation). See also Tallant, "Slavery Controversy in Kentucky," 353-54.

36. Fee to Smith, Jan. 4, 1856, Mar. 10, 1859, Smith Papers; Sears, *Day of Small Things*, 159-63; Fee, "Emigration to Kentucky," 20-21 (1st quotation); Fee, "College in Kentucky," 65-67; Davis, "Shall Kentucky be Free? Emigration Thither," *AMM* 1 (Apr. 1857): 79-80; [Rogers], "Kentucky, Come and See," *AMM* 2 (Oct. 1858): 257-58; John C. Richardson to [Jocelyn], Sept. 16, 1859, in *AMM* 4 (Jan. 1860): 18-19; Fee to Jocelyn, May 1857, West to Jocelyn, Dec. 22, 1857 (2d quotation), AMAA; Fee to *NYTr*, Aug. 17, 1857, in *NASS*, Sept. 12, 1857.

37. Fee, "Emigration to Kentucky," 20-21 (1st quotation); Davis, "Shall Kentucky be Free?" 79-80; Fee to Dear Brother, Nov. 9, 1855, in *AM* 10 (Dec. 1855): 13-14; Fee to [Jocelyn], Mar. 23, 1857, in *AMM* 1 (May 1857): 117 (2d quotation); Waters, "A Christian Colony in Kentucky," *AMM* 1 (May 1857): 104-5 (3d quotation).

38. Davis, "Shall Kentucky Be Free?" 79-80; Waters, "Christian Colony," 104-5 (1st and 3d quotations); Fee to Dear Brother, Nov. 9, 1855, in *AM* 10 (Dec. 1855): 13-14; Davis to [Jocelyn], Feb 28, 1857, in *AMM* 1 (Apr. 1857): 77-78 (2d quotation); Fee, "Emigration to Kentucky," 20-21; Fee, "College in Kentucky," 65-67; Fee to Jocelyn, Apr. 4, 1857, [May 1857], W.E. Lincoln to [Jocelyn], [Oct. 1857], George Candee to Jocelyn, May 12, 1858, AMAA; Rogers, "Kentucky, Come and See," 257-58.

39. McKivigan, *War against Proslavery Religion*, 114-17; C.H. Johnson, "AMA," 181-82, 247-96; AMA, *[9th-12th] Annual Reports*, 9:74, 10:71-72, 11:65, 12:51; *AM* 10 (Dec. 1855)-*AMM* 4 (Jan. 1860).

40. *NASS*, Dec. 15, 1855 (1st quotation); Boynton to Jocelyn, Sept. 15, 1854, AMAA (2d quotation); Fee to Clay, Oct. 21, 1857, Fee-Clay Correspondence (3d quotation); S.A. Johnson, *Battle Cry of Freedom,* 69; R. to Editors, n.d., in *Independent*, Sept. 23, 1858 (4th quotation).

41. Davis, "Shall Kentucky Be Free?" 79; Fee to Jocelyn, Apr. 4, 1857, AMAA; Davis to [Jocelyn], June 29, 1857, in *AMM* 1 (Aug. 1857): 189; Reynolds, "Antislavery Campaign in Kentucky," 113-14; Rogers, "Kentucky, Come and See," 257-58; Tappan to Fee, May 26, 1857, lt. bk. copy, Tappan Papers (quotation); Sears, *Day of Small Things*, 266-70; Fee to Dear Brother, Nov. 9, 1855, in *AM* 10 (Dec. 1855): 13-14; Fee to Jocelyn, June 2, [1857], AMAA.

42. On assaults: *Independent*, July 30, Sept. 10, 1857; *NASS*, Aug. 1, 15, Sept. 5, 1857; *ASB*, Aug. 15, 1857; *Liberator*, Aug. 14, 1857; *NE*, Sept. 3, 1857. On the missionaries assurances of safety: Fee to Jocelyn, Aug. 1857, AMAA; Fee, "Emigration to Kentucky," 21; and Waters, "Christian Colony," 104-5. On the missionaries realization that northerners would not emigrate into such circumstances: West to Jocelyn, Dec. 22, 1857 (1st quotation), Fee to Jocelyn, [Feb. 5, 1858] (3d quotation), AMAA; Fee to editor, Aug. 15, 1857, in *NE*, Sept. 3, 1857 (2d quotation); Fee to *NYTr*, Aug. 17, 1857, in *NASS*, Sept. 12, 1857. On Carpetbaggers during Reconstruction: Degler, *Other South*, 258-60; Foner, *Reconstruction*, 294-97.

43. Lincoln to Whipple, [Oct. 1857], in *AMM* 1 (Nov. 1857): 259.

44. Sears, *Day of Small Things*, 269-70, 296; *ASB*, Jan. 14, 1860 (quotation). The numbers of colonists from the North may be greater than Sears indicates. In 1860 the AMA reported that "a number of families from Ohio and elsewhere were drawn to the place," and Tallant claims, without documentation, that "Berea started to attract a trickle of northern settlers" in late 1855, four years before Sears indicates. See AMA, *Fourteenth Annual Report*, 48; Tallant, "Slavery Controversy in Kentucky," 354.

45. Thayer to Jocelyn, Sept. 16, 1854, AMAA (1st and 2d quotations); Fee to Cassius M. Clay, Oct. 21, 1857, Fee-Clay Correspondence; *Ceredo Crescent*, Jan. 15, 1859; "Annual Meeting, at Worcester, Mass.," in *AMM* 2 (Nov. 1858): 267; Massachusetts to editors, Oct. 11, 1858, in *Independent*, Nov. 4, 1858 (3d and 4th quotations); Thomas C. Upham to Thayer, Apr. 27, 1859, Thayer Papers (5th quotation); Underwood, "Republicans in the Slave States," *NYTr,* Oct. 23, 1860.

7. THE INTERSECTIONAL POLITICS OF SOUTHERN ABOLITIONISM
1. Fee to Julian, Nov. 9, 1852, Joshua R. Giddings-George W. Julian Papers,
LC (quotations); Sewell, *Ballots for Freedom*, 310-14; Blue, *Free Soilers*, 129-30;
Abbott, *Republican Party and the South,* 3-19; *AP*, Feb. 14, 1844, Aug. 26, 1846; *RA*
3 (Aug. 1857): 2-3.
2. Harrold, "Clay and the Garrisonians," 101-19; *TA*, July 8, 15, 1846; Fee to
Clay, Oct. 12, 1844, Fee-Clay Correspondence; *BSV*, Oct. 12, 1844; Clay to Editor
of the *Saturday Visiter*, Jan. 16, 1846, in *NASS*, Feb. 5, 1846; Clay to John C.
Vaughan, Dec. 29, 1847, Cassius M. Clay Papers, WRHS.
3. Fee: Fee to John C. Vaughan, Sept. 13, 1848, Chase Papers, LC; Martin,
Antislavery Movement in Kentucky, 130-32; *NE*, May 10, 17, 1849; Fee to Clay,
Sept. 18, 1849, Fee-Clay Correspondence; Fee to George Whipple, Mar., July 28,
1851, AMAA. Snodgrass: Snodgrass to Editor, Oct. 4, 1848, in *NE*, Oct. 19, 1848;
NE, Oct. 21, 1852, Mar. 15, 1855; *FDP*, Nov. 5, 1852; S.A. Johnson, *Battle Cry of
Freedom,* 67. Bailey: Steely, "Bailey," 274-81.
4. Harrold, *Bailey*; Hickin, "Underwood and the Antislavery Movement in
Virginia," 156-68.
5. M.S. to Cassius M. Clay, Mar. 4, 1846, in *NASS*, Apr. 23, 1846; *LE*, Mar. 3,
1849; P.H. West to Simeon S. Jocelyn, June 2, 1857, George Candee to Jocelyn,
Mar. 2, 1858, Fee to Jocelyn, May 1859, Gamble to Lewis Tappan, Aug. 3, 1852,
Nov. 28, 1856, AMAA; Daniel Keller to James Harlan, Aug. 13, 1856, Blair Family
Papers, LC; Janney to Horace Mann, Oct. 10, 1848, Mann Papers; *AM* 10 (Sept.
1856): 84-85.
6. Goodloe, ms. autobiography, Daniel R. Goodloe Papers, UNC; Lewis
Tappan to Gamaliel Bailey, Nov. 6, 1848, lt. bk. copy, Tappan Papers; *NE*, July 12,
Aug. 8, 1849, Feb. 3, May 12, 1853, Aug. 23, 1855; Goodloe to Lyman Trumbull,
June 15, Sept. 24, 1857, Lyman Trumbull Papers, LC; *DNCB*, s.v. "Goodloe, Daniel
R."; Clephane to Salmon P. Chase, Oct. 31, 1859, Chase Papers, LC; Mayer, *Republican Party*, 51; Degler, *Other South*, 29. Goodloe's fellow-North Carolinian
Benjamin Hedrick gained notoriety in 1856 when he lost his professorship at the
University of North Carolina as a result of his stated preference for Republican
presidential nominee John C. Fremont. But Hedrick does not qualify as a southern political abolitionist. He had not been politically active in the antislavery cause
prior to his endorsement of Fremont, he left the South immediately after he lost
his teaching position, and he had no relationship to northern abolitionism. See
Bassett, *Anti-Slavery Leaders of North Carolina,* 29-47.
7. Lewis Tappan to Danl. R. Goodloe, H.L. Brown, and Lewis Clephane, Mar.
6, 1856, lt. bk. copy, Tappan Papers; Clephane, *Birth of the Republican Party,* 12,
23; *NE*, Mar. 6, 1856; W.E. Smith, *Blair Family*, 2:320-23; Foner, *Free Soil*, 63, 268-
70. Clephane's identification with abolitionism did on occasion place him in danger. See *NASS*, Oct. 29, 1859; Clephane, "Clephane," 267-69.
8. Lewis Tappan to John G. Fee, Feb. 29, 1856, lt. bk. copy, Tappan Papers;
RA, 3 (Mar. 1858): 57; Burritt to Francis P. Blair, June 4, 1858; Smith to Francis P.

Blair Jr., Apr. 7, 1857, Parker to Francis P. Blair Jr., July 26, 1858, Blair Family Papers; *NASS*, Apr. 1, 1857; Gray, "Campbell," 221-37; *Wellsburg Weekly Herald*, Sept. 5, Dec. 12, 1856, Sept. 11, 1857. See also *RA* 3 (Mar. 1858):57; *NASS*, Apr. 1, 1857.

9. Harrold, *Bailey*, 105-8; *ASB*, Mar. 3, 1860; *NE*, Feb. 21, Aug. 14, 1856; Apr. 8, 16, May 14, 1857; Apr. 1, 14, 1859; Tallant, "Slavery Controversy in Kentucky," 160-204; Robert, *Road from Monticello*; A.G. Freehling, *Drift toward Dissolution*; Howard, "Pendleton," 192-215; Keith, "Underwood," 117-32; Fredrickson, *Black Image in the White Mind,* 9-15; Remini, *Clay,* 178-82, 439-40, 617-19, 770.

10. Breckinridge to Charles Hodge, July 2, 1833, Breckinridge Family Papers, LC; *Emancipator*, Oct. 21, 1834, Aug. 11, Sept. 1, 8, 1836; Breckinridge to Payne, Peck, Portie, and others, Mar. 2, 1846, in *NASS*, Apr. 16, 1846; Breckinridge to Sumner, June 11, 1855, in *NASS*, Aug. 4, 1855; *NE*, Aug. 2, 1855; *FDP*, Aug. 3, Nov. 30, 1855; *NASS*, Sept. 8, Nov. 24, 1855; Degler, *Other South*, 78-79.

11. Harrold, "Clay and the Garrisonians," 101-19; Fee to Lewis Tappan, Oct. 30, 1849, AMAA; Snodgrass to Gerrit Smith, June 16, 1848, Smith Papers; Samuel M. Bell to Salmon P. Chase, June 6, 1844, Chase Papers, LC.

12. Fee to Editors, Feb. 20, [1849], in *LE*, Mar. 3, 1849; Fee to George Whipple, Mar. 8, 1849, Fee to Lewis Tappan, Oct. 30, 1849, AMAA; Fee to Cassius M. Clay, Aug. 17, 1849, Fee-Clay Correspondence; Steely, "Bailey," 275; Gilmore, Emery, and Bell to Friends and Fellow Citizens, n.d., in *AP*, Sept. 18, 1844; *Philanthropist*, Apr. 9, 1839; *LE*, June 19, 1847; *LE*, quoted in *NE*, May 3, 1849, Oct. 17, 1850.

13. Gerteis, "Slavery and Hard Times," 316-31; Clay, *Writings*, 187; *LE*, July 10, Aug. 7, 1847, Jan. 6 1848[9], Mar. 10, 1849; Fee to Lewis Tappan, Dec. 27, 1848, Fee to William Jay, May 23, 1854, AMAA; Clay to Salmon P. Chase, Dec. 21, 1842, Chase Papers, HSPa; Fee to Editors, Feb. 20, 1849, in *LE*, Mar. 3, 1849.

14. Clay, *Writings*, 143-44, 232-40 (quotation 233); *NASS*, June 8, 1843. See also Harrold, "Clay on Slavery," 42-56.

15. Clay, *Writings*, 92-460; *Speech of C.M. Clay, at Lexington, Ky., Delivered August 1, 1851,* 11-13; *Liberator*, May 27, 1853.

16. Alan M. Kraut, "Partisanship and Principles: The Liberty Party in Antebellum Political Culture," in Kraut, *Crusaders and Compromisers*, 72-73, 88-89; John G. Fee to Cassius M. Clay, Sept. 18, 1849, Fee-Clay Correspondence; W.W. Freehling, *Road to Disunion*, 1:472.

17. *Emancipator*, Aug. 5, 1841 (1st quotation), Jan. 21, 1846; Clay *Writings*, 59-60, 358-59 (2d and 3d quotations), 441 (4th and 5th quotations); Harrold, "Clay on Slavery," 45-46.

18. "9th Annual Meeting of the New York Anti-Slavery Society," Sept. 13, 1844, unidentified newspaper clipping, Gerrit Smith Papers; MASS, *Eleventh Annual Report,* 62-63; Fee to Clay, May 27, 1847, in *TA*, June 17, 1846; Fee to Clay, Sept. 18, 1849 (quotation), Apr. 28, 1856, Feb. 26, June 1, 1859, Fee-Clay Correspondence; Fee to George Whipple, July 28, 1851, Sept. 24, 1852, Oct. 18, 1853, Mar. 10, 1859, Fee to Simeon S. Jocelyn, Apr. 12, 1856, Feb. 9, 1859, Clay to

Executive Committee, Sept. 1853, AMAA; Fee to George W. Julian, Aug. 31, Nov. 9, 1852, Clay to Julian, Oct. 23, 1853, Giddings-Julian Papers.

19. Clay to the editors of the *LE*, Dec. 25, 1848, in *NE*, Jan. 25, 1849; *Speech of C.M. Clay at Lexington*, 2; Clay to Simeon S. Jocelyn, Dec. 17, 1859, Fee to George Whipple, Mar. 10, 1859 (quotation), AMAA. "My political opinions are part of my religion," Clay told William H. Seward. See Clay to Seward, Aug. 24, 1852, Seward Papers.

20. *AP*, Sept. 11, 1844 (quotation); ERASMUS to Bro. Lee, Nov. 10, 1848, in *TW*, Nov. 25, 1848, McBride to Lee, May 10, 1850, in *TW*, May 25, 1850; Daniel Wilson to Simeon S. Jocelyn, Nov. 30, 1853, E.L. Stevens to Jocelyn, July 28, Aug. 15, 1855, Bassett to [Jocelyn], Dec. 22, 1858, Blanchard to Tappan, Apr. 2, 1860, AMAA.

21. Fee to Clay, Apr. 18, 1856, Fee-Clay Correspondence; *BSV*, 1842-1847; Snodgrass to R.R. Raymond, Sept. 27, 1852, in *Liberator*, Oct. 22, 1852; *Newport News*, quoted in *NASS*, Jan. 3, 1856; Bailey to Francis Jackson, June 29, 1857, in *Liberator*, July 17, 1857.

22. *NE*, Aug. 17, 1854, Apr. 21, July 7, 1859 (1st quotation); Harrold, "Clay on Slavery," 48-51; Clay to R. Vaile, Mar. 15, 1854, in *NASS*, Apr. 8, 1854 (2d quotation); *RA* 2 (May 1857): 87-88; *ASB*, Jan. 28, Mar. 31, May 12, 1860; "Speech of Cassius M. Clay, Esq., at Covington, Ky." [1860], unidentified newspaper clipping, Cassius M. Clay Miscellaneous Papers, Filson Club; *Liberator*, Aug. 22, 1862. Claims by Smiley and others that Clay was an inveterate racist are very questionable. See Smiley, *Lion of White Hall*, 56-57, 91; Pease and Pease, *Bound With Them in Chains*, 63, 74, 76.

23. *Emancipator*, Aug. 5, 1841; *AP*, Mar. 23, 1843; Ohio Anti-Slavery Society, *Report of the Third Anniversary*, 16, 28-30; *Philanthropist*, Mar. 18, 1838, Jan. 19, 1841, Feb. 9, 1842; Bailey to John Scoble, Jan. 19, 1845, in Abel and Klingberg, *Side-Light*, 202; Bailey to Zebina Eastman, June 11, 1847, Zebina Eastman Papers, Chicago Historical Society; Chase to Gerrit Smith, May 14, 1842, Smith Papers. See also Harrold, "Southern Strategy of the Liberty Party," 21-36. The only modern biography of Chase is Blue, *Chase*.

24. *Philanthropist*, quoted in *NASS*, June 8, 1843; *Philanthropist*, Aug. 16, 1843; *Emancipator*, July 13, 1843; Chase to editors of the *Cincinnati Morning Herald*, quoted in *AP*, Jan. 29, 1845; Clay to Chase, Dec. 21, 1842, Chase Papers, HSPa; Chase to Tappan, Feb. 15, 1843, Chase Papers, LC (quotations).

25. Tappan to William Jay, Mar. 16, 1843, Tappan to Clay, Sept. 15, 1843, lt. bk. copies, Tappan Papers; Tappan to Scoble, Mar. 1, 1843, in Abel and Klingberg, *Side-Light*, 119-20.

26. *Liberator*, Feb. 2, Apr. 5, 1844; *Emancipator*, Feb. 15, Apr. 3, 1844; *AP*, Apr. 4, 10, 1844; Stanton to Chase, Feb. 6, 1844, in Bourne, "Chase Diary and Correspondence," 464 (quotation); *Cincinnati Morning Herald*, quoted in *Emancipator*, Apr. 24, 1844.

27. Henry B. Stanton to Salmon P. Chase, Feb. 26, 1844, in Bourne, "Chase

Diary and Correspondence," 464; Harrold, "Clay and the Garrisonians," 101-19; *Liberty Herald* (Utica, N.Y.), quoted in *ASB*, Aug. 22, 1845; Tappan to [Joseph Evans Snodgrass], Aug. 30, 1845, lt. bk. copy, Tappan Papers; *AP*, June 18, 1845 (quotation); *Emancipator*, July 16, 1845.

28. Smiley, *Lion of White Hall*, 28-78; Clay to Salmon P. Chase, Dec. 21, 1842, Jan. 19, 1844, Chase Papers, HSPa; Clay to Giddings, Apr. 22, 1843, Ephraim Brown Papers, WRHS; James Brewer Stewart, "Abolitionists, Insurgents, and Third Parties: Sectionalism and Partisan Politics in Northern Whiggery," in Kraut, *Crusaders and Compromisers*, 25-39; Clay to W.J. M'Kinney, Mar. 20, 1844, in *Liberator*, Apr. 5, 1844; Clay, *Writings*, 160-72.

29. Salmon P. Chase to James G. Birney, Apr. 2, 1844, in Dumond, *Birney Letters*, 2:800; *Boston Morning Chronicle*, quoted in *AP*, May 16, 1844; *Liberator*, Aug. 23, 1844; *AP*, Oct. 2, 1844; *Emancipator*, Sept. 11, 25 (1st quotation), 1844; *Liberty Press* (Utica, N.Y.), quoted in *BSV*, July 13, 1844 (2d and 3d quotations).

30. *Emancipator*, July 30, 1845; *AP*, Aug. 6-Nov. 12, 1845; *CWHP*, Sept. 17-Nov. 2, 1845; W.E.W. to Dr. Bailey, Dec. [Jan.] 12, 1846, in *CWHP*, Jan. 28, 1846; Tappan to Theodore Weld, Jan. 16, 1846, lt. bk. copy, Tappan Papers (quotation).

31. Not all Liberty abolitionists condemned Clay's enlistment. See Salmon P. Chase to Gerrit Smith, Sept. 1, 1846, Smith Papers. On Clay's continued popularity among antislavery advocates: Clay to Chase, Aug. 12, 27, 1851, [Aug. 1, 1854?], Oct. 9, 1856, Chase Papers, HSPa; various unidentified newspaper clippings, in Clay Miscellaneous Papers, Filson Club; *ASB*, Oct 4, 1851, Mar. 3, 1860; *NE*, July 27, 1854; Clay to Bailey, July 5, 1852, in *NE*, July 15, 1852; William Henry Brisbane to Chase, June 22, 1859, Chase Papers, LC; Clay to A.W. Campbell, May 27, 1859, Archibald W. Campbell Papers, West Virginia University.

32. Charles Francis Adams, diary entry, Nov. 29, 1849, Adams Papers; *NS*, Aug. 11, 1848; Snodgrass to Salmon P. Chase, Sept. 26, Oct. 6, Nov. 12, 1848, Chase Papers, LC; JES to editor, Oct. 4, 1848, in *NE*, Oct. 19, 1848; JES to R.R. Raymond, Sept. 27, 1852, in *Liberator*, Oct. 22, 1852.

33. "National Republican Convention . . . Speech of Mr. Underwood of Virginia," unidentified newspaper clipping, scrapbook, p. 1, Underwood Papers; Hickin, "Underwood and the Antislavery Crusade," 52-77, 116-38, and "Underwood and the Antislavery Movement in Virginia," 166 (quotation); Underwood to William H. Seward, Mar. 12, 1860, Seward Papers.

34. Chase to Gerrit Smith, May 14, 1842, Smith Papers; *Philanthropist*, Feb. 9, Aug. 27, 1842, Aug. 16, 1843; *CWHP*, Jan. 15, 22, 1845, July 15, 1846; Chase to Lewis Tappan, June 16, 1844, Bell to Chase, June 6 (quotation), Aug. 4, 1844, Charles Chaney to Chase, June 16, 1844, Chase Papers, LC; SCOBLE to Mr. Leavitt, Aug. 6, 1845, in *Emancipator*, Aug. 20, 1845. Richard H. Sewell mistakenly asserts that "few Liberty partisans were much troubled at the nearly total lack of support from nonslaveholders in the South." He says that, except to encourage the *TA* and *LE*, "they advanced no plans to mobilize it." See Sewell, *Ballots for Freedom*, 87, 314.

35. SPC to Mr. Editor, n.d., in *AP*, Jan. 29, 1845; *CWHP*, Apr. 16, 1845 (1st quotation); *Liberty Herald* (Warren, Ohio), Apr. 30, 1845; Loesch, "Kentucky Abolitionist," 33; Clay to Chase and others, May 15, 1845, in *NASS*, July 10, 1845; Chase, "Address of the Southern and Western Liberty Convention," in Cleveland, *Anti-Slavery Addresses of 1844 and 1845,* 119 (2d and 3d quotations), 121.

36. Gerrit Smith to William H. Seward, Jan. 1, 1845, in *Liberty Herald* (Warren, Ohio), Feb. 20, 1845; *Boston Chronicle*, quoted in *AP*, Feb. 26, 1845; *AP*, Apr. 30, Aug. 27, Sept. 3, 1845 (quotation); *Emancipator*, Feb. 19, July 30, 1845; *Boston Chronicle*, quoted in *CWHP*, Apr. 16, 1845, *AFASR* 2 (Nov. 1845): 73-75; *Christian World*, quoted in *Emancipator*, Oct 28, 1846; Tappan to Joshua Leavitt, Feb. 28, 1847, in ibid., Mar. 10, 1847.

37. Lewis Tappan to Gerrit Smith, Oct. 29, 1846, Smith Papers; Barnes, *Antislavery Impulse*, 177-90; H. Davis, *Leavitt*, 176-97; Joshua Leavitt to Joshua R. Giddings, Aug. 7, 1842, Giddings Papers, Ohio Historical Society; Tappan to Gamaliel Bailey, Jan. 18, 1844, lt. bk. copy, Tappan Papers; *Philanthropist*, Jan. 4, 1843, *CWHP*, Mar. 6, 1844, Jan. 15, 1845.

38. S.A.P. to Joshua Leavitt, Mar. 30, 1845, in *Emancipator*, July 9, 1845; Phelps to Gerrit Smith, Nov. 22, 1845, Smith Papers; *AFASR* 2 (Jan. 1846):93; Lovejoy, *Torrey*, 285; Lewis Tappan to Salmon P. Chase, Mar. 9, 1846, Chase Papers, HSPa; Tappan to J. Bigelow, Jan. 7, 1848, Tappan to [Charles B.] Boynton, Oct. 11, 1847, lt. bk. copies, Tappan Papers; Tappan to Leavitt, Feb. 28, 1847, in *Emancipator*, Mar. 10. 1847; Still, *Underground Railroad*, 174-79. See also Harrold, *Bailey*, 79-83.

39. Tappan to Geo. H. White, Nov. 5, 1846, Autograph File, Houghton Library, Harvard University (quotation); Tappan to Gerrit Smith, Aug. 24, Oct. 29, 1846, Smith Papers; Charles V. Dyer and others, "National Liberty Paper at Washington. Report of the Committee," [Oct. 1846], in *Emancipator*, Nov. 4, 1846; *CWHP*, Nov. 18, Dec. 16, 1846; Tappan to John G. Fee, Nov. 12, 1847, Tappan to Bailey, Nov. 18, 1847, Tappan to Phelps, Jan. 16, 1847, lt. bk. copies, Tappan Papers; Phelps to Tappan, July 20, 1846, AMAA; Moses A. Cartland to Bailey, Dec. 22, 1846, in *NE*, Jan. 7, 1847.

40. *NE*, Jan. 7, 1847.

41. *NE*, Feb. 25, Aug. 26 (quotations), 1847; Nov. 16, 1848.

42. *NE*, June 26, 1851, Dec. 9, 1852, Jan. 13, Oct. 6, 1853, Jan. 19, 1854, Nov. 1, 15, 1855, July 31, 1856, Apr. 8, 15, 1857; Foner, *Free Soil*, 115-23; Lewis Tappan to Amos A. Phelps, Jan. 16, 1847, lt. bk. copy, Tappan Papers; Bailey to John B. Floyd, Dec. 28, 1857, in *NE*, June 3, 1858; Tappan to John G. Whittier, Apr. 21, 1847, Pickard-Whittier Papers, Houghton Library, Harvard University; Tappan to John Scoble, Nov. 14, 1847, in Abel and Klingberg, *Side-Light*, 228 (quotation). See also Harrold, *Bailey*, 139.

43. Harrold, *Bailey*, 125-27, 212; *Southern Press*, July 19, 22, Oct. 17 (1st quotation), 1850; *FDP*, Feb. 25, 1853; *Times*, quoted in *NE*, Jan. 6, 1853 (2d quotation).

44. *Cazenovia Abolitionist,* July 12, 1842, quoted in *Philanthropist,* Aug. 27, 1842; Gerrit Smith to Gamaliel Bailey, Sept. 13, 1842, in *Philanthropist,* Oct. 15, 1842; *Emancipator,* Feb. 19, Apr. 16, 1845; *Liberator,* July 16, 1847; May 5, 12, 1848; Green to James G. Birney, Aug. 2, 1847, in Dumond, *Birney Letters,* 2:1078; *ASB,* Jan. 29, 1847 (quotation), Aug. 2, 30, 1856; *NASS,* Jan. 12, 1847; *Chronotype,* quoted in *AP,* Apr. 26, 1848; *NE,* May 18, 1848, Aug. 15, 1850.

45. *NE,* May 18, 1848 (quotation); Oct. 10, 31, 1851; *Liberty Press* (Utica), quoted in *Emancipator,* June 14, 1848; *Free Presbyterian,* quoted in *NE,* Aug. 29, 1850.

46. Northern abolitionists in general: AFASS, *[8th] Annual Report,* 45-46; *Liberty Press* (Utica), quoted in *Emancipator,* June 14, 1848; B.C. Gilbert to editor, Aug. 5, 1856, in *ASB,* Aug. 16, 1856. Garrisonian and radical political abolitionists: *AP,* Feb. 24, 1847; *NASS,* Jan. 12, 1847; *RA* 1 (May 1856): 75-76; *ASB,* Jan. 12, 1850, Aug. 26, 1856; *Liberator,* quoted in *NE,* Apr. 22, 1852. Southern abolitionists: Janney to Gay, July 27, 1847, Gay Papers, Columbia Univ.; *NE,* Nov. 11, 1852.

47. Clay was less tolerant of criticism from Bailey than he was of criticism from more northerly abolitionists. Fee suspected Bailey and other Yankees of financial sharp dealing. See Fee to editors, Feb. 20, [1849], in *LE,* Mar. 3, 1849; Fee to Lewis Tappan, Aug. 4, 1851, AMAA; Clay to George W. Julian, June 6, 1853, Giddings-Julian Papers; Fee to Editor, Feb. 12, 1858, in *NE,* Mar. 4, 1858. On Bailey as a role model: *LE,* Jan. 6, Mar. 17, 1849; Connolly to Samuel M. Janney, Aug. 7, 1849, Janney Papers; *NE,* Sept. 14, 1854, Jan. 6, Nov. 4, 1858; Lewis Tappan to Bailey, Nov. 6, 1848, lt. bk. copy, Tappan Papers.

48. Fee to John C. Vaughan, Sept. 13, 1848, Fee to Chase, Mar. 12, 1850, Chase Papers, LC; Cassius M. Clay to Chase, Aug. 12, 27, 1851, Chase Papers, HSPa; *NE,* Oct. 26, 1848, Aug. 30, 1849, Dec. 9, 1852, Apr. 20, 1854, Aug. 30, 1855, Aug. 7-21, 1856, Apr. 8, May 14, 1857, Dec. 16, 30, 1858; Seward to John C. Underwood, Nov. 20, 1858, Underwood Papers, LC; Hickin, "Underwood and the Antislavery Movement in Virginia," 160; Harrold, *Bailey,* 105-08; *ASB,* Mar. 3, 1860.

49. Tappan to John G. Fee, July 10, 1855, Feb. 29, 1856, lt. bk. copies, Tappan Papers; William Goodell, Lewis Tappan, Gerrit Smith, and others, to the Radical Political Abolitionists, Apr. 4, 1855, in *FDP,* June 8, 1855; *OE,* Feb. 13, 1856.

50. *AFASR* 2 and 3 (Nov. 1844): 13, (Oct 1845): 66-68, (Dec. 1845): 84-85, (Aug. 1846): 28; *TW,* Aug. 30, 1845, Nov. 13, 1847, Aug. 12, Nov. 4, 1848; *American Citizen,* quoted in *Emancipator,* Sept. 9, 1846 (1st quotation); AFASS, *[8th] Annual Report,* 32-33; *[11th] Annual Report,* 88-89; AMA, *Eighth Annual Report,* 70 (2d quotation).

51. Harrold, "Clay and the Garrisonians," 101-19; MASS, *Fourteenth Annual Report,* 22-23, and *Sixteenth Annual Report,* 25-26 (quotations); *PF,* quoted in *LE,* Mar. 31, 1849.

52. *NASS*, Apr. 10, 1851, Sept. 4, 1857, May 26, 1860; *ASB*, Aug. 16, 1851, Mar. 3, Apr. 14, May 5, 1860; MASS, *Twentieth Annual Report*, 64-65; *Liberator*, May 27, 1853 (quotations); Harrold, "Clay and the Garrisonians," 113-16.

53. Clay's relations with the New York Liberty party were less friendly than with other Liberty groups. See Clay to Gerrit Smith, Oct. 6, 1844, and related newspaper clippings, Gerrit Smith Papers; *AFASR* 2 (Feb. 1846): 101; *AP*, Oct. 2, 1844, Mar. 12, Dec. 3, 1845, Jan. 19, 1848; *NS*, Apr. 28, 1848. In 1845 Smith told William H. Seward that the Liberty party would have to become a proslavery party to gain support in the South. See Smith to Seward, Jan. 1, 1845, in *Liberty Herald* (Warren, Ohio), Feb. 20, 1845. On New York Liberty abolitionist distrust of Gamaliel Bailey: E.S. Gilbert to [?], Dec. 18, 1846, in *AP*, Dec. 30, 1846; Smith to Daniel Dickey and George W. Ellingwood, Mar. 21, 1845, lt. bk. copy, Bailey to Smith, Sept. 2, 1847, Smith Papers.

54. Clay to Smith, Feb. 18, 1845, in *Liberator*, Apr. 4, 1845; Smith to Clay, Aug. 16, 1851 (quotation), Clay to Smith, Mar. 24, 1855, June 14, 1858, Smith Papers; Clay, *Writings*, 209, 242, 281-83, 352-53. See also *RA* 1 (Apr. 1856): 65. Philip J. Schwartz, Department of History and Geography, Virginia Commonwealth University, very kindly sent me a photocopy of an inscription on a copy of *Speeches of Gerrit Smith in Congress* (New York: Mason Brothers, 1855). The inscription is, "Cassius M. Clay from his friend Gerrit Smith, Whitehall June 1, 1857."

55. Clay to Smith, Apr. 24, 1855 (quotation), Nov. 20, 1857, Smith Papers; Clay to Fee, July 8, 1855, Fee-Clay Correspondence.

56. Gerrit Smith to Edmund Quincy, Nov. 23, 1846, in *Emancipator*, Jan. 6, 1847 (1st quotation); Smith to Allan Pinkerton, May 1, 1851, lt. bk. copy (2d quotation), Goodell to Smith, June 8, 1851, Smith Papers; Lewis Tappan to Fee, July 10, 1855, lt. bk. copy, Tappan Papers; Fee to Tappan, Dec. 27, 1848, Fee to George Whipple, June 2, 1850, Feb. 15, 1853, Fee to Simeon S. Jocelyn, [Jan.], Mar. 8, Apr. 12, May 8, June 16, 1856, AMAA; Fee to Clay, Sept. 17, 1857, [Goodell] to Fee, May 1, 1858, Fee Papers; Fee to Goodell, Jan. 10, 1856, in *RA* 1 (Mar. 1856): 57; Fee, *Colonization*, 44.

57. Fee to Goodell, Jan. 10, 1856, in *RA* 1 (Mar. 1856): 57; Lewis Tappan to Fee, Feb. 29, 1856, lt. bk. copy, Tappan Papers; Fee to Clay, May 10, 1856, Clay to Fee, July 8, 1855, Fee-Clay Correspondence; *Kentucky News*, Aug. 25, 1856, clipping, Fee Papers; Fee, *Autobiography*, 102-5; Fee to Simeon S. Jocelyn, July 16, 1856, AMAA. The mob attacks on Fee and his associates are chronicled in AMAA, the Fee-Clay Correspondence, and in northern abolitionist newspapers. An easily accessible account is in Sears, *Day of Small Things*. For Fee's remarks on John Brown see Fee, "The Progress of Emancipation in Kentucky," *Principia*, Nov. 26, 1859.

58. Challenges legitimacy of slavery: Fee to Jocelyn, July 16, 1856, AMAA; Fee to Editors of the *Cincinnati Gazette*, Apr. 9, 1860, in *Liberator*, May 11, 1860.

Attempt to influence Clay: Fee to Clay, Apr. 18, 1856, Aug. 27, 1857, Fee-Clay Correspondence. Martyrs: *Principia*, Jan. 7, 1860; Fee et al., "Exiles of Kentucky to the People of the United States," in *NASS*, Jan. 21, 1860.

59. On Fee and Clay's distrust of Bailey: Fee to George Whipple, Feb. 15, 1853, Fee to D.S. Newton, Feb. 4, 1859, AMAA; [Clay], to *NYTr*, Apr. 30, 1860, in *ASB*, May 20, 1860. On Bailey's appeals for financial aid: *RA* 2 (Feb. 1857): 63; Rebecca Bailey to Charles Harvey, Jan. 10, 1859, Adams Papers, MHS; *Liberator*, Feb. 23, 1860. On Bailey's special relationship with the radical political abolitionists: Goodell to Gerrit Smith, Dec. 31, 1856, Smith Papers; Bailey to Simeon S. Jocelyn, Dec. 11, 1856 (printed), AMAA; *RA* 3 and 4 (Aug. 1857): 2-3, (Mar. 1858): 58.

60. *RA* 3 and 4 (Mar. 1858): 57-58, (Apr. 1858): 67 (quotations), (Nov. 1858): 30; *Principia*, Mar. 31, 1860.

8. LEGACIES

1. Fairbank, *Fairbank*, [i] (1st quotation), [iii] (2d quotation), 173-92.

2. Rhodes, *History*, 1:62-63; Pressly, *Americans Interpret Their Civil War*, 270-71, 283, 301-5, 316; Dillon, "Abolitionist Historiography," 500; Craven, *Coming of the Civil War*, 134-50; Friedman, "'Historical Topics,'" 177-94; Stewart, "Young Turks and Old Turkeys," 226-32; Huston, "Experiential Basis," 609-40.

3. Foner, "Causes of the Civil War," 198; Friedman, *Gregarious Saints*; Walters, *Antislavery Appeal*.

4. Stewart, "Young Turks and Old Turkeys," 226-32.

5. Huston, "Experiential Basis," 610-20.

6. Hart, *Slavery and Abolition*, 315; Wyatt-Brown, "Abolitionists' Postal Campaign," 227-38; Dillon, "Abolitionist Historiography," 506-9. There is certainly evidence for an abolitionist determination to concentrate on the North. However, conflicting evidence in favor of a continued abolitionist commitment to converting the South has been overlooked. Aside from the undertakings described in this book, abolitionists in the late 1830s, 1840s, and 1850s continued to endorse seeking a southern audience. See, for example, *Emancipator*, Apr. 5, 1838; Gerrit Smith to Nathaniel Crenshaw, Dec. 30, 1841, Smith to Virginia Mason, Jan. 7, 1849, lt. bk. copies, Smith Papers; W. Phillips, *Speeches, Lectures, and Letters* (3d ed.), 82-83; AFASS, *Thirteenth Annual Report*, 182.

7. McPherson, *Struggle for Equality*, 3. Friedman, *Gregarious Saints*, 1; Friedman, "'Historical Topics,'" 186-87. Giddings served as the Ohio Anti-Slavery Society manager for Ashtabula County in 1836 and 1837. Chase was a corresponding member of the AFASS executive committee in 1848 and 1849. But William E. Gienapp, in his monumental history of the Republican party, generally ignores the question of abolitionist influence on that organization. See Price, "Ohio Anti-Slavery Convention of 1836," 182; Ohio Anti-Slavery Society, *Report of the Second Anniversary,* 9; AFASS, *[8th] Annual Report*, 3; Gienapp, *Origins of the Republican Party*.

8. Aptheker, *Abolitionism*; Dillon, *Slavery Attacked*, 230-42.

9. Fredrickson, *Arrogance of Race*, 13, 75-76; U.B. Phillips, *Course of the South to Secession*, 114 (1st quotation); W. Phillips, *Speeches, Lectures, Letters* (1884 ed.), 136 (2d quotation); Friedman, *Gregarious Saints*, 4-5 (3d and 4th quotations); Barney, *Road to Secession* and *Secessionist Impulse*; Channing, *Crisis of Fear*; W.W. Freehling, *Prelude to the Civil War*, 306-60, esp. 358.

10. Milton, *Eve of Conflict*, 39-40.

11. W.W. Freehling, *Road to Disunion*, 1:473, and "Editorial Revolution," 68-71.

12. Publicola, "Present Aspects of Abolitionism," 434; David Johnson to John C. Calhoun, Oct. 18, 1848, in Boucher, "Correspondence Addressed to John C. Calhoun," 481-82; [John C. Calhoun], "The Address of the Southern Delegates in Congress to Their Constituents," in Cralle, *Works of Calhoun*, 6:290-313 (hereafter cited as Calhoun, "Southern Address"); Dumond, *Southern Editorials*, 178-81, 357-60.

13. Holst, *Constitutional and Political History*, 3:429-35; W.W. Freehling, "Editorial Revolution," 68-71; Foner, "Causes of the American Civil War," 209-10; W.W. Freehling, *Road to Disunion*, 1:33-35, 162-210, 481; Fields, *Slavery and Freedom on the Middle Ground*; Levine, *Half Slave and Half Free*, 39-45.

14. *Baltimore Ray*, quoted in *BSV*, July 19, 1845 (1st-3d quotations); *New Era*, quoted in *TW*, Oct. 23, 1847 (4th-6th quotations).

15. *NYH*, Apr. 20, 1848 (1st quotation); *CG*, 30 Cong., I sess., 501-9 (2d-4th quotations, 501 and 505); Calhoun, "Southern Address," 290-309.

16. *RE*, Dec. 4 (1st quotation), 28 (2d quotation), 1849.

17. McBride to Luther Lee, Aug. 23, 1851, in *TW*, Sept. 13, 1851 (1st quotation); Fee to Simeon S. Jocelyn, June 23, 1855, George Clark to Jocelyn, Nov. 19, 1855, AMAA; D.B. Davis, *Slave Power Conspiracy*, 37-50 (2d quotation); Channing, *Crisis of Fear*, 77-78.

18. On the Kentucky AMA missionaries efforts to expand into Virginia: AMA, *Sixth Annual Report*, 46-47, *Tenth Annual Report*, 69; George Rye to Simeon S. Jocelyn and Lewis Tappan, Dec. 13, 1855; James Scott Davis to Jocelyn, Jan. 21, Apr. 22, 1856, AMAA.

19. R.G. Williams to Editors, Aug. 27, 1853, unidentified newspaper clipping, John G. Fee, "Mt. Vernon Resolutions vs. Free Speech," July 18, 1855, AMAA; Jacob Crooks to Luther Lee, Oct. 18, 1850, in *TW*, Nov. 19, 1850; Jesse McBride to Lee, May 3, 1851 (quoting a letter in the *Greensborough Patriot*), in *TW*, June 7, 1851 (quotation); AMA, *Fourteenth Annual Report*, 49-54; C.H. Johnson, "AMA," 546.

20. *NASS*, April 12, 19, 26, May 10, 1849; Savage, *Controversy over the Distribution of Abolitionist Literature*, 112-13; Davis to Malcolm D. Haynes, Aug. 18, 1849, in Crist, *Papers of Jefferson Davis*, 4:34-37; Roland, *Davis*, 1:251-52 (quotations).

21. *CM*, Oct. 4, 1856; Dew, "Black Ironworkers and the Slave Insurrection Panic," 321-38.

22. *RE*, quoted in *Liberator*, Apr. 24, 1857 (quotation); *Richmond Whig*, quoted in *NYH*, Mar. 10, 1857; *South* (Richmond), Apr. 21, [1857], quoted in *NE*, May 7, 1857; G.W. Smith, "Ante-Bellum Attempts," 204-5.

23. *South Side Democrat* (Petersburg, Va.), Mar. 9, 1857, quoted in F.P. Rice, "Thayer," chap. 20:14-15; *New Orleans Delta*, Apr. 29, 1857, quoted in F.P. Rice, "Thayer," chap. 21:6-7 (quotation).

24. *CM*, Mar. 5, 1857.

25. Hickin, "Antislavery in Virginia," 699-72, 720, 747; Abbott, *Republican Party and the South*, 3-19.

26. *Wheeling Daily Intelligencer*, Oct. 1, 1856; *Wellsburg Weekly Herald*, Dec. 12, 1856, Sept. 11, 1857, May 11, Sept. 28, 1860; *RA* 3 and 4 (Mar. 1858): 57-58, (Apr. 1858): 67, (Nov. 1858): 30; Hickin, "Antislavery in Virginia," 723-26; Sewell, *Ballots for Freedom*, 316-17; Foner, *Free Soil*, 63, 268-70; *NE*, 1854-1860; Harrold, *Bailey*, 184-215; Abbott, *Republican Party and the South*, 12-17.

27. Barney, *Secessionist Impulse*, 37; W.W. Freehling, *Road to Disunion*, 1:473; *Savannah Georgian*, quoted in *CM*, Sept. 20, 1856; *Columbia Guardian*, quoted in *CM*, Oct. 17, 1860; Foner, "Causes of the Civil War," 210.

28. The southern-rights advocates' confusion of abolitionists and Republicans was pervasive. For indications that the southerners were quite aware of the distinction between the two groups, see Roland, *Davis*, 1:479-80; Publicola, "Present Aspects of Abolitionism," 430; Ruffin, "Consequences of Abolition Agitation," 587-88; Wilson, *Letters and Speeches of Hammond*, 350; Channing, *Crisis of Fear*, 78-82. On conservative southern Republican advocacy of emancipation: *Wellsburg Weekly Herald*, Dec. 12, 1856, Sept. 28, 1860; Hickin, "Antislavery in Virginia," 723-26.

29. *RE*, July 10, 1860, in Dumond, *Southern Editorials*, 141 (quotation); *CM*, Oct. 11, 1860; *Columbus [Ga.] Times*, quoted in *RE*, Oct. 19, 1860; W.W. Freehling, "Editorial Revolution," 69-70; M.P. Johnson, *Toward a Patriarchal Republic*, 43-45; Foner, *Free Soil*, 119-23.

30. *CM*, Oct. 11 (quotations), 17, 19, 1860; *RE*, Oct. 19, 1860; *Louisville Daily Courier*, Dec. 20, 1860, in Dumond, *Southern Editorials*, 357-60. See also *NYH*, quoted in *CM*, Sept. 8, 1860.

31. McPherson, *Struggle for Equality*, 72, 156; Oates, *To Purge this Land with Blood,* 361; Cornish, *Sable Arm*, 12-13.

32. Cornish, *Sable Arm*, esp. 156, 290; Glatthaar, *Forged in Battle*; Foner, *Reconstruction*, 3-4, 78-123.

33. *NASS*, Mar. 14, Apr. 4, 1857; Lydia Maria Child to John C. Underwood, Dec. 6, 1860, in Child Collected Correspondence.

34. Mrs. H.P. Blanchard to Simeon S. Jocelyn, Jan. 14, 1861, A Free Soil Resident to Jocelyn, Feb. 1, 1861, Stephen Blanchard to [Jocelyn], Dec. 10, 1862,

AMAA; McPherson, *Struggle for Equality*, 69-70 (quotation), 158-75, 394-407, 413-18; AMA, *Fifteenth Annual Report,* 7, 46-49, *Sixteenth Annual Report,* 37-49, *Seventeenth Annual Report,* 36-46, and *Eighteenth Annual Report,* 10-27; Richardson, *Christian Reconstruction.*

35. Maryland and North Carolina Files, AMAA; Mrs. H.P. Blanchard to Jocelyn, Jan. 14, 1861, Stephen Blanchard to Jocelyn, May 12, Dec. 10, 1862, AMAA; Jocelyn to Fee, Apr. 28, 1862, Fee Papers; McPherson, *Ordeal by Fire,* 394.

36. Sears, *Day of Small Things,* 375-414; Fee, *Autobiography,* 161-83; Sears, "Fee," 29-45; Fee to William Lloyd Garrison, May 13, 1866, Garrison Papers; E.H. Fairchild and others to the Editor of the *Louisville Commercial,* Apr. 12, 1871, in *NASS,* Apr. 22, 1871; Simeon S. Jocelyn to Fee, Feb. 14, Apr. 28, May 14, 1862, June 6, 1864, Fee Papers; AMA, *Sixteenth Annual Report,* 38. On Fee's depression: *AMM* 2 (June 1858): 138-39; Fee to Gerrit Smith, Mar. 29, 1862, Smith Papers; Fee to Cassius M. Clay, July 25, 1886, Fee-Clay Correspondence.

37. Fee to Wendell Phillips, n.d., in *Liberator,* Mar. 18, 1864; Fee to Editor, n.d., in *Liberator,* June 17, 1864 (1st and 2d quotations); Fee to Julian, Oct. 6, 189[7], Giddings-Julian Papers (3d quotation).

38. *DAB,* s.v. "Nelson, David"; Fladeland, *Birney,* 293; Harrold, *Bailey,* 211-15; Tolbert, "Worth," 303: Fredrickson, *Arrogance of Race,* 95; *New Bedford Standard,* quoted in *NE,* July 9, 1857; Nicholson, *Wesleyan Methodism,* 76.

39. Burr to Lewis Tappan, June 21, 1858, Work to H.W. Hubbard, Jan. 1, 1878, AMAA; Coleman, *Slavery Times in Kentucky,* 241n; Jackson to Gerrit Smith, Apr. 24, 1855, Thayer to Smith, Apr. 4, 1862, Smith Papers; *Cortland [N.Y.] Standard,* May 2, [1871], quoted in *New National Era,* May 11, 1871; Charles B. Hoard to Thayer, June 15, Aug. 15, 1870, Apr. 24, 1871, Thayer Papers; Foner, *Free Soil,* 204-5; Thayer, *Kansas Crusade,* 88-116, 146-201.

40. Thompson to Gerrit Smith, Oct. 11, 25, Nov. 8, 20, 1865, Smith Papers; Redpath, *Roving Editor,* xv, 269; Plummer, *Frontier Governor,* 56-63.

41. Walker to William Lloyd Garrison, n.d., in *Liberator,* Sept. 2, 1864 (quotation); Walker to [?], n.d., in *Liberator,* Apr. 22, 1853; *DAB,* s.v. "Fairbank, Calvin"; Fairbank, *Fairbank,* 149-81; Fairbank to Editor, Feb. 24, 186[5] and Thomas Garrett to Oliver Johnson, Feb. 27, 1865, in *NASS,* Mar. 11, 1865; Fairbank to Editor, Dec. 1868, in *NASS,* Dec. 26, 1868; Fairbank to Editor, Jan. 1869, in *NASS,* Feb. 27, 1869; Fairbank to William Lloyd Garrison, Feb. 7, 1865, Garrison Papers.

42. Snodgrass to Salmon P. Chase, Mar. 28, 1861, Chase Papers, LC; R.E. Fenton to Snodgrass, n.d., in *NASS,* Oct. 12, 1867; Snodgrass to Editor, n.d., in *NASS,* June 17, 1865; Snodgrass to J.M. Wood, n.d., in *NASS,* Feb. 20, 1869 (quotation); Snodgrass to Gerrit Smith, Nov. 11, 1871, Bailey to Smith, Jan. 19, May 13, 1864, Dec. 23, 1866, Smith Papers; Snodgrass to Rutherford B. Hayes, Jan. 27, 1878, Hayes Papers, Hayes Presidential Center. John C. Underwood and

Cassius M. Clay also recognized that blacks had to own land to succeed in freedom. See Underwood to Charles Sumner, Mar. 1, 1865, Sumner Papers, Houghton Library, Harvard University; Clay, *Life*, 423.

43. Lydia Maria Child to Underwood, July 30, Oct. 13, Nov. 15, Dec. 8, 1860, Child to [Robert Folger] Walcutt, Nov. 5, Dec. 5, 1860, in Child Collected Correspondence; Underwood to Abraham Lincoln, Feb. 17, 1862, Underwood Papers; Underwood to Gerrit Smith, May 2, 1863, Smith Papers; Underwood to the *Union Republic* (Norfolk, Va.), July 24, 1867, in *NASS*, Aug. 10, 1867; Calvin Fairbank to Editor, Jan. 1869, in *NASS*, Feb. 27, 1869; Lowe, *Republicans and Reconstruction in Virginia*, passim (quotation 159).

44. Thompson to Gerrit Smith, Nov. 20, 1865, Smith Papers (quotation). For a recent analysis of Republican political calculations and black suffrage see Abbott, *Republican Party and the South,* passim.

45. Underwood to Smith, May 2, 1863, Smith Papers (1st quotation); Snodgrass to Editor, n.d., in *NASS*, June 17, 1865 (2d quotation); Fairbank to Convention at Framingham, July 2, 1865, in *NASS*, July 15, 1865 (3d quotation).

46. McPherson, *Struggle for Equality*, 302, 397; Curry, "Abolitionists and Reconstruction," 527-45; Foner, *Reconstruction*, 67-68; Underwood to Gerrit Smith, Oct. 18, 1868, Smith Papers (1st quotation); Fairbank to Editor, Jan. 1869, in *NASS*, Feb. 27, 1869 (2d quotation).

47. Walker to William Lloyd Garrison, n.d., in *Liberator*, Sept. 2, 1864.

48. Steelman, "Goodloe," 66-90; *DNCB*, s.v. "Goodloe, Daniel Reeves"; Smiley, *Lion of White Hall*, 215-37; Clay to Editor of the *Sun*, Nov. 16, [1884], unidentified newspaper clipping, Clay Misc. Papers, Filson Club (quotation). Unlike Goodloe, Clay continued to oppose legal restrictions on the social and educational interaction of the races. See Clay, *Life*, 594-98.

49. Steelman, "Goodloe," 79-80, 84-87; Clay to Gen. William Larimer, Aug. 2, 1871, unidentified newspaper clipping, Clay to Liberal Republican Convention held in Jefferson City, Jan. 20, 1872, in *[St. Louis] Republican*, [Jan. 27, 1872], clipping, Clay Misc. Papers, Filson Club; Gerteis, *Morality and Utility*, 191-210. Clay's biographer, David L. Smiley, neglects factors other than Clay's political ambitions in explaining his motivation.

50. Steelman, "Goodloe," 66-67, 84, 90; Clay, *Life*, 594-600; Clay to [Elliot C.] Cowdin, Mar. 19, 1862, Speech of Clay to the Kentucky legislature, "reported in the Cincinnati Gazette, August 31, 1862" (typed script), Clay to Liberal Republican Convention, Jan. 20, 1872, Clay Misc. Papers, Filson Club; Clay to Abraham Lincoln, Sept. 27, 1861, Lincoln Papers, LC; *Evening Post* (New York), quoted in *NASS*, Aug. 16, 1862; Wendell Phillips to Clay, Aug. 19, 1862, Clay Papers, Lincoln Memorial University; *NASS*, Aug. 23, 1862.

51. *Liberator*, Aug. 22, 1862 (1st and 2d quotations); *NYH*, Nov. 2, 1862, clipping, Clay Misc. Papers, Filson Club (3d quotation).

52. Clay to William H. Seward, Feb. 9, 1867, in *NASS*, Apr. 10, 1869.

BIBLIOGRAPHY

Manuscript Collections

Charles Francis Adams Papers, Massachusetts Historical Society, Boston. Microfilm.

American Missionary Association Archives, Amistad Research Center, Tulane University, New Orleans. Microfilm.

Antislavery Collection, Cornell University Library, Ithaca, N.Y.

Autograph File, Houghton Library, Harvard University, Cambridge, Mass.

Blair Family Papers, Library of Congress.

Breckinridge Family Papers, Library of Congress.

Archibald W. Campbell Papers, West Virginia University, Morgantown, W.Va.

Maria Weston Chapman Papers, Boston Public Library.

Salmon P. Chase Papers, Historical Society of Pennsylvania, Philadelphia.

Salmon P. Chase Papers, Library of Congress. Microfilm.

Lydia Maria Child Collected Correspondence. Microfilm edition assembled from a number of collections by Patricia G. Halland and Milton Meltzer.

Cassius M. Clay Miscellaneous Papers, Filson Club, Louisville, Kentucky.

Cassius M. Clay Papers, Lincoln Memorial University, Harrogate, Tenn.

Cassius M. Clay Papers, Western Reserve Historical Society, Cleveland, Ohio.

Zebina Eastman Papers, Chicago Historical Society.

John G. Fee-Cassius M. Clay Correspondence, Berea College Archives, Berea, Ky.

John G. Fee Papers, Berea College Archives, Berea, Ky.

William Lloyd Garrison Papers, Boston Public Library.

Sydney Howard Gay Papers, Columbia University, New York.

Joshua R. Giddings Papers-George W. Julian Papers, Library of Congress.

Joshua R. Giddings Papers, Ohio Historical Society, Columbus, Ohio.

Daniel Reeves Goodloe Papers, Southern Collection, University of North Carolina, Chapel Hill, N.C.

Rutherford B. Hayes Papers, Hayes Presidential Center, Fremont, Ohio.

Benjamin P. Hunt Collection, Boston Public Library.

Samuel M. Janney Papers, Friends Historical Library, Swarthmore College, Swarthmore, Pa.

Abraham Lincoln Papers, Library of Congress. Microfilm.

Horace Mann Papers, Massachusetts Historical Society, Boston, Mass.

Amos A. Phelps Papers, Boston Public Library.

Samuel Thomas Pickard-John Greenleaf Whittier Papers, Houghton Library, Harvard University, Cambridge, Mass.

William Henry Seward Papers, University of Rochester. Microfilm.
Gerrit Smith Papers, George Arents Research Library, Syracuse University, Syracuse, N.Y. Microfilm.
Lysander Spooner Papers, Boston Public Library.
Alvan Stewart Papers, New York Historical Society, New York.
Charles Sumner Papers, Houghton Library, Harvard University, Cambridge, Mass. Microfilm.
Lewis Tappan Papers, Library of Congress. Microfilm.
Eli Thayer Papers, Brown University Library, Providence, R.I.
Charles T. Torrey Papers, Congregational Library, Boston.
George Truman Papers, Friends Historical Library, Swarthmore College, Swarthmore, Pa.
Lyman Trumbull Papers, Library of Congress.
John C. Underwood Papers, Library of Congress.

Newspapers and Periodicals
Albany Patriot, 1843-1848.
American and Foreign Anti-Slavery Reporter, 1844-1846.
American Missionary, 1847-1856.
American Missionary Magazine, 1857-1860.
Anti-Slavery Bugle (Salem, Ohio), 1845-1860.
Anti-Slavery Reporter, 1835.
Baltimore Saturday Visiter [sic], 1842-1846.
Ceredo Crescent, 1859.
Charleston Mercury, 1857-1860.
Cincinnati Weekly Herald and Philanthropist, 1844-1846.
DeBow's Review, 1857.
Emancipator (New York and Boston), 1833-1848.
Frederick Douglass Paper (Rochester, N.Y.), 1850-1857.
Genius of Universal Emancipation (Philadelphia), 1830-1834.
Independent (New York), 1855-1858.
Liberator (Boston), 1831-1860.
Liberty Herald (Warren, Ohio), 1845.
Examiner (Louisville), 1847-1849.
National Anti-Slavery Standard (New York), 1841-1869.
National Era (Washington), 1847-1860.
New National Era (Washington), 1871.
New York Herald, 1848-1857.
New York Tribune, 1846-1856.
North Star (Rochester, N.Y.), 1848-1850.
Oberlin Evangelist, 1855-1859.
Pennsylvania Freeman (Philadelphia), 1851.
Philanthropist (Cincinnati), 1838-1843.

Principia (New York), 1859-1860.
Radical Abolitionist, 1856-1858.
Richmond Enquirer, 1849-1860.
Southern Literary Messenger, 1847.
Tocsin of Liberty (Albany, N.Y.), 1842.
True American (Lexington, Ky.), 1845-1846.
True Democrat (Cleveland), 1847.
True Wesleyan (New York), 1845-1860.
Wellsburg Weekly Herald, 1856 1860.
Wheeling Daily Intelligencer, 1856.

Contemporary Publications and Published Documents
Abel, Annie H., and Frank J. Klingberg, eds. *A Side-Light on Anglo-American Relations, 1839-1850; Furnished by the Correspondence of Lewis Tappan and Others with the British and Foreign Anti-Slavery Society.* Lancaster, Pa.: Association for the Study of Negro Life and History, 1927.

American and Foreign Anti-Slavery Society. *Address to the Non-Slaveholders of the South, on the Social and Political Evils of Slavery.* New York: S.W. Benedict, 1843.

American and Foreign Anti-Slavery Society. *Annual Reports.* New York: AFASS, 1847-51, 1853.

American Anti-Slavery Society. *Second Annual Report.* New York: AASS, 1835.

American Missionary Association. *Annual Reports.* New York: AMA, 1846-64.

Aptheker, Herbert, ed. *A Documentary History of the Negro People in the United States.* 5th paperback ed. 2 vols. New York: Citadel, 1968.

Barnes, Gilbert H., and Dwight L. Dumond, eds. *The Letters of Theodore Weld, Angelina Grimke Weld, and Sarah Grimke, 1822-1844.* 2 vols. 1934. Reprint, Gloucester, Ma.: Peter Smith, 1965.

Bassett, George. *Slavery Examined in the Light of Nature.* Washington: privately printed, 1858.

Bell, Howard H., ed. *Minutes and Proceedings of the National Negro Conventions, 1830-1864.* New York: Arno, 1969.

Blassingame, John W., ed. *The Frederick Douglass Papers.* 4 vols. New Haven: Yale Univ. Press, 1979-86.

Boucher, Chauncy S., ed. "Correspondence Addressed to John C. Calhoun, 1837-1849." *Annual Report of the American Historical Association for the Year 1929.* 2 vols. Washington,D.C.: G.P.O., 1930.

Bourne, Edward G., et al., eds. "Diary and Correspondence of Salmon P. Chase." *Annual Report of the American Historical Association for the Year 1902.* 2 vols. Washington, D.C.: G.P.O., 1903.

By-Laws of the Webster Kentucky Farm Association: With a Brief Description of Its Origins and Object. Boston: Geo. C. Rand and Avery, 1858.

The Case of William L. Chaplin. Boston: Chaplin Committee, 1851.

Clay, Cassius M. *Speech of C.M. Clay, at Lexington, Ky., Delivered August 1, 1851.* Lexington: privately printed, 1851.

Cleveland, Charles Dexter, ed. *Anti-Slavery Addresses of 1844 and 1845.* Philadelphia: J.A. Bancroft, 1867.

Congressional Globe.

Cralle, Richard K., ed. *The Works of John C. Calhoun.* 6 vols. New York: D. Appleton, 1874-1888.

Crist, Lynda Lasswell, ed. *The Papers of Jefferson Davis.* 7 vols. to date. Baton Rouge: Louisiana State Univ. Press, 1971-85.

Drayton, Daniel. *Personal Memoirs of Daniel Drayton.* New York: Bela Marsh, 1855.

Dumond, Dwight L., ed. *The Letters of James G. Birney.* 2 vols. New York: Appleton-Century, 1938.

——. ed. *Southern Editorials on Secession.* 1931. Reprint, Gloucester, Ma.: Peter Smith, 1964.

Fee, John G. *Colonization: The Present Scheme of Colonization Wrong, Delusive, and Retards Emancipation.* Cincinnati: American Reform Tract and Book Society, [1854].

Filler, Louis, ed. *Wendell Phillips on Civil Rights and Freedom.* New York: Hill and Wang, 1965.

Garnet, Henry Highland. *The Past and Present Condition and Destiny of the Colored Race.* 1848. Reprint, Miami: Mnemosyne, 1969.

Garrison, William Lloyd, comp. *The New "Reign of Terror" in the Slaveholding States, for 1859-60.* New York: AASS, 1960.

Goodell, William. *Slavery and Antislavery: A History of the Great Struggle in Both Hemispheres.* 1852. Reprint, New York: Negro Univs. Press, 1968.

Greeley, Horace, ed. *The Writings of Cassius Marcellus Clay.* 1848. Reprint, New York: Negro Univs. Press, 1969.

Griffiths, Julia. *Autographs for Freedom.* 2 vols. 1853. Reprint, Miami: Mnemosyne, 1969.

[Hammond, Jabez D.]. *Life and Opinions of Julius Melbourne.* Syracuse, N.Y.: Hall and Dickson, 1847.

Helper, Hinton Rowen. *The Impending Crisis of the South: How to Meet It.* New York: Burdick Brothers, 1857.

[Higginson, Thomas Wentworth]. "Nat Turner's Insurrection." *Atlantic Monthly* 8 (Aug. 1861): 173-87.

Higginson, Thomas Wentworth. "Physical Courage," *Atlantic Monthly* 2 (Sept. 1858):728-37.

[Janney, Samuel M.]. *The Yankees in Fairfax County, Virginia.* Baltimore: Snodgrass and Wehrly, 1845.

Lovejoy, J[oseph] C. *Memoir of Rev. Charles T. Torrey.* 2d ed. 1848. Reprint, New York: Negro Univs. Press, 1969.

Marsh, Luther Rawson, ed. *The Writings and Speeches of Alvan Stewart on Slavery*. 1860. Reprint, New York: Negro Univs. Press, 1969.

Martineau, Harriet. *The Martyr Age in the United States*. 1839. Reprint, New York: Arno, 1969.

Massachusetts Anti-Slavery Society. *Annual Reports*. 1835-56. Reprint, Westport, Conn.: Negro Univs. Press, 1970.

Matlack, Lucius C. *The History of American Slavery and Methodism, from 1780 to 1849; and History of the Wesleyan Connection of America*. New York: privately printed, 1849.

Merrill, Walter M., and Louis Ruchames, eds. *The Letters of William Lloyd Garrison*. 6 vols. Cambridge, Ma.: Harvard Univ. Press, 1971-81.

Minutes of the State Convention of the Colored Citizens of Ohio: Convened at Columbus, Jan. 16, 17, and 18th, 1851. [Columbus]: E. Glover, 1851.

Narrative of Facts Respecting Alanson Work, Jas. E. Burr, and Geo. Thompson. Quincy, Ill.: *Quincy Whig*, 1842.

New England Anti-Slavery Society. *Annual Reports*. 1833-34. Reprint, Westport, Ct.: Negro Univs. Press, 1970.

Ohio Anti-Slavery Society. *Report of the Second Anniversary*. Cincinnati: OASS, 1837.

——. *Report of the Third Anniversary*. Cincinnati: OASS, 1838.

Phelps, Amos A. *Lectures on Slavery and Its Remedy*. Boston: NEASS, 1834.

Phillips, Wendell. *Speeches, Lectures, and Letters*. 3d ed. Boston: J. Redpath, 1863; and Boston: Lee and Shepard, 1892.

Pickard, Kate. *The Kidnapped and the Ransomed*. 1856. Reprint, New York: Negro Univs. Press, 1968.

Publicola. "Present Aspects of Abolitionism." *Southern Literary Messenger* 8 (July 1847): 429-34.

Redpath, James. *The Roving Editor: Or, Talks with Slaves in the Southern States*. 1859. Reprint, New York: Negro Univs. Press, 1968.

Ripley, C. Peter, ed. *The Black Abolitionist Papers*. 5 vols. Chapel Hill: Univ. of North Carolina Press, 1985-92.

Rogers, Nathaniel P. *Collections from the Miscellaneous Writings of Nathaniel P. Rogers*. 2d ed. Manchester, N.H.: W.H. Fisk, 1849.

Roland, Dunbar, ed. *Jefferson Davis, Constitutionalist: His Letters, Papers, and Speeches*. 10 vols. Jackson, Miss.: Mississippi Dept. of Archives and History, 1923.

Ruffin, Edmund. "Consequences of Abolitionist Agitation." *DeBow's Review* 22 (June 1857): 587-88.

Sanborn, Franklin B. *The Life and Letters of John Brown*. 1885. Reprint, New York: Negro Univs. Press, 1969.

Stowe, Harriet Beecher. *Uncle Tom's Cabin; Or, Life Among the Lowly*. Boston: Jewett, 1852.

Thompson, George. *Prison Life and Reflections.* 1847. Reprint, New York: Negro Univs. Press, 1969.

Walker, David. *David Walker's Appeal.* Ed. Charles M. Wiltse. New York: Hill and Wang, 1965.

Walker, Jonathan. *Trial and Imprisonment of Jonathan Walker.* 2d ed. 1848. Reprint, New York: Negro Univs. Press, 1970.

Webster, Delia A. *Kentucky Jurisprudence: A History of the Trial of Miss Delia A. Webster.* Vergennes, Vt.: E.W. Blaisdell, 1845.

Whittier, John Greenleaf. *The Conflict with Slavery, Politics, and Reform: The Inner Life Criticisms.* New York: Houghton Mifflin, 1889.

Wilson, Clyde N., ed. *Selections from the Letters and Speeches of Hon. James H. Hammond of South Carolina.* 1866. Reprint, Spartanburg, S.C.: Reprint Company, 1977.

Memoirs, Reminiscences, and Autobiographies

Clay, Cassius M. *The Life of Cassius Marcellus Clay.* 1886. Reprint, New York: Negro Univs. Press, 1969.

Coffin, Levi. *Reminiscences of Levi Coffin, the Reputed President of the Underground Railroad.* 3d ed. 1898. Reprint, New York: Arno, 1968.

Fairbank, Calvin. *Rev. Calvin Fairbank during Slavery Times.* 1890. Reprint, New York: Negro Univs. Press, 1969.

Fee, John G. *The Autobiography of John G. Fee.* Chicago: National Christian Assoc., 1891.

Mathews, Edward. *The Autobiography of the Rev. E. Mathews, the "Father Dickson" of Mrs. Stowe's "Dred."* 1866. Reprint, Miami: Mnemosyne, 1969.

May, Samuel J. *Some Recollections of Our Anti-Slavery Conflict.* 1869. Reprint, New York: Arno, 1968.

Pillsbury, Parker. *Acts of the Anti-Slavery Apostles.* 1883. Reprint, Miami: Mnemosyne, 1969.

Stanton, Henry B. *Random Recollections.* New York: Harper, 1887.

Thayer, Eli. *A History of the Kansas Crusade, Its Friends, and Its Foes.* New York: Harper, 1889.

Books

Abbott, Richard H. *The Republican Party and the South, 1855-1877: The First Southern Strategy.* Chapel Hill: Univ. of North Carolina Press, 1986.

Adams, Alice Dana. *The Neglected Period of Anti-Slavery in America, 1808-1832.* 1908. Reprint, Gloucester, Ma.: Peter Smith, 1964.

Aptheker, Herbert. *Abolitionism: A Revolutionary Movement.* Boston: Twayne, 1989.

——. *American Negro Slave Revolts.* New Edition. New York: International Publishers, 1974.

——. *Anti-Racism in U.S. History: The First Two Hundred Years*. New York: Greenwood, 1992.

Bailey, Hugh C. *Hinton Rowan Helper: Abolitionist Racist*. Montgomery: Univ. of Alabama Press, 1965.

Barnes, Gilbert H. *The Antislavery Impulse, 1830-1844*. 1933. Reprint, Gloucester, Ma.: Peter Smith, 1973.

Barney, William L. *The Road to Secession: A New Perspective on the Old South*. New York: Praeger, 1972.

——. *The Secessionist Impulse: Alabama and Mississippi in 1860*. Princeton: Princeton Univ. Press, 1974.

Bassett, John Spencer. *Anti-Slavery Leaders of North Carolina*. 1898. Reprint, Spartanburg, S.C.: Reprint Company, 1971.

Benson, Lee. *The Concept of Jacksonian Democracy: New York as a Test Case*. Princeton: Princeton Univ. Press, 1961.

Berlin, Ira. *Slaves without Masters: The Free Negro in the Antebellum South*. New York: Random House, 1974.

Birney, William. *James G. Birney and His Times: The Genesis of the Republican Party with Some Account of the Abolitionist Movement in the South before 1828*. 1890. Reprint, New York: Negro Univs. Press, 1969.

Blue, Frederick. *The Free Soilers: Third Party Politics, 1848-54*. Urbana: Univ. of Illinois Press, 1973.

——. *Salmon P. Chase: A Life in Politics*. Kent, Ohio: Kent State Univ. Press, 1987.

Boles, John B. *Masters and Slaves in the House of the Lord: Race and Religion in the American South, 1740-1870*. Lexington: Univ. Press of Kentucky, 1988.

Boyer, Richard O. *The Legend of John Brown: A Biography and a History*. New York: Knopf, 1973.

Bracy, John H., et al. eds. *Blacks in the Abolitionist Movement*. Belmont, Cal.: Wadsworth, 1971.

Brandt, Nat. *The Town that Started the Civil War*. Syracuse, N.Y.: Syracuse Univ. Press, 1990.

Bruce, Dickson D. *Violence and Culture in the Antebellum South*. Austin: Univ. of Texas Press, 1979.

Channing, Steven A. *Crisis of Fear: Secession in South Carolina*. New York: Norton, 1974.

Cheek, William F., and Aimee L. Cheek. *John Mercer Langston and the Fight for Black Freedom*. Champaign: Univ. of Illinois Press, 1989.

Clephane, Lewis. *Birth of the Republican Party*. Washington: Gibson Bros., 1889.

Coleman, J. Winston. *Slavery Times in Kentucky*. Chapel Hill: Univ. of North Carolina Press, 1940.

Commager, Henry Steele. *Theodore Parker*. Boston: Beacon, 1947.

Cornish, Dudley T. *The Sable Arm: Negro Troops in the Union Army*. 1956. Reprint, New York: Norton, 1966.

Cover, Robert M. *Justice Accused: Antislavery and the Judicial Process.* New Haven, Conn.: Yale Univ. Press, 1975.

Craven, Avery O. *The Coming of the Civil War.* 2d ed. Chicago: Univ. of Chicago Press, 1957.

Crooks, Elizabeth W. *The Life of Rev. A. Crooks, Written and Compiled by His Wife.* Syracuse, N.Y.: Wesleyan Methodist Publishing, 1875.

Cross, Whitney R. *The Burned-over District: The Social and Intellectual History of Enthusiastic Religion in Western New York, 1800-1850.* Ithaca: Cornell Univ. Press, 1950.

Current, Richard N. *Northernizing the South.* Athens: Univ. of Georgia Press, 1983.

Davis, David Brion. *The Problem of Slavery in the Age of Revolution.* Ithaca, N.Y.: Cornell Univ. Press, 1975.

——. *The Problem of Slavery in Western Culture.* Ithaca, N.Y.: Cornell Univ. Press, 1966.

——. *The Slave Power Conspiracy and the Paranoid Style.* Baton Rouge: Louisiana State Univ. Press, 1961.

Davis, Hugh. *Joshua Leavitt: Evangelical Abolitionist.* Baton Rouge: Louisiana State Univ. Press, 1990.

D'Entremont, John. *Southern Emancipator, Moncure Conway: The American Years.* New York: Oxford Univ. Press, 1987.

Degler, Carl N. *The Other South: Southern Dissenters in the Nineteenth Century.* New York: Harper and Row, 1974.

Dillon, Merton L. *The Abolitionists: The Growth of a Dissenting Minority.* New York: Norton, 1974.

——. *Benjamin Lundy and the Struggle for Negro Freedom.* Urbana: Univ. of Illinois Press, 1966.

——. *Slavery Attacked: Southern Slaves and their Allies, 1619-1865.* Baton Rouge: Louisiana State Univ. Press, 1990.

Donald, David. *Lincoln Reconsidered: Essays on the Civil War Era.* 2d ed. 1956. Reprint, New York: Random House, 1961.

Duberman, Martin, ed. *The Antislavery Vanguard.* Princeton: Princeton Univ. Press, 1965.

Dumond, Dwight L. *Antislavery Origins of the Civil War in the United States.* 1939. Reprint, Ann Arbor: Univ. of Michigan Press, 1969.

——. *Antislavery: The Crusade for Freedom in America.* New York: Norton, 1961.

Eaton, Clement. *The Freedom-of-Thought Struggle in the Old South.* New York: Harper and Row, 1964.

Edelstein, Tilden G. *Strange Enthusiasm: A Life of Thomas Wentworth Higginson.* New Haven, Conn.: Yale Univ. Press, 1968.

Egerton, Douglas B. *Gabriel's Rebellion: The Virginia Slave Conspiracies of 1800 and 1802.* Chapel Hill: Univ. of North Carolina Press, 1993.

Fields, Barbara Jeanne. *Slavery and Freedom on the Middle Ground: Maryland During the Nineteenth Century*. New Haven: Yale Univ. Press, 1985.

Filler, Louis. *The Crusade Against Slavery, 1830-1860*. New York: Harper and Row, 1960.

Fladeland, Betty. *James Gillespie Birney: Slaveholder to Abolitionist*. Ithaca, N.Y.: Cornell Univ. Press, 1955.

Floan, Howard R. *The South in Northern Eyes, 1831-1861*. Austin: Univ. of Texas Press, 1958.

Foner, Eric. *Free Soil, Free Labor, Free Men: The Ideology of the Republican Party before the Civil War*. New York: Oxford Univ. Press, 1970.

——. *Politics and Ideology in the Age of the Civil War*. New York: Oxford Univ. Press, 1980.

——. *Reconstruction: America's Unfinished Revolution, 1863-1877*. New York: Oxford Univ. Press, 1988.

Fredrickson, George M. *The Arrogance of Race: Historical Perspectives on Slavery, Racism, and Social Inequality*. Middleton, Conn.: Wesleyan Univ. Press, 1988.

——. *The Black Image in the White Mind: The Debate on Afro-American Character and Destiny, 1871-1964*. New York: Harper and Row, 1971.

Freehling, Alison Goodyear. *Drift Toward Dissolution: The Virginia Slavery Debate of 1831-1832*. Baton Rouge: Louisiana State Univ. Press, 1982.

Freehling, William W. *Prelude to the Civil War: The Nullification Controversy*. New York: Harper and Row, 1966.

——. *The Road to Disunion*. 2 vols. projected. New York: Oxford Univ. Press, 1990.

Friedman, Lawrence J. *Gregarious Saints: Self and Community in American Abolitionism, 1830-1870*. New York: Cambridge Univ. Press, 1982.

Gara, Larry. *The Liberty Line: The Legend of the Underground Railroad*. Lexington: Univ. of Kentucky Press, 1961.

Garrison, Wendell Phillips, and Francis Jackson Garrison. *William Lloyd Garrison, 1805-1889: The Story of His Life Told by His Children*. 4 vols. New York: Century, 1885-89.

Genovese, Eugene D. *From Rebellion to Revolution: Afro-American Slave Revolts in the Making of the Modern World*. Baton Rouge: Louisiana State Univ. Press, 1979.

——. *Roll, Jordan, Roll: The World the Slaves Made*. New York: Pantheon, 1974.

Gerteis, Louis S. *Morality and Utility in American Antislavery Reform*. Chapel Hill: Univ. of North Carolina Press, 1987.

Gienapp, William. *The Origins of the Republican Party, 1852-1856*. New York: Oxford Univ. Press, 1987.

Glatthaar, Joseph T. *Forged in Battle: The Civil War Alliance of Black Soldiers and White Officers*. New York: Free Press, 1990.

Greeley, Horace. *The American Conflict: A History of the Great Rebellion in the United States, 1860-1865*. 2 vols. Hartford, Conn.: O.D. Case, 1867.

Hallowell, Anna Davis. *James and Lucretia Mott: Life and Letters*. Boston: Houghton Mifflin, 1885.

Harlow, Ralph V. *Gerrit Smith, Philanthropist and Reformer*. New York: Holt, 1939.

Harrison, Lowell H. *The Antislavery Movement in Kentucky*. Lexington: Univ. Press of Kentucky, 1978.

Harrold, Stanley. *Gamaliel Bailey and Antislavery Union*. Kent, Ohio: Kent State Univ. Press, 1986.

Hart, Albert Bushnell. *Slavery and Abolition, 1831-1841*. 1906. Reprint, New York: New American Library, 1969.

Higham, John. *History: The Development of Historical Studies in the United States*. Englewood Cliffs, N.J.: Prentice-Hall, 1965.

Holst, Herman E. von. *Constitutional and Political History of the United States*. 8 vols. Chicago: Callaghan, 1877-1902.

Howard, Victor B. *Conscience and Slavery: The Evangelistic Domestic Missions, 1837-1861*. Kent, Ohio: Kent State Univ. Press, 1990.

——. *Religion and the Radical Republican Movement, 1860-1870*. Lexington: Univ. Press of Kentucky, 1990.

Howe, Daniel Walker. *The Political Culture of the American Whigs*. Chicago: Univ. of Chicago Press, 1979.

Hunt, Alfred N. *Haiti's Influence on Antebellum America: Slumbering Volcano in the Caribbean*. Baton Rouge: Louisiana State Univ. Press, 1988.

Jacobs, Donald J., ed. *Courage and Conscience: Black and White Abolitionists in Boston*. Bloomington: Indiana Univ. Press, 1993.

James, Howard. *Mutiny on the "Amistad": The Saga of a Slave Revolt and Its Impact on American Abolition, Law, and Diplomacy*. New York: Oxford Univ. Press, 1986.

Johnson, Michael P. *Toward a Patriarchal Republic: The Secession of Georgia*. Baton Rouge: Louisiana State Univ. Press, 1977.

Johnson, Oliver. *William Lloyd Garrison and His Times: Or Sketches of the Anti-Slavery Movement in America*. 1881. Reprint, Miami: Mnemosyn, 1969.

Johnson, Samuel A. *The Battle Cry of Freedom: The New England Emigrant Aid Company in the Kansas Crusade*. Lawrence: Univ. of Kansas Press, 1954.

Jones, Howard. *Mutiny on the "Amistad": The Saga of a Slave Revolt and Its Impact on American Abolition, Law, and Diplomacy*. New York: Oxford Univ. Press, 1986.

Kraditor, Aileen S. *Means and Ends in American Abolitionism: Garrison and His Critics on Strategy and Tactics*. New York: Random House, 1967.

Kraut, Alan M., ed. *Crusaders and Compromisers: Essays in the Relationship of the Antislavery Struggle to the Antebellum Party System*. Westport, Conn.: Greenwood, 1983.

Lerner, Gerda. *The Grimké Sisters from South Carolina: Rebels against Slavery*. Boston: Houghton Mifflin, 1967.

Levine, Bruce. *Half Slave and Half Free: The Roots of the Civil War*. New York: Hill and Wang, 1992.

Litwack, Leon. *North of Slavery: The Negro in the Free States, 1790-1860*. Chicago: Univ. of Chicago Press, 1960.

Litwack, Leon, and August Meier, eds. *Black Leaders of the Nineteenth Century*. Urbana: Univ. of Illinois Press, 1988.

Lowe, Richard C. *Republicans and Reconstruction in Virginia, 1856-1870*. Charlottesville: Univ. Press of Virginia, 1991.

Mabee, Carlton. *Black Freedom: The Nonviolent Abolitionists from 1830 through the Civil War*. London: Macmillan, 1970.

Martin, Asa Earle. *The Antislavery Movement in Kentucky Prior to 1850*. 1918. Reprint, New York: Negro Univs. Press, 1970.

Mayer, George E. *The Republican Party, 1854-1964*. New York: Oxford Univ. Press, 1964.

McFeely, William S. *Frederick Douglass*. New York: Simon and Schuster, 1991.

McGowan, James A. *Station Master on the Underground Railroad: The Life and Letters of Thomas Garrett*. Moylan, Pa.: Whimsie Press, 1977.

McKivigan, John R. *The War Against Proslavery Religion: Abolitionism and the Northern Churches, 1830-1865*. Ithaca, N.Y.: Cornell Univ. Press, 1984.

McLeister, Ira F., and Roy S. Nicholson. *Conscience and Commitment: the History of the Wesleyan Methodist Church of America*. 4th ed. Marion, Ind.: Wesley, 1976.

McMaster, John Bach. *History of the People of the United States, from the Revolution to the Civil War*. 8 vols. New York: D. Appleton, 1883-1913.

McPherson, James M. *The Struggle for Equality: Abolitionists and the Negro in the Civil War and Reconstruction*. Princeton: Princeton Univ. Press, 1964.

———. *Ordeal by Fire: The Civil War and Reconstruction*. 2d ed. New York: McGraw-Hill, 1992.

Merkel, Benjamin. *The Antislavery Controversy in Missouri, 1819-1865: Abstract of a Dissertation*. St. Louis: Washington Univ., 1942.

Messerli, John. *Horace Mann, A Biography*. New York: Knopf, 1972.

Milton, George F. *The Eve of Conflict: Stephen A. Douglas and the Needless War*. New York: Houghton-Mifflin, 1934.

Nash, Gary B., and Richard Weiss, eds. *The Great Fear: Race in the Mind of America*. New York: Rinehart and Winston, 1970.

Nicholson, Roy S. *Wesleyan Methodism in the South*. Syracuse: Wesleyan Methodist Publishing, 1933.

Nye, Russell B. *Fettered Freedom: Civil Liberties and the Slavery Controversy, 1830-1860*. East Lansing: Michigan State Univ. Press, 1963.

Oates, Stephen B. *The Fires of the Jubilee: Nat Turner's Fierce Rebellion*. New York: Harper and Row, 1975.

———. *To Purge this Land with Blood: A Biography of John Brown*. 2d. ed. Amherst: Univ. of Massachusetts Press, 1984.

Pease, Jane H., and William H. Pease. *Bound With Them in Chains: A Biographical History of the Antislavery Movement*. Westport, Conn.: Greenwood, 1972.

——. *They Who Would Be Free: Blacks' Search for Freedom, 1830-1861*. New York: Athenaeum, 1974.

Perry, Lewis. *Radical Abolitionism: Anarchy and the Government of God in Antislavery Thought*. Ithaca, N.Y.: Cornell Univ. Press, 1973.

——. and Michael Fellman, eds. *Antislavery Reconsidered: New Perspectives on the Abolitionists*. Baton Rouge: Univ. of Louisiana Press, 1979.

Phillips, Ulrich B. *The Course of the South to Secession*. New York: Appleton-Century, 1933.

Plummer, Mark A. *Frontier Governor: Samuel J. Crawford of Kansas*. Lawrence: Univ. Press of Kansas, 1971.

Pressly, Thomas J. *Americans Interpret Their Civil War*. 2d ed.; New York: Free Press, 1965.

Pugh, David G. *Sons of Liberty: The Masculine Mind in Nineteenth-Century America*. Westport, Conn.: Greenwood, 1983.

Quarles, Benjamin. *Black Abolitionists*. New York: Oxford Univ. Press, 1969.

Quint, Howard H., and Milton Cantor, eds. *Men, Women, and Issues in American History*. 2 vols. Homewood, Ill.: Dorsey, 1980.

Randall, James G. *The Civil War and Reconstruction*. New York: Heath, 1937.

Remini, Robert V. *Henry Clay: Statesman for the Union*. New York: Norton, 1991.

Rhodes, James Ford. *History of the United States*. 8 vols. 1892-1928. Reprint, Port Washington, N.Y.: Kennikat Press, 1967.

Richardson, Joe M. *Christian Reconstruction: The American Missionary Association and Southern Blacks, 1861-1890*. Athens: Univ. of Georgia Press, 1986.

Robert, Joseph Clarke. *The Road from Monticello: A Study of the Virginia Slavery . Debates of 1832*. Durham, N.C.: Duke Univ. Press, 1941.

Rossbach, Jeffery S. *Ambivalent Conspirators: John Brown, the Secret Six, and a Theory of Slave Violence*. Philadelphia: Univ. of Pennsylvania Press, 1982.

Savage, William Sherman. *The Controversy over the Distribution of Abolitionist Literature, 1830-1860*. Washington, D.C.: Assoc. for the Study of Negro Life and History, 1938.

Scarborough, Ruth. *The Opposition to Slavery in Georgia Prior to 1860*. 1933. Reprint, New York: Negro Univs. Press, 1968.

Schor, Joel. *Henry Highland Garnet: A Voice of Black Radicalism in the Nineteenth Century*. Westport, Conn.: Greenwood, 1977.

Sears, Richard D. *The Day of Small Things: Abolitionism in the Midst of Slavery, Berea, Kentucky, 1854-1864*. Lanham, Md.: Univ. Press of America, 1986.

Sewell, Richard H. *Ballots for Freedom: Antislavery Politics in the United States, 1837-1860*. New York: Oxford Univ. Press, 1976.

Siebert, Wilbur H. *The Underground Railroad from Slavery to Freedom*. 1898. Reprint, New York: Arno, 1968.

Smiley, David L. *Lion of White Hall: The Life of Cassius M. Clay*. Madison: Univ. of Wisconsin Press, 1962.

Smith, H. Shelton. *In His Image, But . . . : Racism in Southern Religion, 1780-1910*.
Durham, N.C.: Duke Univ. Press, 1972.

Smith, Theodore Clarke. *The Liberty and Free Soil Parties of the Northwest*. 1897. Reprint, New York: Arno, 1969.

Smith, William E. *The Francis Preston Blair Family in Politics*. 2 vols. New York: Macmillan, 1933.

Sorin, Gerald. *The New York Abolitionists: A Case Study of Political Radicalism*. Westport, Conn.: Greenwood, 1971.

Stanton, William R. *The Leopard's Spots: Scientific Attitudes toward Race in America, 1815-1859*. Chicago: Univ. of Chicago Press, 1960.

Stern, Madelene B. *The Patriarch: A Biography of Stephen Pearl Andrews*. Austin: Univ. of Texas Press, 1968.

Stewart, James Brewer. *Holy Warriors: The Abolitionists and American Slavery*. New York: Hill and Wang, 1976.

——. *Joshua R. Giddings and the Tactics of Radical Politics*. Cleveland: Case-Western Reserve Univ. Press, 1970.

——. *Wendell Phillips, Liberty's Hero*. Baton Rouge: Louisiana State Univ. Press, 1986.

Still, William. *The Underground Railroad*. 1871. Reprint, Chicago: Johnson Publishing, 1970.

Sundquist, Eric J., ed. *Frederick Douglass: New Literary and Historical Essays*. New York: Cambridge Univ. Press, 1990.

Takaki, Ronald. *Iron Cages: Race and Culture in Nineteenth-Century America*. New York: Knopf, 1979.

Thomas, Benjamin P. *Theodore Weld: Crusader for Freedom*. New Brunswick, N.J.: Rutgers Univ. Press, 1950.

Tise, Larry E. *Proslavery: A History of the Defense of Slavery in America, 1701-1840*. Athens: Univ. of Georgia Press, 1987.

Trefousse, Hans. L. *The Radical Republicans: Lincoln's Vanguard for Racial Justice*. Baton Rouge: Louisiana State Univ. Press, 1968.

Tuckerman, Bayard. *William Jay and the Constitutional Movement for the Abolition of Slavery*. 1893. Reprint, New York: Negro Univs. Press, 1969.

Tyler, Alice Felt. *Freedom's Ferment: Phases of American Social History from the Colonial Period to the Outbreak of the Civil War*. New York: Harper and Row, 1944.

Volpe, Vernon L. *Forlorn Hope of Freedom: The Liberty Party in the Old Northwest, 1838-1848*. Kent, Ohio: Kent State Univ. Press, 1990.

Walker, Peter. *Moral Choices: Memory, Desire, and Imagination in Nineteenth-Century American Abolitionism*. Baton Rouge: Louisiana State Univ. Press, 1978.

Walters, Ronald G. *The Antislavery Appeal: American Abolitionism after 1830.* Baltimore: Johns Hopkins Univ. Press, 1976.

Ward, John William. *Andrew Jackson—Symbol for an Age.* 1953. Reprint, New York: Oxford Univ. Press, 1962.

Whitfield, Theodore M. *Slavery Agitation in Virginia, 1829-1832.* Baltimore: Johns Hopkins Univ. Press, 1930.

Wiecek, William W. *The Sources of Antislavery Constitutionalism in America.* Ithaca, N.Y.: Cornell Univ. Press, 1977.

Willey, Austin. *The History of the Antislavery Cause in State and Nation.* 1886. Reprint, New York: Negro Univs. Press, 1969.

Wilson, Henry. *History of the Rise and Fall of the Slave Power in America.* 3d ed. 3 vols. Boston: James R. Osgood, 1876.

Wolf, Hazel C. *On Freedom's Altar: The Martyr Complex in the Abolitionist Movement.* Madison: Univ. of Wisconsin Press, 1952.

Wood, Forrest G. *The Arrogance of Faith: Christianity and Race in America from the Colonial Era to the Twentieth Century.* New York: Knopf, 1990.

Wyatt-Brown, Bertram. *Lewis Tappan and the Evangelical War Against Slavery.* Cleveland: Case-Western Reserve Univ. Press, 1969.

——. *Southern Honor: Ethics and Behavior in the Old South.* New York: Oxford Univ. Press, 1982.

——. *Yankee Saints and Southern Sinners.* Baton Rouge: Louisiana State Univ. Press, 1985.

Yacavone, Donald. *Samuel Joseph May and the Dilemmas of the Liberal Persuasion, 1797-1871.* Philadelphia: Temple Univ. Press, 1991.

Zilversmit, Arthur. *The First Emancipation: The Abolition of Slavery in the North.* Chicago: Univ. of Chicago Press, 1967.

Articles

Abzug, Robert H. "The Influence of Garrisonian Abolitionists' Fear of Slave Violence on the Antislavery Argument, 1829-1840." *Journal of Negro History* 55 (Jan. 1970): 15-28.

Aptheker, Herbert. "Militant Abolitionism." *Journal of Negro History* 26 (Oct. 1941): 438-84.

Batson, C. Daniel, et al. "Is Empathic Emotion a Source of Altruistic Motivation?" *Journal of Personality and Social Psychology* 40 (Feb. 1981): 290-302.

Bentley, Nancy. "White Slaves: The Mulatto Hero in Antebellum Fiction." *American Literature* 65 (Sept. 1993): 501-22.

Clephane, Walter C. "Lewis C. Clephane: A Pioneer Washington Republican." *Records of the Columbia Historical Society* 21 (1918): 263-77.

Curry, Richard O. "The Abolitionists and Reconstruction: A Critical Appraisal." *Journal of Southern History* 34 (Nov. 1968): 527-45.

——, and Lawrence B. Goodheart. "'Knives in their Heads': Passionate Self-Analysis and the Search for Identity in American Abolitionism." *Canadian Review of American Studies* 14 (Winter 1983): 401-14.

Davis, David Brion. "Antislavery or Abolition?" *Reviews in American History* 1 (Mar. 1973): 95-99.

Demos, John. "The Antislavery Movement and the Problem of Violent 'Means.'" *New England Quarterly* 37 (Dec. 1964): 501-26.

Dew, Charles B. "Black Ironworkers and the Slave Insurrection Panic of 1856." *Journal of Southern History* 41 (Aug. 1975): 321-38.

Dillon, Merton L. "The Abolitionists: A Decade of Historiography, 1959-1969." *Journal of Southern History* 35 (Nov. 1969): 500-22.

——. "Three Southern Antislavery Editors: The Myth of the Southern Antislavery Movement." *East Tennessee Historical Society Publications* 17 (1970): 47-56.

Eaton, Clement. "The Resistance of the South to Northern Radicalism." *New England Quarterly* 8 (June 1935): 215-31.

Fellman, Michael. "Theodore Parker and the Abolitionist Role in the 1850s." *Journal of American History* 61 (Dec. 1974): 66-84.

Finnie, Gordon E. "The Antislavery Movement in the Upper South before 1840." *Journal of Southern History* 35 (Aug. 1969): 319-42.

Foner, Eric. "The Causes of the Civil War: Recent Interpretations and New Directions." *Civil War History* 20 (Sept. 1974): 197-214.

Formisano, Ronald P. "Political Character, Antipartyism, and the Second American Party System." *American Quarterly* 21 (Winter 1969): 683-709.

Freehling, William W. "The Editorial Revolution, Virginia and the Coming of the Civil War: A Review Essay." *Civil War History* 16 (Mar. 1970): 64-72.

Friedman, Lawrence J. "'Historical Topics Sometimes Run Dry': The State of Abolitionist Studies." *Historian* 43 (Feb. 1981): 177-94.

Gerteis, Louis S. "Slavery and Hard Times: Morality and Utility in American Antislavery Reform." *Civil War History* 29 (Dec. 1983): 316-31.

Gray, Myra Gladys. "Archibald W. Campbell—Party Builder." *West Virginia History* 7 (Ap. 1946): 221-37.

Green, Fletcher M. "Northern Missionary Activities in the South, 1846-1861." *Journal of Southern History* 21 (May 1955): 147-72.

Harrison, Lowell H. "The Anti-Slavery Career of Cassius M. Clay." *Register of the Kentucky Historical Society* 59 (Oct. 1961): 259-317.

——. "Cassius Marcellus Clay and the *True American.*" *Filson Club History Quarterly* 22 (Jan. 1948): 30-49.

Harrold, Stanley. "Cassius M. Clay on Slavery and Race: A Reinterpretation." *Slavery and Abolition* 9 (May 1988): 42-56.

——. "The Intersectional Relationship between Cassius M. Clay and the Garrisonian Abolitionists." *Civil War History* 35 (June 1989): 101-19.

——. "The Southern Strategy of the Liberty Party." *Ohio History* 87 (Winter 1978): 21-36.

——. "Violence and Nonviolence in Kentucky Abolitionism." *Journal of Southern History* 57 (Feb. 1991): 15-38.

Hesseltine, W[illiam] B. "Some New Aspects of the Pro-Slavery Argument." *Journal of Negro History* 21 (Jan. 1936): 1-14.

Hickin, Patricia. "Gentle Agitator: Samuel M. Janney and the Antislavery Movement in Virginia, 1842-1851." *Journal of Southern History* 37 (May 1971): 159-90.

——. "John C. Underwood and the Antislavery Movement in Virginia, 1847-1860." *Virginia Magazine of History and Biography* 73 (Apr. 1965): 156-68.

Higginson, Thomas Wentworth. "Anti-Slavery Days." *Outlook* 60 (Sept. 3, 1898): 47-57.

Hoganson, Kristan. "Garrisonian Abolitionists and the Rhetoric of Gender, 1850-1860." *American Quarterly* 45 (Dec. 1993): 558-95.

Howard, Victor B. "Cassius M. Clay and the Origins of the Republican Party." *Filson Club Historical Quarterly* 45 (Jan. 1971): 49-71.

——. "James Madison Pendleton: A Southern Crusader Against Slavery." *Register of the Kentucky Historical Society* 74 (July 1976): 192-215.

Huston, James L. "The Experiential Basis of the Northern Antislavery Impulse." *Journal of Southern History* 56 (Nov. 1990): 609-40.

Johnson, Clifton H. "Abolitionist Missionary Activities in North Carolina." *North Carolina Historical Review* 40 (July 1963): 295-320.

Johnson, Oliver. "Charles Osborn's Place in Anti-Slavery History." *International Review* 13 (Sept. 1882): 191-206.

Jones, Howard. "The Peculiar Institution and National Honor: The Case of the *Creole* Slave Revolt." *Civil War History* 21 (Mar. 1975): 28-50.

Julian, George W. "The Genesis of Modern Abolitionism." *International Review* 12 (June 1882): 533-55.

Keith, Jean E. "Joseph Rogers Underwood, Friend of African Colonization." *Filson Club History Quarterly* 22 (Ap. 1948): 117-32.

Mathews, Donald G. "The Abolitionists on Slavery: The Critique Behind the Social Movement." *Journal of Southern History* 33 (May 1967): 163-182.

McClintic, Elizabeth K. "Ceredo: An Experiment in Colonization and a Dream of Empire." *West Virginia Review* 15 (Mar., May 1938): 168-90, 198-200, 233-54.

McKivigan, John R. "Antislavery 'Comeouter' Sects: A Neglected Dimension of the Abolitionist Movement." *Civil War History* 26 (June 1980): 142-60.

——. "The Gospel Will Burst the Bonds of the Slave: The Abolitionists' Bibles for Slaves Campaign." *Negro History Bulletin* 45 (July-Sept. 1982): 62-64, 77.

Pease, Jane H., and William H. Pease. "Antislavery Ambivalence: Immediatism, Expediency, Race." *American Quarterly* 17 (Winter 1965): 682-95.

——. "Confrontation and Abolition in the 1850s." *Journal of American History* 58 (Mar. 1972): 923-37.

——. "Ends, Means, and Attitudes: Black-White Conflict in the Antislavery Movement." *Civil War History* 18 (June 1972): 117-28.

Phillips, Ulrich B. "Conservatism and Progress in the Cotton Belt." *South Atlantic Quarterly* 3 (Jan. 1904): 1-10.

——. "The Plantation as a Civilizing Factor." *Sewanne River Review* 12 (July 1904): 257-67.

Price, Robert. "The Ohio Anti-Slavery Convention of 1836." *Ohio State Archaeological and Historical Quarterly* 45 (Apr. 1936): 173-88.

Rice, Otis K. "Eli Thayer and the Friendly Invasion of Virginia." *Journal of Southern History* 37 (Nov. 1971): 575-96.

Sears, Richard D. "John G. Fee, Camp Nelson, and Kentucky Blacks." *Register of the Kentucky Historical Society* 85 (Winter 1987): 29-45.

Simms, Henry H. "A Critical Analysis of Abolitionist Literature." *Journal of South ern History* 6 (Aug. 1940): 368-82.

Simpson, Lewis P. "Slavery and the Cultural Imperialism of New England." *Southern Review* 25 (Jan. 1989): 1-29.

Smiley, David L. "Cassius M. Clay and Southern Industrialism." *Filson Club History Quarterly* 28 (Oct. 1954): 315-27.

Smith, George W. "Ante-Bellum Attempts of Northern Business Interests to 'Redeem' the Upper South." *Journal of Southern History* 11 (May 1945): 177-213.

Stampp, Kenneth M. "The Fate of the Southern Anti-Slavery Movement." *Journal of Negro History* 28 (Jan. 1943): 10-22.

Steelman, Joseph F. "Daniel Reeves Goodloe: A Perplexed Abolitionist during Reconstruction." *East Carolina College Publications in History* 2 (1965): 66-90.

Steely, Will Frank. "William Shreve Bailey, Kentucky Abolitionist." *Filson Club History Quarterly* 31 (July 1957): 274-81.

Stewart, James Brewer. "Evangelicalism and the Radical Strain in Southern Antislavery Thought during the 1820s." *Journal of Southern History* 39 (Aug. 1973): 379-96.

——. "Peaceful Hopes and Violent Experiences: The Evolution of Reforming and Radical Abolitionism, 1831-1837." *Civil War History* 17 (Dec. 1971): 293-309.

——. "Young Turks and Old Turkeys: Abolitionists, Historians, and Aging Processes." *Reviews in American History* 11 (June 1983): 226-32.

Tapp, Hambleton. "Robert J. Breckinridge and the Year 1849." *Filson Club History Quarterly* 12 (July 1938): 125-50.

Thompson, Priscilla. "Harriet Tubman, Thomas Garrett, and the Underground Railroad." *Delaware History* 22 (Sept. 1986): 1-21.

Tolbert, Noble. "Daniel Worth: Tar Heel Abolitionist." *North Carolina Historical Review* 39 (Su. 1962): 284-304.

Weeks, Stephen B. "Anti-Slavery Sentiment in the South." *Southern Historical Association Publications* 2 (1898): 87-130.

Weiss, Robert F., William Buchanan, and John F. Lombardo. "Altruism Is Rewarding." *Science* 171 (Mar. 1971): 1262-63.

Wish, Harvey. "The Slave Insurrection Panic of 1856." *Journal of Southern History* 5 (May 1939): 206-27.

Wyatt-Brown, Bertram. "The Abolitionists' Postal Campaign of 1835." *Journal of Negro History* 50 (Oct. 1965): 227-38.

Dissertations, Theses, and Other Unpublished Studies

English, Philip Wesley. "John G. Fee: Kentucky Spokesman for Abolition and Educational Reform." Ph.D. diss., Indiana Univ., 1973.

Hickin, Patricia P. "Antislavery in Virginia, 1831-1861." 3 vols. Ph.D. diss., Univ. of Virginia, 1968.

——. "John C. Underwood and the Antislavery Crusade, 1809-1860." Master's thesis, Univ. of Virginia, 1961.

Johnson, Clifton H. "The American Missionary Association, 1846-1861: A Study of Christian Abolitionism." Ph.D. diss., Univ. of North Carolina, 1958.

Loesch, Robert K. "Kentucky Abolitionist: John Gregg Fee." Typescript, Berea College Archives, 1969.

Reynolds, Todd Armstrong. "The American Missionary Association's Antislavery Campaign in Kentucky, 1848-1860." Ph.D. diss., Ohio State Univ., 1979.

Rice, Franklin P. "The Life of Eli Thayer." Typescript. Eli Thayer Papers, Brown Univ. Library, undated.

Tallant, Harold D., Jr. "The Slavery Controversy in Kentucky, 1829-1859." Ph.D. diss., Duke Univ., 1986.

INDEX

abolitionism. *See* abolitionists

abolitionists (*see also* antislavery), 1-4, 16-17, 151; and abolitionist missionaries, 84-86; and blacks, 46-54, 62, 93, 96-97, 163, 185 n 17; and North, 11; and Reconstruction, 149; and sectional conflict, 3, 11, 15, 65-66; and violent means, 46, 59-61; historiography, 2-4, 9-26, 64-66, 85-86, 91, 105, 108, 133, 149-54; on slave rescuers, 56

abolitionists, black, 5, 7-8; and slave rescuers, 67, 145, 149, 167; on slave revolt, 53, 46-48, 61

abolitionists, border, 53, 80, 119-20, 129

abolitionists, church-oriented, 6-7, 27, 89, 144-45

abolitionists, evangelical. *See* abolitionists, church-oriented

abolitionists, Garrisonian, 6, 39; and Civil War, 163; and slaves, 61-62; and South, 8; on northern antislavery initiatives in South, 104-5, 116-19, 142-43; on southern abolitionists, 27, 38, 44, 136-37, 144-45; on U.S. Constitution, 75

abolitionists, gradual, 45

abolitionists, Liberty. *See* Liberty party

abolitionists, northern, 4-5, 15; and American Colonization Society, 30; and antislavery initiatives in South, 24, 28, 38, 66-67, 74-90, 104-7, 109, 116-18, 121, 125, 142-43; and Civil War causation, 149-61; and racism, 23, 48-49; and revivalism, 11, and South, 4, 6, 9-10, 27; and southern abolitionists, 20, 23-44, 137; and southern

antislavery politics, 127-30; and violent means, 44, 55, 78-79; on blacks, 41, 50, 55, 62-63; on slave revolt, 45-63; postal campaign of, 25, 43, 66, 85, 93, 151

abolitionists, political (*see also* Liberty party), 7; on U.S. Constitution, 75; in upper South, 127-29

abolitionists, radical political, 7; and Civil War, 163; and Republican party, 147; and slave violence, 59-60; and southern antislavery politics, 144-48; and southern abolitionists, 27, 29, 44, 128, 146-48; on antislavery initiatives in South, 74-75, 81, 91, 117-19, 142-43; on U.S. Constitution, 75-76

abolitionists, second-generation: 7-8, 119-20

abolitionists, southern, 1-2, 4-6, 13, 15, 16-20, 39; and black rights, 35-36, 134-35, 167-71; and northern abolitionists, 19-44, 51, 131-33, 135, 148, 178-79 n 6; and racism, 21-23; and religion, 133-34; appeal to whites, 35, 132; on *National Era*, 143

abolitionists, white, 5; and blacks, 46-49, 67, 72-73; on slave revolt, 47-48, 58, 61

Abzug, Robert H., 46-47

Adams, Alice Dana, 12-15, 17-18

Adams, John Quincy, 82

African Americans (*see also* blacks), 28, 163-63

Albany Patriot, 68, 70

Albany Vigilance Committee, 74

American Abolition Society, 147